MEANING &
MITZVAH

DAILY PRACTICES
for
RECLAIMING JUDAISM
through
PRAYER,
GOD,
TORAH,
HEBREW,
MITZVOT *and*
PEOPLEHOOD

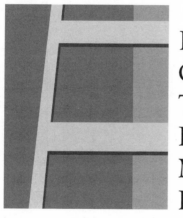

D1441664

RABBI GOLDIE MILGRAM

JEWISH LIGHTS Publishing
Woodstock, Vermont

MAY 2006

Meaning & Mitzvah:
Daily Practices for Reclaiming Judaism through Prayer, God, Torah, Hebrew, Mitzvot and Peoplehood

2005 First Printing
© 2005 by Goldie Milgram

For information regarding permission to reprint material from this book, please write or fax your request to Jewish Lights Publishing, Permissions Department, at the address / fax number listed below, or e-mail your request to permissions@ jewishlights.com.

Library of Congress Cataloging-in-Publication Data
Milgram, Goldie, 1955–
Meaning & mitzvah : daily practices for reclaiming Judaism through God, Torah, mitzvot, Hebrew, prayer and peoplehood / Goldie Milgram.
   p. cm.
Includes bibliographical references and index.
ISBN 1-58023-256-6 (quality pbk.)
1. Spiritual life—Judaism. 2. Jewish way of life. 3. Judaism—Doctrines. I. Title.
BM723.M46 2005
296.7—dc22

10 9 8 7 6 5 4 3 2 1

Manufactured in the United States of America
Cover Design: Sara Dismukes

Published by Jewish Lights Publishing
A Division of LongHill Partners, Inc.
Sunset Farm Offices, Route 4, P.O. Box 237
Woodstock, VT 05091
Tel: (802) 457-4000   Fax: (802) 457-4004
www.jewishlights.com

This book is dedicated
to my beloved hubbatzin,
Barry "Ben Tzion" Bub

CONTENTS

ACKNOWLEDGMENTS

This book has been made possible by a grant from the Nathan Cummings Foundation with the support and encouragement of Dr. Ruth Durchslag.

Meaning and Mitzvah was written over the course of four years of teaching in more than thirteen countries and fifty-three cities. A team of stunningly loving, bright, and perceptive family members, friends, publishing professionals, colleagues, and students provided the support that is making this book and its companion volume possible and successful in reaching those seeking spirituality and meaning for living through a Jewish lens. As this book is released, *Reclaiming Judaism as a Spiritual Practice: Holy Days and Shabbat* has made its way into the homes of seekers as well as both congregational and college classrooms, where understanding Judaism and its applications to daily living are matters of study and compelling interest.

I am tremendously grateful to my beloved "hubbatzin," Barry Bub, who so freely contributed his amazing mind, great deep soul, hundreds of hours of driving, and attention to the logistics and activities of daily living during the writing of this work.

The concept for these two books began at the recommendation of Rabbi Nancy Fuchs-Kreimer, who reached out to me upon reviewing the original ReclaimingJudaism.org website. Her encouragement and sharing of her contact with her agent, Anne Edelstein, greatly helped to set this process in motion. Nancy is my esteemed colleague; and in rabbinical school, as a professor of Contemporary Jewish Philosophy, she was among the first to incorporate the vision, views, values, and voices of Jewish women into the seminary curriculum as well as to engage our attention and depth of learning through effective experiential techniques.

Giving freely of their time and acumen have been the dedicated focus group readers and consultants for *Meaning and Mitzvah:* Ania Bien, Carola de Vries Robles, Rabbi Kevin Haley, Rabbi Burt Jacobson, Tzeitl Locher, Dr. Lenore Mennin, Dr. Samuel Milgram, Lara Rosenthal, Ellen Triebwasser, Dr. Sharon Ufberg, Dr. Laura Vidmar, and Ellen Weaver.

The smooth flow of the text is directly the result of the professional editing of Judith Kern and Emily Wichland. Stuart M. Matlins, publisher of Jewish Lights, thank you for envisioning and captaining a publishing house of such high caliber and creativity that supports an author with excellence at every step of the publishing process.

The following teachers and colleagues have been primary sources of professional inspiration to me. I hope readers will seek out these remarkable individuals and their works: Anne Brener; Rabbi Samuel Barth; Dr. Judith Baskin; Sylvia Boorstein; Rabbis Marcello Bronstein, David A. Cooper, Julie Hilton-Danan, and Gail Diamond; Dr. Marcia Falk; Dr. Harold Frank; Dr. Tikveh Frymer-Kensky; Rabbi Nancy Fuchs-Kreimer, Cindy Gabriel, and Rabbis Yaacov Gabriel and Elliot Ginsberg; Dr. David Golomb; Rabbis Lynn Gottlieb, Arthur Green, Shefa Gold, Victor and Nadia Gross, Jill Hammer, Linda Holtzman, Irving Greenberg, and Raachel Jurovics; Dr. Aaron Katcher; Hazzan Richard Kaplan; Rabbis Burt Jacobson, Myriam Klotz, Jonathan Kligler, Arthur Kurzweil, Isaac Mann, and Natan Margalit; Dr. George McClain; Dr. Shulamit Magnus; Rabbis Itzchak Marmorstein, Yitchak Mann, Roly Matalon, and Leah Novick; Dr. Peter Pitzele; Dr. Judith Plaskow; Rabbis Marcia Prager and Geelah Rayzl Raphael; Dr. Simcha Paull Raphael; Rabbis Jeff Roth, Zalman M. Schachter-Shalomi, Robert Scheinberg, and Peninnah Schram, David Seidenberg, Rami Shapiro, and Daniel Siegel; Dr. Edward Shils; Rabbis Jacob Staub, Margot Stein, Adin Steinsaltz, David Teutsch, and Shawn Zevit; Rabbis Arthur Waskow, Shohama Wiener, and David Zaslow; and Dr. Noam Zohar. And for this volume, in particular, Rabbi David Wolfe-Blank of blessed memory.

And finally, deepest appreciation to the board and faculty members of Reclaiming Judaism, the teaching and research educational nonprofit that is the primary vehicle for my work in the world—Sara Harwin, Lynn Hazan, Janice Rubin, Dr. Sharon Ufberg, and Rabbi Shohama Wiener. And also to the leadership of the ever-inspiring Project Kesher—Karen Gerson, Sallie E. Gratch, Natasha Slobodyanik, and Svetlana

Yakimenko. And to my students everywhere—thank you for your stimulating questions and creative responses: You are the best teachers.

With love and appreciation from my heart to yours,
R'Goldie Milgram

INTRODUCTION

Quality of life is a phrase that's bandied about all too easily these days, but I believe that the true quality of your life depends greatly on your daily preparations for living. Consider, for example, the difference between awakening to birdsong and awe, and awakening to traumatic world news spilling from your bedside clock radio. Awakenings come more easily when the "you" who loves, learns, remembers, reacts, and yearns also trusts that you will begin each day with a spiritual stretch. Awakenings could be called periods of "threshold consciousness," tender times for spiritual practice. The word *adonai*—often translated in the language of the old paradigm as "Lord" or "Master"—appears frequently in Jewish prayer practice. Through the mystery of Hebrew's remarkable nature as a uniquely spiritual language, one root word of *adonai* is *ehden*, "threshold." Perhaps this is why one of our practices for awakening, as well as for going to sleep and dying, is to say the biblical prayer verse known as the *shema*. *Shema* means "listen." So if waking, sleeping, and dying are all threshold times, saying this prayer (found in every mezuzah, the prayer box Jews place on our doorposts) is like putting up a mezuzah of spirit. Saying the *shema* draws a "line of intention," a *kavannah*, to enter your day listening, enter your dreams listening, and enter death listening, which might be termed one of the *penimiut*, "inner," spiritual meanings of mezuzah practice.

The emphasis in Jewish spiritual practice is on the magnificence of what can be experienced and the good that can be accomplished while your soul is in this lifetime, in this body, in this world—because the only "world to come" of which Jews claim certainty is the one we leave to the children. And even proponents of those strands in our tradition that accept reincarnation or resurrection emphasize that hell is not an otherworldly destination; it is, in the words of Rebbe Nahman of Breslov (eighteenth century), "how people are suffering now." Spiritual practice reveals that the Garden of Eden is right where you are standing and helps you to be here, now. Therefore, Jewish spiritual practices cultivate joy, hope, resilience, and understanding so that you can undertake your soul's work in this lifetime with vision, passion, and integrity.

Perhaps this is not the way Judaism sounded if you went to religious school. As a post–World War II people who had been subjected to an attempted extinction—whose books, homes, safe havens, sacred places, and sages had mostly been incinerated or overtaken for use by others—our Jewish ancestors' immediate needs were for physical survival and data storage. While they labored to create social welfare networks in new lands, they also built religious schools and synagogues that functioned as places where the knowledge of our traditions and history was stuffed into our youth. It was a primitive uploading from one generation to the next. We, their children and grandchildren, became human hard drives carrying a sacred trust. But while they faithfully passed on to us the texts and traditions, our parents and grandparents were, for the most part, too wounded to show us how to turn on the light carried by Judaism as a living spiritual path.

Spiritual education, however, is quite different from what you might remember as religious education. Once you become familiar with the ingredients of a practice—the steps, contexts, symbols, metaphors, and technical language—spiritual education continues as a guiding, sharing, and maturing of experience. Like any acquired skill—be it sailing, meditating, playing an instrument, or growing healthy roses—spiritual practice may seem awkward or burdensome at first. But as it is cultivated and becomes more familiar, you get to the point where you can improvise, explore, and, with persistence, sometimes exceed what you imagined possible.

Meaning and Mitzvah makes accessible Judaism's daily spiritual pathways, principles, and applications, and empowers you to test their value and impact within and upon your own life. Each chapter provides step-by-step, recipe-like guides to a particular spiritual practice or group of practices, gives examples of how they might unfold inside your life and spirit, and shows how each recipe fits into a healthy menu of spirit for your day. In these pages, you will learn how to reach for the *penimiut*, "inner faces" of prayer, God, Torah, Hebrew, mitzvot, and peoplehood.

We will begin with prayer practices for "when you are at home, when you walk upon the way, for when you lie down and when you rise up"(Deuteronomy 6:7). Judaism as a spiritual path starts with the individual *adam* (pronounced ah-dahm), "earthling," that is, you, your self—your physical, emotional, intellectual, and spiritual development, enjoyment, and health. Why? Because our tradition teaches that we are co-creating the world with God every day. Accordingly, chapter 1, "Finding Meaning in Jewish Prayer," teaches prayer practices and sequences for embracing the body and creation with awe, limbering up your mind, preparing for compassionate action and innovation. It also offers pathways for refueling your spirit throughout the day.

Chapter 2, "Reclaiming God with Integrity," concerns relating to the "G" word, but primarily in its many Hebrew manifestations, because fixed-image Western models of a judgmental-old-guy God or a resurrected-young-one, which were projected by generations before phenomena like the invention of the Hubble telescope, are the opposite of Judaism's most basic practice—allowing no specific image to represent the mystery of the Source of Life. Instead, Judaism's synergistic spiritual practices lead to a perception of the unity of all life so that you can move from *mohin d'katnut,* "small mind" or "personal consciousness," to *mohin d'gadlut,* expanded consciousness.

That said, we are complex beings, able to consider diametrically opposing perceptions—in this case, awareness of the self as individual and also as part of the unified whole—as equally valuable. It is, therefore, a very powerful and precious moment when a person first feels what in Western language would be expressed as God's inquiring presence and is able to respond—*"hineini*—Here I am" (Genesis 21:1). It might happen to you when you are presented with an opportunity to help an elder reach an item on the top shelf in the supermarket, when you are dispensing food in a soup kitchen, or when you are in a city park and a stranger listens to you speak about your day. Or perhaps your *hineini* happens in a planetarium beholding the birth of a galaxy, or under a *huppah* (wedding canopy) entering a committed relationship and feeling the ritual braid your soul with another, or in synagogue when you find yourself rising for an *aliyah* to "ascend" as a witness to a Torah reading that touches you deeply. Chapter 2 will consider how our system of practices draws sustenance from the Great Mystery, the inexplicable and unknowable Source of Life so awkwardly termed *God* in English.

If the Jewish people were viewed as a book club, we would be a club whose members love mining the same book over and over for gems of meaning that beckon to each generation. The Torah, the Hebrew Scriptures, is the sacred starting place of Jewish spiritual practice. Through commentary and encounter, Torah is the meeting place of the ancestors, one of which you, too, will become. Some ask, Why Torah? Why not some other book or books? Or why don't we also annex Native American symbols or adopt Buddha, Krishna, or Jesus? Because every spiritual path has its own inner integrity, and in order to maintain the depth of our ancient wisdom tradition, the Jewish people ground our primary sacred imagery in Torah. This is a conscious practice.

In the third chapter, "Taking Torah Personally," you will learn how to go behind the scenes to mine the stories, commentaries, symbols, metaphors, and even the letters in the texts for meaning. Torah study means entering a 3,400-year-long conversation across the generations about the nature of families, societies, leadership, challenges, vision, ethics, and change. In Judaism, the text is a sacred starting place for awareness to arise. The layers of meaning in Torah, as far as we know, are infinite. It is a Jewish spiritual practice to *shema*, or deeply listen, to the life wisdom the Torah stories have evoked from others, to incorporate an understanding of our ancestors' views into our studies, and to make our own known as well.

For example, in Genesis 24:64 when Rebecca looks up and sees a man on the horizon (Isaac) and senses her destiny coming toward her, she gets so excited that she *va-teepole mae al ha-gamal*, "falls off her camel." So this verse might lead you to contemplate and share your own understanding of the difference between falling in love and growing in love.

As another example, Abraham and Sarah never speak again after he comes so close to sacrificing their son Isaac. One year you might recognize in this how actions can wound and traumatize families for generations. Another year you might know it to be a complex act of mutual faith. The next year you might understand the incident as a male rite of transition, the knife symbolically raised, father and son leaving the ritual scene separately.

In chapter 3, you will also be introduced to Midrash and Talmud, traditional activist texts that reveal the responsibility of every generation to advance the tradition by adding new visions, views, and voices. Chapter 3 will show you how to create your own *divrei Torah*, "words" of insight and interpretation, and enter into the sacred dialogue of the generations. Your interpretations are holy, too.

Chapter 4, "Hebrew Is a Spiritual Practice," explains why, when you look in a Bible, you may find that the term *va-teepole* is not so plainly translated as "falls"; you might see "she gets down" or "she alights from her camel," or, as the sage Saadia Gaon put it, "she almost falls." Every printed translation is the interpretation of an individual or a commission, and hence a political document. Prior generations cleaned up Rebecca's act in their "translations," not wanting a future matriarch to appear undignified or immodest. So translations are opportunities to see the Torah stories from one particular perspective, often the perspective traditionally accepted by the group behind the volume's publishers. But translations are not truths. Gradually developing the capacity to formulate your own interpretations is a wonderful step to take toward your own spiritual empowerment. Accordingly, in chapter 4 you will learn the origins of Hebrew, a uniquely spiritual language, and be assisted in developing your vocabulary so that you can move beyond the *p'shat*, apparent meanings, to new levels of possible meaning that perhaps only you were born to discover.

Did you hear the joke about the student who cheated on a metaphysics exam? He was caught looking into the soul of the person sitting next to him. Well, spirituality is different from philosophy; no one can earn a grade or take a final in spirituality. In Jewish spiritual education, awareness of others isn't cheating, it is spirituality in action! You will know authentic spirituality is afoot when you feel the light of awe and connection safely growing deep inside you and your relationships.

In Jewish spiritual practice, it is more than okay to be happy. Achieving a positive outlook on life, *lih'yote b'simhah tamid*, is deemed a mitzvah, and living a mitzvah-centered life is the core of Judaism as a spiritual path. We have hundreds of mitzvot—actions and attitudes to be undertaken with curiosity and consciousness and to be continuously explored so that we can access and activate their many spiritual health benefits. Often mistakenly viewed as fixed forms and formulas, many of our mitzvot, "practices to be done with focused consciousness" when viewed through a spiritual lens, will help you move beyond surviving to thriving.

Chapter 5, "Living a Mitzvah-Centered Life," introduces more than fifty mitzvot for you to view through a spiritual lens.

With exploration and practice, the particular mitzvot you choose can become meaningful, compelling parts of your life.

Mitzvot are not opiates for the masses; they are guidelines for right action. One of the mitzvot is *tzaar baalei ḥayyim*, "to ensure that no unnecessary pain comes to sentient beings." Its activation is both a personal and a social process. The mitzvah of *haḥnassat orḥim* asks you to look at your life through a spiritual lens and recognize it as a guesthouse into which you welcome the inner parts of your self as well as everyone you meet out in the world. How different it is to perceive others as your guests rather than to live with a consumer consciousness that inherently expects to be treated as everyone else's guest.

Does every verse of the thousands of volumes of Jewish religious thought and law reflect all these higher-self aspirations? Any knowledgeable Jew can point to some interpretations and traditions that make us cringe in light of contemporary values. No matter; that was then. We live in a time when the highest principles of Judaism are vitally needed on this planet. *Teshuvah*—"turning" toward what is important, vital, life-affirming, relationship-building—is itself a mitzvah to be done in the passionate spirit of all mitzvot, *b'ḥol l'vav'ḥah, u'v'ḥol nafsh'ḥah, u'v'ḥol m'o-deh-ḥah*—with all your heart, soul, and ability.

Peoplehood is the subject of our final chapter, chapter 6, "The Positive Power of Peoplehood." The Jewish people can be viewed as a precious human resource; you might say we are humanity's most resilient and experienced research and development group. The Exodus, our foundational story as a nation, serves as a primal motif for many who seek freedom from domination by family members, employers, governments, addictions, and all oppressors. We brought with us from Egypt the idea of monotheism. We survived the era of temples and sacrificial systems, and in our exile every home became a *mikdash m'aht,* a small sacred center where instead of atoning through animal sacrifice, we created change through ego sacrifice, by sitting down to dine together and working through the psychodynamics to make our relationships evolve and thrive. Instead of perpetuating the edifice complex of Temple times, we learned to create our most important temples in the time we take as radical refugees from employers and the stresses of work called Sabbath and holy days.

Judaism is, in the words of Rabbi Mordecai Kaplan, an evolving civilization. In every age we harmonize and upgrade our practices to account for innovations and changes in the world around us. Organ donation, for example, was once eschewed and is now considered a mitzvah. Even our conscious eating practices are shifting as eco-kosher labels begin to appear on foods.

We are and have always been a diverse people. Just as there is no single variety of rose or bird, Jews truly comprise a bouquet of pluralism. We experiment with different operating systems for our spiritual traditions. Lately we have given these systems labels like Renewal, *Havurah,* Reconstructionist, Reform, Conservative, Orthodox, Chabad, Breslov, and more, while in earlier times they were Karraite, Rabbanite, Hasidei Ashkenaz, Beit Hillel, Beit Shammai, and many, many more. Nothing destroys us—not intermarriage, Inquisition, or Holocaust. Our numbers vary greatly across history, but numbers are not the source of our impact; we are more like a pinch of baking soda in the cake of creation, small in numbers yet bringing something powerful and essential to the mix of nations and to the principles for living that liberate, cultivate, and elevate the human spirit when applied with integrity.

Exile, persecution, hope, curiosity, despair, and wonder have led Jews to reside in every country on earth. Our dispersion makes us a litmus test to the nations of the world—can they imagine a (w)holy shareable earth, freedom of religion and movement, global joint citizenships? Can we? Today almost half the world's total Jewish population struggles daily to survive and figure out how to coexist peacefully with neighboring peoples in the Middle East. Once again we are incredulous that triumphalist religious fundamentalism and anti-Semitism are in resurgence so soon after so much recent suffering. For centuries we had little experience of self-governance in our own land and are discovering ethical nationhood in Israel and America. As has long been the case for longer-established nations, this is difficult to determine and attain. And yet, ours is a spirituality of optimism. We figured out how to make the desert bloom, and we will work with what's on our path at this time, too. How is it possible to be so resilient? That is our subject throughout this series: the remarkable practices of our people, which *sheheheyanu, v'kimanu, v'higeeyanu, la-z'man ha-zeh*, "give us life, sustain us and bring us to this season." Welcome to *Meaning and Mitzvah: Daily Practices for Reclaiming Judaism through Prayer, God, Torah, Hebrew, Mitzvot and Peoplehood.*

TRANSLITERATION AND FORMATTING DECISIONS

1. Transliterations are done with a schema created to make it as easy as possible for the reader to sound out a passage. In Hebrew the letters *haf* and *het* have a sim-

ilar guttural sound, much like clearing your throat or saying "kh." Often depicted as "ch" and mispronounced accordingly, these letters are both transliterated in this series as "<u>h</u>."

2. Since Hebrew has no capital letters, from this point forward Hebrew words will not be capitalized unless they appear at the beginning of an English sentence. This intends no disrespect in writing out names of God, matriarchs, or patriarchs; it is to convey just a bit of what it is like to experience the absence of capitalization that is the reality of all Hebrew text.

3. Keeping God as an infinite mystery with many facets that we numerously name, while recognizing that none could ever fully define this category of awareness—this is a core Jewish spiritual practice. Out of respect for this, G*d will be the symbolic term used throughout the rest of this book.

RECLAIMINGJUDAISM.ORG

The nonprofit companion website for this book has over six hundred pages of additional information on Jewish spiritual practice and links to teachers, retreats, and courses that will support your understanding and experience of Judaism through a spiritual lens. You are also encouraged to make contact with the author, Rabbi Goldie Milgram, to offer feedback, for guidance, or to ask her about giving workshops, retreats, or talks for your school or community. She responds to e-mail sent through www.ReclaimingJudaism.org.

Finding Meaning in Jewish Prayer

Have you heard the joke about the young person reading a list of names on the memorial wall in the synagogue? She asks a member, "Why are so many names up there?" Noting that it is a memorial plaque for those who perished in World War II, the member answers, "It's for those who died in the service." "Which service?" inquires the young person. "Friday night or Saturday morning?"

This chapter will be your antidote to religious boredom, so you will never need "to die in services" again. Here you will study and have opportunities to try out prayer methods that transform the words on the page and inside your heart into portals of healing for you, your relationships, and the world.

The Jewish prayer service is a carefully crafted inheritance intended to guide and nourish your soul on its journey. When they are understood through a mystical lens, the various Jewish prayer forms work together like a multivitamin, conditioning you to live in balance, be of service, cultivate and calibrate what you need in order to feel healthy, holy, and happy.

If you are willing to apply yourself with focus and discipline, these practices can also bring you into the unforgettable, life-enhancing realm of full mystical experience, allowing you to feel a part of something vast and grand, while at the same time catching glimpses both of the importance of your own brief presence in creation and of what it means to be a Jew.

FINDING THE PRAYER OF YOUR HEART

In Judaism, existence is meaningful, even as you feel humble in the face of it. The place you occupy in the fabric of creation—your voice, your thoughts, your desires, your potential, your decisions, *you*, and the prayer of your heart—all of these matter. In the biblical Book of Samuel, a story is told of a woman named Hannah, who, devastated by her infertility, takes the unprecedented step of going into the ancient Temple in Jerusalem on her own. The Temple priests assume that any woman found in there whispering to herself must be drunk. But they are wrong. It is the prayer of her breaking heart that Hannah is so softly voicing, and the story indicates that her prayer is heard and answered.

Our sages cited Hannah's incentive to personal prayer with approval. And, in so doing, they illustrated awareness that the sacrificial system, based on the rituals surrounding animal sacrifice and agricultural offerings, which was the formal way of relating to G*d at that time, was not the only effective method of spiritual expression. They understood what is being widely documented with research today: The prayer of the heart can be very effective. Allow me to illustrate with a story from my own experience.

A girl who had recently become bat mitzvah at our synagogue was riding with her family when they were in a terrible car accident. The car rolled over and over, and in it the bat mitzvah girl and her family were being slammed about. They were all miraculously alive when the vehicle came to a halt, but two of the daughters required surgery and "my" recent bat mitzvah girl was in a deep, unresponsive coma. Even these many years later, the memory of watching the parents, who were traumatized themselves, going from one child's room to another brings a rush of tears to my eyes.

Looking back, I remember my love for that congregation, which I served for almost ten years, and for this particular family. My anxiety and sense of hopelessness grew as I saw the hospital staff, hour by hour, appear to be giving up hope for the girl in a coma. My intellectual and cultural understanding of Judaism was no longer enough. During those days I truly prayed for the first time, many years after graduating as a "trained rabbi."

The nurses said it was good to massage the girl's twitching legs. As I did that, I tried to sense a presence in her, to feel her consciousness. My soul kept trying to find hers. After a while, I couldn't sense my own body at all.

Gradually, soft, healing-sounding songs from the Psalms came through me, filling the lengthening hours, hopefully offering a counterpoint to the infernal beeping of the monitoring equipment with which she was surrounded. Then, I found myself just talking to her, as if she could hear, about this and that. I taught her parents the prayer of Moses for his sister Miriam when she became ill:

ana	Please
el	G*d
na	Please
r'fa	heal
na	[another "please"]
la	her

Despairing inside, professional on the outside, I just couldn't leave and so stayed on. An adventure story began to replace the psalm songs. A story came through me to her wherein a gorgeous teenage boy snatched her up to travel the medieval world with him by ship to Jerusalem. Their mission was to sketch an accurate picture of the Wailing Wall and bring it back to the boy's grandfather while he was still alive. The hospital monitor caught my eye during the telling. Was there a change in blood pressure? Or was that line the heart rate? Did the tiny fluctuation mean something? The staff all said, "No, it just happens." Finally, I went home exhausted.

I returned the next night and continued the story, slipping in the image of a kiss between her and the young man. Her heartbeat began to race and her blood pressure did increase, but still, the doctors were solemn and sad, their faces showing how foolish they considered my efforts. The nurses were kind, but talking to her less and less. I understood them to be shutting down emotionally, protecting themselves.

Meanwhile, as I recall, her sisters each underwent a major surgery with a good prognosis. Any sick child is a spiritual challenge to loving parents, but to have three all at once!

Somehow, they couldn't leave the bat mitzvah girl to the loving attendance of other family members, friends, or the numerous willing congregants who had gathered. I hoped that if they knew I'd napped earlier in the day they might agree to go home and try to get some rest. I was glad when they ultimately did go home for a brief rest, allowing me to stay with their daughter.

At 2:00 a.m. I took advantage of a "code" for another Intensive Care Unit patient to cover the girl with my rainbow-hued *tallit* (prayer shawl). I felt the pulse of her life force and, as I rested lightly over her with my full body, my heart broke open and my soul flew up in desperation toward an untapped Source. Soundless petitions poured out from me, pleas for her healing. Time lost meaning, and then I felt a probing in my awareness, nothing physical. I lifted my head in a daze and pulled back the *tallit*, surprised I'd had the <u>h</u>*utzpah* to cover her face.

She was looking right at me, a large tear slipping down her face. Her broken jaw had been wired shut; she had a tracheotomy tube and was receiving oxygen. We communicated with our eyes and our tears, then I remembered I *could* talk and very quickly said: "Don't try to talk. You had an accident. Your jaw is wired shut. You are healing. We'll be a team for recovery, okay?" She squeezed my hand and then fell back into the jerking coma. Caught between hope and despair, I called a nurse who cheered me as she whooped in joy and decided to wake a doctor with the news. We looked at the girl again; the coma had shifted to visibly deep sleep. "Go home, Rabbi," the nurse said. "By now that room must be draped in angels."

At the end of the first week our congregation held our very first healing service. The bat mitzvah girl had been in and out of a coma several times by then. Usually I led services, but this time the service led us. I closed my eyes and simply let the traditional chain of melodies, prayer, and movement come. The deep structure of the service, imprinted by training, supported us in our hope, terror, grief, and fear. We brought out the Torah and held it horizontally like a body, as the peers of the parents and the three girls pressed in close. Tears flowed freely as we chanted Moses' prayer together, *ana el na r'fa na la*.

With the family's permission, I described to the community the week of terror and hope that had just passed. We became a radiant mass, broadcasting through the cosmos our loving concern, healing hopes, and prayers. As my gaze touched them, others whispered the names of those in their intimate worlds who needed healing. The river of caring energy was passionately palpable. We chanted *ana el na* over and over and then sang another prayer of healing for ourselves as well as for the family, asking in the words composed by Rabbi Shohama Wiener: "May the waters of healing flow through our souls … our minds … our hearts … our forms." We were all huddled around the Torah and stayed there in silent prayer long after setting it back in the ark.

Our closing *aleynu* prayer held a remarkable sense of richness and connection that day. I had promised a talking circle after services during which people could share their thoughts and feelings. But the moment was too holy to talk about just then. Congregants said they wanted to take the experience of the service home inside themselves, to savor and consider the healing they'd sent and received. I, too, was relieved, enlivened, healed.

Today that bat mitzvah girl is a lovely, successful, healthy young woman. When I sent her this chapter to read, she wrote back that her only memory of the accident and the whole hospital experience was of waking up with me leaning over her wearing a rainbow.

Jewish prayer practice is very powerful. When you incline your heart steadily toward your hopes, eventually you can attain the momentum that's necessary to create change. You can dampen, refocus, or enhance your mood, your immune system, your words, and your actions depending on how you send your energy outward into what I have heard my teacher, Rabbi Zalman Schachter-Shalomi, call the "G*d field."

Jewish theology does not provide any expectation of a precise response to our prayers. The cosmos has far greater considerations than what is going on individually with each of us. So I don't take what happens personally. I don't imagine that my prayer healed that young woman, although it did change me and perhaps created a shift in the field of possibility. And I do take notice of Chaos Theory, from which we can take hope that the way we direct our energy might encourage a particular outcome.

Praying in a group, as well as privately, matters. Even if each of us in that healing service had been praying for a different relative, friend, or for ourselves, by including Moses' prayer for his sister, we connected to the universal anguish of the human condition. Hurting, hoping, and human, by taking those words from his story as ours, we experienced the benefit of liturgy as a group. Even without retelling the whole Moses/Miriam story at the service, the *ana el na* verse served to identify, unify, and give voice to our prayer. We were not alone, either in the moment or in eternity.

Judaism teaches that, through the power of your prayer and the amplification of that prayer in community, you can generate a landslide of new possibilities—perhaps not always what you expect, yet often enough to make a great difference.

RECLAIMING LITURGY

Jewish liturgy is an ever-growing collection of spiritual delicacies to which every generation contributes. You've likely noticed that trying to recite the liturgy of a full service can be toxic to some, and has proved terminal to the Jewish connection of many.

What has prayer been like for you—
privately and at services?
When you prayed, who else was there?
What were they doing?
Was the experience boring? Energizing?
Comforting? Transformative?

Many of us have suffered the stultifying effects of participating in congregations where saying every word of the written prayers, often as quickly as possible by rote, seemed to be the right thing for a "good" Jew to do. Some of us didn't even know how to translate more than a word or two we spoke during those express-train prayer experiences. Dependent on archaic translations, we were alienated, mouthing words we didn't believe and had not been taught to understand. We learned Hebrew without realizing that it is a language full of spiritual nuances. Without access to the levels of meaning that allow a person to be supported and touched by Jewish prayer, we were given a jealous G*d needing our praise in order for "Him" to feel validated and for us to be redeemed.

Alternatively, perhaps you look back fondly on sitting beside a parent or grandparent in synagogue. Perhaps you recall flirting as a teen with those in nearby rows or up in the balcony. Perhaps your mastery of Hebrew characters was a matter of pride, and your pages of thin blue-lined notebook paper with square Hebrew characters were posted on the refrigerator. While tears slid down a parent's face in anticipation of *yizkor*, the memorial service of the dead, were you sent outside at the High Holy Days to play in the yard or the hall? Do Shabbat candles burning brightly bring warm memories, and do the melodies of their blessings come easily to you even today? If you are new to Judaism, do you have similar memories from your tradition of origin?

> What prayers or prayer melodies
> do you remember?
> What memories arise with them?
> Hum aloud; go for it!

Go ahead and send a blessing to the chapters of your life you have just remembered. Save those melodies and the memorized words on the hard drive of your spiritual consciousness; you will want them later. The recipes in this chapter are intended to reawaken the possibility of meaningful prayer, to restore the spice of spirituality to your inheritance, and to stir things up!

A host of Jewish contemplative practices long lost to most of us have recently been recovered and made available across the full spectrum of Judaism. These practices are becoming important methods for bringing meaning to the experience of prayer and for infusing its nutrients into your soul stream.

RECIPE #1:
Exploring
Traditional
Prayer
through a
Mystical Lens

The goal here is to gradually expand your ability to find and enter the portals of Jewish prayer. This recipe teaches a method of encountering traditional prayer so that it can enter your heart from several perspectives. It is a method that can be applied to any of our sacred texts.

Our study example is from *l'hah dodi*, "To You My Beloved," an ode to Shabbat that is joyfully sung during Friday night services. It was written by the sixteenth-century kabbalist Rabbi Shlomo HaLevy Alkabetz. Our ancestors loved this prayer and preserved it for us. To read even one line in modern idiom can be quite surprising. Here is a verse for your contemplation:

hit-o-r'ri, hit-o-r'ri   Wake yourself up! Wake yourself up!
mae ah'far kumi   From dust arise! [Dust yourself off; get up!]

Do you find it odd that this verse is in a prayer said in the evening, usually a time to put yourself to sleep? That it's a Sabbath practice? Why would our ancestors preserve a practice of waking yourself up at the beginning of the "day of rest"? When I consider these questions, one connection that comes to mind is that there may be parts of ourselves that are kept asleep, repressed, or hidden during the work week with which we might dearly want to reconnect.

Take some time to contemplate and write in your journal, or discuss with a friend the question: How is the soul's waking up different from the body's waking up?

Is there anyone in your life to whom you might want to address this study verse? "Wake yourself up! Wake yourself up! Dust yourself off; get up!" Out loud, as if the person you've chosen were present, say the words again, perhaps again, now again. Now whisper or sing them with that person in mind. Does doing this change your relationship to the verse?

Now or at a future time, direct the verse to *yourself*. Notice any difference between ranting it at yourself and making it into a prayer for yourself? What images, memories, or feelings rise to the surface of your consciousness when you do one rather than the other?

> Take time to contemplate your responses,
> because revelation can occur when
> you listen to the way your life intersects
> with the words of sacred texts and prayers.

Recently, after Shabbat services, a volunteer at the Rose Science and Space Center in New York City came over to me and whispered: "You ask what it means to 'arise from the dust'? Rabbi, we *are* stardust. We are all composed of and will return to being stardust. Consider that when praying the *l'hah dodi*."

Imagine yourself looking through the lens of the Hubble Telescope, beholding stars being born. Whisper our study verse very softly, "Wake up, wake up, from dust arise." What is it like to pray as a soul wrapped around stardust?

Rumi, a thirteenth-century Sufi mystic, wrote: "Wake up, wake up, don't go back to sleep!" In what ways do people go back to sleep even after waking up spiritually? Has this happened to you? One of my students suggested that such phrases may be our ancestors' way of shaking us awake, of saying: "Wake up, wake up! Your soul is a gift. You are designed to be more than stardust. Notice the gift! Wake up!"

Now see if this contemplative exploration of a single verse will change the prayer as a whole when you encounter it in its original context. Imagine it is Friday night in synagogue. Let's try our verse of *l'hah dodi* in the manner of its author's generation, by opening the doors of the synagogue, slipping outside under a darkening, star-filled sky, and singing it out: *hit-o-r'ri, hit-o-r'ri, mae ah'far kumi!* "Wake up! Wake up! From dust arise!" Add body English (body Hebrew?)—gesture with your arms; see if this piece of liturgy has awakened for you.

Perhaps the recipe above gave you a new appetite for *l'hah dodi* and the possibilities inherent in Jewish prayer. I hope so. This experience is only a *forshpeis* (Yiddish for "appetizer") for our studies. We have so much more to reclaim!

NUTRIENTS ARE BURIED IN EVERY PRAYER AND SERVICE

Recognizing that your spirit is deeply affected by the events of any given day and season, Judaism offers a range of daily prayer practices, including prayer sessions for the morning, afternoon, and evening known respectively as *shaharit, minhah,* and *ma'ariv.* Like tiny time capsules releasing spirit-restoring nutrients, the infrastructure of the services are similar, with changes or additions that address the time of day, season, and whether it happens to be Shabbat and/or a holiday.

The thirteenth-century Spanish kabbalist Joseph Gikatilla wrote that the service may be thought of as a ladder "reaching up to heaven." Our goal is to reach the highest rung, to experience the unity of being that is pure peace. If this does not correlate with your experience, it is understandable. Few of us have been taught how to climb up that ladder, or how to come back down, and most of the existing directions are in rabbinic Hebrew. I want to help you get started. Here is a basic menu of spirit for a morning service followed by a diagram of the ladder of prayer. We will then go on to explore several courses to create a taste of satisfying personal and collective prayer possibilities.

A MENU OF SPIRIT: THE INFRASTRUCTURE OF A JEWISH SERVICE

Menu Note: Items in italics on the left are part of morning services only. Except for the Torah service, which is held only on Monday, Thursday, and Saturday, the rest of the menu is the form for almost every service.

Intent	Associated Traditional Prayer
Awakening to a new day	*modeh [m] modah [f] ani*
Becoming conscious of your body	*asher yatzar*
Incorporating the intellect [mind]	*la-asok b'divrei torah*
Acknowledging your pure soul [spirit]	*elohai neshamah*
Morning blessings	*birhot ha-shahar*
Getting in touch with feelings; raising energy	*tehillim*—"psalms"
Awe at the coherence of creation	*borhu*
Giving and receiving love	*shema* and adjacent blessings

Liberation from our concern with history	*ga-al yisrael*
Expressing the prayer of your heart	*amidah*
Receiving guidance and healing	Torah service
Committing to engaged living	*aleynu*
Fulfilling the mitzvah of remembrance	*kaddish*
Emerging spiritually revitalized	*adon olam*

Do you known the term *daven* (dah-vehn)? Daven is the Yiddish word for really praying from your heart and with your whole body, to connect you to what feels "divine." Davenology, then, is the study of how Jewish prayer becomes meaningful so as to touch your spirit. To do that, let's look at the flow of services from a viewpoint inspired by Rabbi David Wolfe-Blank, of blessed memory.

RECIPE #2:
The
Davenology
Ladder

Following is a diagram showing the intended flow of a traditional prayer service viewed as a ladder. Note the movement up and down through four dimensions of experience: physical grounding, emotional satisfaction, intellectual expansion, and spiritual connection.

Are there any surprises for you on the ladder? You can raise questions about this view of the service with your teachers and online at www.ReclaimingJudaism.org.

People often ask why the *amidah*, personal prayer, is at the top of the ladder while the Torah service is one *madrega*, "step," down. This bears reflection. One reason might be that

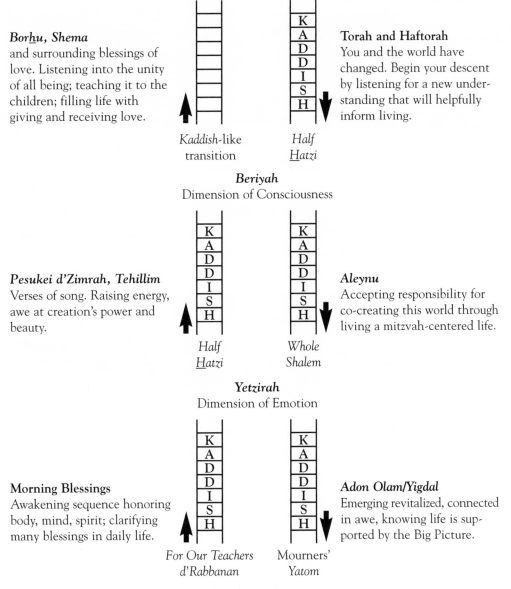

Atzilut
Dimension of Being

Amidah
Finding and Expressing the Prayer of Your Heart

Borhu, Shema
and surrounding blessings of love. Listening into the unity of all being; teaching it to the children; filling life with giving and receiving love.

Kaddish-like transition

K
A
D
D
I
S
H

Half Hatzi

Torah and Haftorah
You and the world have changed. Begin your descent by listening for a new understanding that will helpfully inform living.

Beriyah
Dimension of Consciousness

Pesukei d'Zimrah, Tehillim
Verses of song. Raising energy, awe at creation's power and beauty.

Half Hatzi

Whole Shalem

Aleynu
Accepting responsibility for co-creating this world through living a mitzvah-centered life.

Yetzirah
Dimension of Emotion

Morning Blessings
Awakening sequence honoring body, mind, spirit; clarifying many blessings in daily life.

For Our Teachers d'Rabbanan

Mourners' Yatom

Adon Olam/Yigdal
Emerging revitalized, connected in awe, knowing life is supported by the Big Picture.

Assiyah
Dimension of Physical Manifestation

Figure 1.1 Ladder of Meaning and Spirit: Jewish Morning Prayer Practice

finding and expressing the prayer of your heart is your highest ascent, where your soul flies up inside you, whispering your hopes and needs. This prepares you to be a somewhat new person when you leave the privacy of your *amidah* to rejoin those around you in welcoming the Torah. Each of you will have changed, so the meaning of what you hear in Torah will have changed. First your heart flies up and then you come back a step to earth to listen for answers to the immediate questions of your life.

The experience of the ladder of davening can be described as a process innate to all of creation, *ratzo v'shov*, "running and returning." *Ratzo* likens the soul to a flame. The kindled candle flame rushes upward, its energy consumed in merging with the unity of all being. And the body is the wick that requires the soul to also *shuv*, "return." Just as evaporated water returns in the form of rain to nourish the earth, so too your soul returns to be of service in the vital physical dimension of action in this life. In this model "intellect" is likened to water and "emotions" to flame. Figure 1.1, the Ladder of Meaning and Spirit, shows the balance of passing through emotion and entering intellect, and then doing the reverse, ultimately returning to a grounded state of active being. This is the nutrient cycle of Jewish daily prayer beginning with Morning Blessings.

PREPARATION FOR PRAYER

In chapter 5, "Living a Mitzvah-Centered Life," you will find teachings about the *tallit*—a special prayer shawl—and the ritual headcovering known as a yarmulke (Yiddish) or *kippah* (Hebrew) that can support and amplify your Jewish prayer experience. In addition to putting on these special garments, however, in the talmudic period the sages would prepare for prayer by meditating for one hour before the formal prayer service. Serious instructors use prep-time to become emotionally and intellectually ready for class. Artists and athletes have many ways to stretch and prepare themselves. *Your* preparation for prayer will positively affect the quality of your experience. I have found that cultivating a Jewish morning practice can be very valuable. This section offers a guide for how to do that.

While you might be inclined to enter the day with a *kvetch*, Judaism offers a spiritual stretch in the form of liturgy for guiding your awakening into an expression of gratitude and praise for the gift of another day of soulful life inside the miracle we call a body, surrounded by the blessings of creation.

The items in italics on the left side of the menu of spirit (see pp. 13–14) highlight a beautiful preparatory part of morning prayer that begins with awakening.

RECIPE #3:
Contemplative
Awakening

The starting point for Jewish morning practice is to awaken into a sense of wonder and appreciation for creation and the mystery of renewed life via the prayer portal known as *modeh ani*. You might do this from your bed, in a comfortable sitting position, or perhaps in a garden or park. While it can also be done in synagogue, traditional congregations generally assume that members have already completed this prayer at home. The following method can also be applied to any verse of Torah or prayer.

- Settle yourself into a comfortable position with a copy of the following verse from the morning *modeh ani* prayer on the table or floor in front of you.

modeh ani [m] modah ani [f]	I am praising
l'fanehah	into Your face [or before You]
meleh [some prefer "*ruah*"]	King/organizing principle [some prefer "breath"]
hai	of life
v'kayam	sustaining all.

- Allow yourself the luxury of getting acquainted with the verse. Think about what the words might mean to you. Let as many permutations as possible arise.
- What does it feel like to pray *l'fanehah*, "into the face," of G*d? Historically this phrase was translated as "before G*d," as in "before a king," but we can take the equally available translation of "into Your face" and experience a different face of what you might call G*d. Begin to notice what can be praised around and within you. What are the praiseworthy faces of G*d in your life?
- When you feel ready, leave your study of the verse and take some time to relax. Notice and follow your breathing.
- Gently set free any emotions and any distracting or even interesting images or thoughts that might arise as this recipe continues. You might imagine that such thoughts are hot-air balloons and let

them drift upward and out of sight. Or, imagine them as a sound like the whistle of a train that fades out of earshot. Being gentle with your spirit is essential. Don't punish yourself for being distracted. Instead, lovingly set the errant thought aside for another time. Even really interesting thoughts are distractions from this process; bless them to return on a different occasion.

- It usually helps to keep your eyes open but unfocused. Closing your eyes just might put you to sleep. Begin to repeat the verse in a tone that is comfortable for you, or as a familiar chant or melody.

- Let yourself fill with the emotions that are evoked by repeating this verse. Keep reciting or chanting the phrase over and over. (Sound files for verses of prayer cited in *Meaning and Mitzvah* are posted at www.ReclaimingJudaism.org).

- Keep going. Take regular breaths from deep in your abdomen. At some point you'll probably become bored. That's normal. Push through the boredom and keep chanting until you are one with the chant; until it's pouring through you like the air you are breathing; until you *become* the chant.

- Now is the most precious time. After perhaps five minutes, or however long you can continue, gradually slow the pace of your prayer until you cease to vocalize the words and simply hear them inside yourself.

- Gradually bring your internal chant to an end. You will be filled with a kind of energy that will now begin to affect your consciousness further. Keep breathing normally. Remain still and silent.

- In the silence, note your physical and emotional state. This process of contemplation based on an attitude of praise may lead to openings in your awareness that come in the form of a comforting color, a clear sound, a skin sensation, or, for some, a great feeling of peaceful centeredness. Dwell in and with tender curiosity explore this rich silence a while longer.

- To emerge, begin to notice your breathing. Send a blessing to the Source of Life for constructing you so magnificently that you are able to have this experience, for sending you awareness and blessing. Take note of the amount of time you took to complete this process; as runners do, you might gradually want to stretch for the duration of your practice.

CHERISH THE SILENCE

You have just been introduced to one form of Jewish meditation. As an experience, it is quite different from what many people fear meditation will be; namely, a tedious session of sitting in silence. In this practice, silence provides a vessel for spirit you have constructed by studying and contemplating a verse that lets the experience of authentic praise come to life within you.

The Torah relates: "To You silence is praise" (Psalm 65:2). You could never figure this out from most translations, the word-filled prayer book, or most sermons. Is a heartwarming insightful silence your first association with most Jewish gatherings?

Many people who were left unsatisfied by the dominant forms of Judaism in the twentieth century are very happy about the current restoration of meditation as a Jewish practice. When services are full of responsive or congregational readings, the value of the prayers tends to be lost, run over without the space necessary to connect with their meaning in a way that makes it possible to gain insight or enter into *devekut*, "intimacy," with the Source of Life. It's like trying to read a book of poetry in one brief sitting and expecting to get very much out of it. Jewish meditation is one of the most recently recovered reagents for bringing our traditions alive.

Silence as a route to holiness is still unusual,
unfamiliar, and even uncomfortable for many of us.
In our media and work-saturated culture,
silence is rare—a luxury really.

Is the silence in your home cold and lonely?
Is someone shutting you out?
Or being shut out by you?
Do you often keep the TV or radio on
so that you don't feel so alone?

What was the quality of silence
in your home growing up?
Have you ever experienced
a warm silence?

What might Torah mean by the verse:
"To You silence is praise"?

The healing, warm silence at the end of a Jewish chanting meditation can be a very precious feeling. It does, however, require some personal discipline—that you temporarily cease multitasking, remain in the moment, and train your spiritual muscles through repetition. Note that meditation is not an end in itself, but rather a way to connect with the depth of the prayers and recognize the abundance and eternity of which we are all a part.

The goal of Jewish meditation practice is not to transcend the body in order to spend as much of our lives as possible in an altered state, outside of family and community life. It is rather to provide insight and energy for the fullest expression of life, including the grounding, inspiration, and moral strength required to work on yourself and the world. Personally, I resisted a long time before trying anything labeled meditation. It was as if I feared I would die or fall into some ecstatic state, never to return. The word *fear* is an acronym for *False Evidence Appearing Real*.

There are many myths that can create the fears that get in the way of our benefiting from the ancient practice of Jewish meditation. You may have heard it said that whether you meditate using Hebrew or, let's say, Sanskrit, it doesn't matter; or, that if you simply chant any mantra-like formula, do the movements, or follow your breath, the practices will work their magic. This is only superficially true. Each element on the "menu" of a Jewish prayer service contains particular nutrients and is part of a very deliberate, integrative order of experience. With practice, it has become clear to me that our tradition's specific prayers *do* matter if you want to truly experience the gift of Judaism as a spiritual path. This form of meditation is one way to gradually develop a deep relationship with the prayers. I recommend that you expand your repertoire gradually, rather than risk choking on the whole enchilada.

A PRODUCT LABEL WARNING

Like anything that stimulates pleasure, meditation can be overdone. I do not recommend the extensive practice of meditation without a balanced complement of practices that include your work in the world, Torah study, prayer, mitzvot, and the celebration of holy days and life-cycle events. Sometimes meditation will bring up very strong feelings or a new awareness that deserves serious consideration. This may prove a good indicator that it is time to seek the guidance of a spiritually aware therapist or a clinically trained clergy person. As personal issues emerge, get worked through, and melt away, your Jewish spiritual practices will serve as both a mirror for your evolving self and a source of connection to the awesomeness of being alive.

BECOMING CONSCIOUS OF YOUR BODY

Jewish morning practice includes a prayer of appreciation for the body. Judaism teaches that the body is a temple, a vessel to be cared for and treasured. Rabbi Zalman Schachter-Shalomi describes the body as "the marvelous instrument on which the soul plays life for G*d."

The *asher yatzar* prayer for the body is generally invoked after you finish your first trip to the bathroom. Despite the delicacy of most "translations," the language of this prayer is very direct:

Let us bless that which fashioned the human
with wisdom and created within:
n'kah-veem, n'kah-veem   Openings, openings!
halooleem, halooleem Hollows, hollows!
It is revealed and well known
before the *keesay,* "seat" of Your glory
*["keesay" also refers to toilet; the ancients were likely
aware of some humor here]*
that if one of them would be ruptured or sealed
it would be impossible to sustain life
or to stand before You even one hour.
baruh atah adonai   Blessed is G*d [Threshold of Awareness]
rofei hawl bah-sahr   Healing all flesh
u'maflee la-ah-sote   Making of wonders [like us!]

INCORPORATING THE INTELLECT

The traditional prayer service offers a bit of text study at this point in morning practice, helping you to move from appreciation of your body into appreciation of the power of the mind. Before such contemplation study, however, there is the blessing for study.

baruh atah adonai	Blessed is Adonai, [Threshold of Awareness]
eloheynu	Our G*d,
meleh ha-olam	Organizing Principle of the Universe
asher	which
kidshanu	makes us holy
b'mitzvotav	through mitzvot, "sacred acts of consciousness"
v'tzivanu	guiding us

la-asok	to be occupied
b'divrei	in matters/words of
torah	Torah.

Classical commentaries on the practice of blessing suggest that all can be lost by neglecting to pray this particular blessing. Why? Because we are on a slippery slope that begins with taking Torah for granted and leads to taking each amazing facet of creation for granted, right up to our slipping into imagining that *we* are the source of the abundance and diversity of creation.

Judaism offers a view of creation as full of abundance and "very good." Not perfect, but very good. And humans are described in Genesis as created "in the image of G*d," meaning that we are responsible for the quality of life around us. So it is our practice to become a source of blessing by contributing to the flow of abundance through cultivating the attitude and practice of generosity each day.

RECIPE # 4:
Generosity
Practice

For your contemplation, here is an interpretive translation of a text taken from the Mishnah that is one of the texts in the daily prayer book traditionally studied at this point in morning practice:

These are the matters upon which there is no upper limit: the size of the corner of your field which you leave for the poor to glean from [*What does this mean in modern terms; how can a corporation leave gleanings?*], giving away the first fruits of your trees [*Could this mean donating the first fruits or proceeds of your efforts? The first dividend, the first sale, the first prize won?*], the elevation offering [*In the Temple this was an offering connected with making a trip to Jerusalem. Hold up your hands and make a plan to offer up something of yours for a higher purpose. Does the physical movement increase the power of your intention?*] and deeds of loving-kindness [*in Judaism giving time is a mitzvah distinct from giving goods or money*], and learning Torah [*or, you might say, "talmuding Torah"—making our own commentary, comprising reactions, thoughts, and practices on the concepts we receive when reading Torah*].

To all of these the sages could imagine no limits. If you journal, you might make note of when you incorporate reflection on this text into your regular morning practice and see, after some months, what the effect of this nutrient has been.

THE BLESSING OF HAVING A SOUL

The primary metaphor for the soul in Jewish literature is the light of a flame. We are adjured by the sages to be tender when near another soul, lest our words or actions dim or extinguish this precious gift that defines life. Our liturgy teaches that each body serves as the vessel for a pure soul. This purity is renewable; each day the soul receives another pure white page of possibility on which to inscribe its choices. Connecting with the presence of your pure soul is the next step in a traditional Jewish morning practice.

You might begin by contemplating and chanting the following phrase from the morning prayer for the soul. You can use the meditative technique that was illustrated for the *modeh ani*.

elohai neshamah sheh	My G*d the soul you have
nah-tah-tah bi te-ho-rah hee	placed in me, pure is she.

I discovered another way to contemplate the soul during one of my spiritual adventures, a tour of the headquarters of the Lubavitch H̲asidim. An Orthodox community with many mystical traditions, they also separate men and women during prayer. My guide escorted me many levels up to the empty women's balcony. From there, I peered down through the one-way glass partition upon a sea of men, clustered in groups of ten or more, praying the weekday morning prayers. Each cluster was vigorously and tunefully praying a different part of the service. How intriguing! Upon arriving, a few of the men planted and lit five candles in their own individual shoe boxes of sand. (The sand is for fire safety.) Each then began meditating in front of the candles as a start to his weekday morning prayer practice. Why five candles?

Those candles represent the Jewish mystical tradition of the five levels of the soul. The following recipe is one of several variant models for this practice.

You can engage in this flame practice on your own or lead it for a group. If you do this with a group, let your guests know you have a guided visualization to share that will involve some chanting first and some silence afterward. Tell them you will

RECIPE #5:
The Five
Levels of Soul

let them know when to emerge from the silence, which will last for a few minutes.

- Light one candle or five—in candleholders or sand trays, or just place the idea of the flame in your own and any participants' imaginations.
- Focusing softly on the flames, begin to chant the *elohai neshamah*. Recite this together slowly, over and over; let it become a chant.
- Very slowly describe each of the levels of soul. (To view a diagram of the five levels of the soul, visit www.rebgoldie.com/flame.htm.) Be sure to leave quiet time between each one. Reflecting upon and feeling each level can be interesting and pleasurable. Each level deserves time.
  - ✦ *Nefesh*. The blue core of the flame is the first level of soul. This is where you sense your soul and body connect, your center of vitality. Imagine where this place of soul and body connection is for you.
  - ✦ *Rua<u>h</u>*. The yellow band of the flame is the layer of anger, joy, sadness—your feelings.
  - ✦ *Neshamah*. The orange band of the flame. You are more than merely your feelings; you have another level of soul: your personality, thoughts, memories, opinions, and innovations.
  - ✦ *<u>H</u>ayah*, the black farfrizzlings that come off into the air as the flame burns, represent your intuition. This is also the quality of soul that helps you to stay alive during times when it feels as if you are clawing at the ground with your fingernails to survive, to tolerate the pains of life.

✦ *Ye<u>h</u>idah*, the candle's heat and light. Who can say where this begins and ends? This is where your soul is unified and undifferentiated from All Being. This is where you occupy space in creation, where you are needed in particular. You contribute uniquely and at the same time you are in *ye<u>h</u>idut*, "unity," as the drop of water is with the ocean, as the leaf is with the tree, as the heat and light of the flame are simultaneously part of the shining of the original light of creation.

• Let a warm silence prevail.

• When you feel ready, chant the *elohai neshamah* prayer softly again. Has its meaning begun to shift as a result of this flame practice?

Sometimes when leading the flame visualization for a community, I sense the flame of each soul in the room expanding along with mine, radiating through shining faces and great hearts far beyond each physical body, a light that comes through us from the Source of all energy and creation, and, suddenly, the menorah of humanity is revealed. Still, reading about my mystical experiences isn't having your own. Hopefully, reading about my mystical experiences is pleasurable and stimulates useful thoughts, possibilities, and feelings. Even so, it is much like showing a postcard of a fountain or picture of someone flying a plane—the words on the back are "Having a great time. Wish you were here." Now it's your turn to try the flame.

RECIPE #6:
Recounting
Your Blessings

One central aspect of Jewish prayer practice is to express blessings that put you in touch with the awe and joy of being alive. Some of these blessings, such as those before meals or candlelighting, may be quite familiar to you, while others will serve you in surprising ways.

For example, the next step in morning prayer practice is to bless the Mystery of the Design of Life, which makes possible such transformations as:

ha notayn la'yah-ayf [m]	Giving strength to the weary
la-yah-ayfah [f] koah	
pokei-ah ivrim	Opening the eyes of the blind
ha-mayhin m'tzadei	Guiding a person's footsteps
gah-ver [m] g'veret [f]	

The traditional list of blessings is well worth looking up in a *siddur,* "prayer book." For today, let's just do one *iyyun tefillah,* or focused prayer study, by looking at the verse "Opening the eyes of the blind." Why include this prayer for all of us? Because it is essential to explore prayer on many levels, from the literal to the metaphorical and mystical. The meaning of each line of any prayer will become more accessible when you keep asking, "How does this phrase apply to me in my own life?"

With regard to *pokei-ah ivrim,* "opening the eyes of the blind":

- Have you been metaphorically blind recently?
- What has come to enhance your awareness?
- Have you achieved a new vision of someone or something?
- Have your eyes been opened to an injustice?

- If so, how will this change the way you live at
  home, at work, or in society?

The power of such a focused study of each morning blessing is that gradually all the meanings you uncover for it will reside on the hard drive of your mind.

For some, cultivating the steps we've studied thus far will suffice as a morning practice. Others will wish to continue with the full range of morning practices at home or in synagogue.

RAISING EMOTIONS

Now we can continue our ascent by entering the level of the psalms, where emotion is aroused and supported.

Did you notice that the order of morning practice begins in a very individual way—with *your* awakening, and *your* reintegration of awareness and gratitude for body, mind, and spirit? You then stayed in personal consciousness during the morning blessings. During a community service, you connect with your own feelings during the next step, chanting of psalms, while also becoming attuned to the spirit of the community within which you pray. The melodies and chants for the psalms will tend to bring your spirit and the group energy into greater harmony.

Psalms express the full range of emotions. When you review the psalms at this point in your practice, key words and phrases may leap out as speaking to you about your inner life. Trust this effect and contemplate the verses to which your soul cleaves. To get you started, here are some verses from traditional psalms that Rabbi Shefa Gold has set to powerful meditative chants she's composed and recorded.

Psalm 23	My cup is full to the brim.
Psalm 30	You established it.
	You have made my mountain strong.
Psalm 30	In the evening one goes to sleep crying,
	but in the morning there is joy.
Psalm 51	Create a pure heart in me.
Psalm 68	As smoke is driven away, so drive them
	[your fears/enemies] away.
Psalm 92	How great are Your works, G*d,
	how very deep are Your designs.
Psalm 119	I have called out with all my heart. Answer me!

Now, let's ascend yet another rung on the davenology ladder. It is time to hear yourself called as a member of an ancient collective consciousness, Israel, that carries the memory of the Oneness of All Being. In a communal service there is first an antiphonal blessing called the *borhu* and then comes the *shema*, derived from Torah, where Moses calls out to gather the people together in the wilderness. *Shema*—listen in on the party line of All Being and know All is One.

SHEMA AND HER BLESSINGS

In addition to being a part of every service, the *shema* is also written on the scroll inside every mezuzah and in the meditative aids known as *tefillin* and it is the meditation for going to sleep and when the soul is preparing to leave the body at death. The *shema* first appears in Deuteronomy 6:4:

| *shema* | Listen [put your consciousness online] |
| *yisrael* | the part of you that wrestles with awareness |

	[*yisrael* is the name Jacob receives after wrestling with an "angel" in the night]
adonai	*yud hey vav hey*—the Process of All Being
eloheynu	our G*d
adonai	*yud hey vav hey*—
ehad	is one
v'ahavtah et	so love
adonai eloheh'hah	based on your G*d understanding
b'hol l'vav'hah	with all your heart
u'v'hol nafsh'hah	with all your soul
u'v'hol m'o-deh'hah	and with all your ability.

The prayer just before the *shema* in each service talks about the experience of being loved, a precondition for the ability to listen fully. The prayer just after says, now knowing the Oneness, teach this to your children, and stay connected to this awareness throughout your day.

Note: Find more on the *shema* in chapter 5, "Living a Mitzvah-Centered Life."

It is customary after saying the last words of the section of Deuteronomy that contains the *shema* to continue into the first word of the next prayer, *emet*, "truth." So these three words are:

RECIPE #7:
What Is
Truth?

adonai eloheyhem emet	*yud hey vav hey*, your G*d is truth.

Many religious seekers are looking for "the truth," and many religions claim to offer "the truth." Of what value could it be to say that G*d is truth? *Emet*, the Hebrew word for truth, is composed of precisely the first, middle, and last letters of the Hebrew alphabet. There is a Jewish mystical tradition that *aleph* represents your past, *mem* your present, and *taf* your future. So truth is the combination of what was, what is, and what will be. In this prayer the name given for G*d is the tetragrammaton, the four letters of the most sacred name, which is made up of all forms of the verb "to be," for "what was, what is, and what will be." So G*d is not a fixity in Judaism: G*d is a process, life is a process, and truth is a process composed of your past, present, and future.

Why is this prayer located right here? You are at the rung of prayers for preparing yourself for the highest level of the service, finding and expressing the prayer of your heart. Letting go of attachments to what the truth is and opening your heart to new awareness is crucial to achieving a beneficial prayer state. Here is a movement meditation to help this section of morning prayer take hold more fully in your consciousness.

- Take the form of the letter *aleph* by lifting your hands above your head and opening your stance slightly wider than normal. In some way connect with the sweep of your past in your imagination.
- Allow your fingers to touch and lower your arms so they are in front of you. Now you are a letter *mem*, containing this moment, the present, what is.
- Bend down and became a *taf* by gracefully opening your arms outward. Give birth, yield, release into your future.

As this becomes a familiar movement sequence, you might slowly chant *eh-mmm-meht, eh-mmmm-meht*. A sequence of emotional states may fill you as the expansive power of this approach to G*d and truth so carefully preserved for us by our ancestors continues to reveal itself to you. Should you weep, allow this to happen fully for you; it is a very holy moment. *Emet* contains two Hebrew words, *em*, "mother" and *met*, "death." Certain illusions die during this meditation, and something feeling much like truth may be born.

BEYOND LITURGY

Congratulations, you have reached the apex of morning practice, the center of the *shaḥarit* service. Here there is the *amidah*, a safe, supportive opportunity for you to whisper your truth out loud or inside your head. This interval of white space is a gift that Jewish tradition suggests you give yourself three times a day. During the *amidah* your own thoughts, hopes, pleas, and aspirations get to take center stage in your consciousness. What a sane notion for the multitasking times in which we live!

Recently while I was serving as guest rabbi at a Reform synagogue, a woman came up to me after services to ask if it was all right to cry during services. Overhearing her, another woman exclaimed that she had felt the same way, that she had been afraid her heart was going to break open. Then, her face breaking into a gentle smile, she changed her words: "No, not afraid. Turning my worries into hopes and prayers, I felt a good kind of sad, and then a hopeful kind of happy."

Did anyone ever encourage you to pray more than just what the words say on the page? Looking back on your life,

what might have been the prayer of your heart
had you been given support to express it?

The term *pray* does not have to mean praying to G*d. For
some, the concept of G*d is actually an impediment to prayer.
Expressing the prayer of your heart can seem awkward at first.
What could you possibly add, after all, to the flow of words in
the Jewish prayer book? But your whole body, mind, and soul
will feel different afterward. In fact, the siddur itself actually
offers some eighteen printed sequential prayers, often chanted
aloud by the service leader, to serve as springboards for shaping
the prayer of your heart during the *amidah*. Of the over one
hundred traditional blessings available for each day, the three
daily repetitions of these eighteen make up more than half.
The next recipe translates those eighteen springboards into a
starter model for personal prayer. Later, as your Hebrew skills
improve, and should you take time to study each of the *amidah*
prayers, you will find them individually subtle and important,
much like the equalizer adjustments on your sound system.

RECIPE #8:
Finding Your
Inner *Amidah*

You might try the practice below at home, or, as an experiment, take this section with you to synagogue.

- Remember specific ancestors—creative ones, patriarchs, matriarchs, teachers. Send your awareness to
  the ancestor(s) you feel has/have been guiding your
  steps most recently. Ask for his/her/their blessing.
- Begin to envision, one by one, those in your family

who have been specially blessed this week and/or those who need guidance. Imagine blessings and love going from your heart to theirs. Pray that they notice the warning signs and hidden supports that line the paths of their lives. Pray that they receive the guidance and blessings they need.

- Touch your own heart with your hand. Let the ways in which you may feel blessed and/or desire support and guidance enter your awareness. Imagine the blessings you need, the qualities you hope to develop in yourself; whisper these aloud. Ask for guidance and support for yourself.

- Take a satellite view of the planet into your aware-ness. Recall specific moments of peace—perhaps the end of apartheid in South Africa or the removal of the Berlin wall. Zoom in on those specific coun-tries and neighborhoods where war, disease, and weather have provoked tragedies. Send blessings and love from your heart to those tragic regions. Ask that all creation be able to experience *oseh shalom*—comfort, guidance, support, and peace.

Add these four *amidah* nutrients to your life up to three times daily. If you continue the practice, you will likely notice subtle changes occurring in your relationships with those for whom you have prayed. With practice, it will become more and more natural and helpful to review the key members of your inner circle and pray for them to receive the help and support they need. It will also become natural to do this for yourself. If you are a parent, a grandparent, or an educator, you are also in position to be a spiritual mentor, to help our youth clarify their hopes and dreams by expressing them through regular personal prayer.

BRIDGES FOR LOSS AND HOLINESS

Our religious services contain a recurring prayer known as the *kaddish*, from the same root as *kedushah*, "holiness." There are several forms of *kaddish* in every service, the most common being *kaddish shalem*, "a whole Kaddish," *hatzi kaddish*, "partial" *kaddish*, the *kaddish d'rabbanan*, which honors learned teachers, and *kaddish yatom*, the Mourners' *kaddish*. Each of these provides a segue of spirit from one major section of the service to the next.

In *Kohelet* (Ecclesiastes) 12:16, our sages offer the image of a silver thread that connects each individual soul to All Being in this life and, if there is one, the next. If you have recited *kaddish* as a mourner, perhaps you sensed how it embroiders a gradual patch of holiness over the raw hole in your life. Even while engaged in their own dying, many people express comfort in the knowledge that their children or friends will attend services to say *kaddish* in their memory. The gentle rhythmic words of the prayer come to form a mantra of comfort for mourners.

All the forms of *kaddish* are written in Aramaic, the daily language of our people when we lived under the Greeks and Romans. The prayer was deliberately put in the vernacular so that people could understand what they were saying even if they weren't literate in Hebrew. Every *kaddish* begins by emphasizing awe and the ongoing process of creation:

yitgadal, v'yitkadash, *sh'may rabbah*	May "The Name" [all the amazing, combined facets of creation; That Which Is Becoming] grow greater and holier.

Kaddish is about holiness in all its manifestations. It is essentially a Jewish definition and affirmation of G*d as the "Big Picture" we will never be able to back up far enough from our location within creation to "see" or comprehend as a whole. It is intended to help us hold onto the mystery and awe of That Which Makes Life. What any human can see and understand of "It" is limited, in the words of the *kaddish*, because "It":

l'aylah mi-kawl bir<u>h</u>atah	is really higher than any blessings,
v'sheerahtah, toosh b'<u>h</u>ah-tah	songs, praises,
v'neh-<u>h</u>eh-mah-tah	and comfort
dah'ahmee-rahn b'ahl-mah	utterable in this world.

One of the functions of daily services is to create a place for hearts broken open with grief, hearts leaping in joy, hearts reaching for connection to come together in a group of people with common interests and mutual understanding, who share a desire for grounding, strength, and connection. It is traditional not to say the Mourners' *kaddish* except in community, with at least ten Jews, a minyan, present.

Many people feel incomplete when a death goes unmarked by some form of this ritual. A "delay-mourning-now, pay-in-emotional-perpetuity" problem develops. Although some persistently patriarchal Jewish communities prevent women from standing to say this as a public prayer, many welcome all who mourn to engage in the healing supported by the congregational saying of *kaddish*. In fact, the Mourners' *kaddish* is embedded in every service to help transform the pain of loss that results from a loved one's dying into a mitzvah, a "sacred act of consciousness," honoring the way she or he lived and will continue to live in your memory as a source of love, learning, and inspiration. In the beginning, the Aramaic words may feel foreign and awkward, but by the end of a healthy term of mourning, the phrases will be familiar friends.

In addition to those for whom we grieve personally, there are also those who have no one to say *kaddish* for them, or whose deaths are so radical and public that we need to deal with them as a community. Not too long ago, while I stood sadly on the deck of the memorial for those who lie beneath the waters at Pearl Harbor, the natural response for a Jewish person came through. I began to whisper in the old European Ashkenazi pronunciation still in use in my childhood, *yisgadal, v'yiskadash, sh'may* … and there seemed to be an echo coming back at me, carrying the words. It wasn't an echo. Among the hundreds of tourists present in that one moment, scattered about the platform, other Jews were joining me. Softly a minyan of memory linked up in that dark place, inviting holiness. While in a large crowd at Ground Zero of the former World Trade Center, I whispered *kaddish* again, with the same response. The silver cord bringing holiness into the heaviness connected us all. (For a guide to Jewish mourning practices, visit www.ReclaimingJudaism.org.)

MOVEMENT AS A FORM OF JEWISH PRAYER PRACTICE

Concerned about how the neighbors would interpret our religious practices (one word about how Native Americans were treated was hint enough), most Jews, upon arriving in America, increasingly emphasized the importance of decorum—pews, hushed tones, music relegated to hidden choirs, and much more. Even earlier, conditioned by frequent periods of having to pray while huddled and hiding, our prayer movements were reduced to a *shuckle*, a form of fervent swaying or bending in rhythm to our prayer plus the occasional bow.

In the Talmud, however, Rabbi Akiva is described as having moved across the room by means of numerous "bowings and prostrations." Also, in the Bera<u>h</u>ot section of the Talmud we find a residual yoga-like instruction to bow during prayer "by hyperextending your spine" in such a way that you could "read the face of a coin were it to be placed at your feet." In many communities it is customary at one point in the Yom Kippur service for the leader(s) to lie flat, prostrate on the floor. Creative communities sometimes invite everyone to experience this deference to the Flow of Life, a deeply physical form of awe and relief at releasing into the Great Stream of Experience.

The passionate theater of full-body prayer is also expressed in the Torah, as when, for example, the prophet Miriam leads the women with her tambourine in a prayer dance of joy after the Israelites have crossed the sea. Perhaps you recall the scene in the movie version of *The Chosen* where the rebbe dances in ecstasy?

> To dance in prayer, to move in prayer,
> for those who are able,

can bring the prayer, you, and the community
so fully into life that you enter *hitgashmiut,*
the experience of being transported into pure spirit,
far beyond *gashmiut,* "materiality."

Rebbe Naḥman of Breslov (1720–1810) recognized the ecstasy of *hitgashmiut* as an essential nutrient for human healing, especially for and to prevent depression. "Acquire the habit of singing a tune. It will give you new life and fill you with joy. Take on the habit of dancing. It will displace depression and dispel hardship."

Those who attend Congregation B'nai Jeshurun in New York City will find more than one thousand people—singles, moms and dads with new babies, couples, elders—singing and dancing in joy in the midst of the Friday night service. In another part of the city, some Breslov Ḥasidic congregations have the tradition of engaging in ecstatic dance for an entire hour after the formal service. Hebrew letter-based movement meditation practices called Ophanim, Otiyot Ḥayyot, and *Aleph-Bet* Yoga are also now widely taught privately and in retreat settings.

RECIPE #9:
Beyond Self
through
Dance and
Song

You don't have to join the dancers to lift prayer to new heights at services. Let all who can join in, and the rest of us will benefit from drinking in the sight.

Dance as a form of prayer at services benefits from planning:

• Organize a regular congregational *ruaḥ,* "spirit,"
corps, to try out new melodies, prayer interpreta-

tions, and dances in order to recommend which
ones to introduce at services and special programs.
The *ruaḥ* corps members (of various ages) can then
be among the first to leap up and begin the
dancing, offering their hands to others, helping the
energy of the prayer to build.

> Guidance also comes through
> this vessel, the body
> as song and poetry.
> As the words and music
> reach into our hearts,
> they remind us of our Source
> and reconnect us to our purpose
> —*Rabbi Hannah Tiferet Siegel*

- Select simple steps and try to find a way for dance or
  prayer melodies to become known to the community
  before they are introduced at services. Send tapes to
  congregants so they can boogie to new melodies
  during commutes and at home, and if their practice
  is to drive on Shabbat or holidays, to sweeten the
  spirit of the drive to synagogue. If there is a religious
  school or club for various ages in the congregation,
  arrange for *ruaḥ* corps members to stop in during the
  week for a brief rally of song and dance so that by
  the time everyone gathers for prayer, the melody will
  feel comfortable.
- Build a vocabulary of spirit by teaching—in your
  newsletter, at classes, or on your website—a group
  of words that is part of the prayer to which the

dance is performed. Invite various interpretations of the prayer's meaning and post these on your congregational website or in your newsletter.

- To enter into the state of *hitgashmiut*, to "dematerialize" all aches and pains of body and soul and feel part of the Great Unity of Spirit, the dance must go on past the initial awkwardness, into fun; past boredom, until you don't want to stop. Eventually your physical limitations or the constraints of time will call you back to earth, where you will land, in my experience, quite high and expanded. To a certain extent, this can even be accomplished alone.

- It's important to keep the same dances and melodies in your community's service repertoire for an extended period of time. Most people love what is familiar in services, and when they feel that familiar place satisfied, they will be more open to innovation. At year's end, when you honor the multitudes of volunteers it takes to have a spiritually vital congregation, remember to include the *rua<u>h</u>* corps, even though, surely, the dance itself will be its own reward.

BODY-CENTERED PRACTICES

In addition to dance, *shuckling*, bowing, and the morning prayer for the body, Judaism has many other powerful body-centered prayers and movement practices. There are mystical phrases for a couple to say before making love; *mikvah*, a "full-body immersion" practice (page 158); and hand-washing practices. The last of these actually saved Jewish lives when, long before germ theory and sanitation practices, we were blessed with the guidance to wash our hands before eating.

Before eating, it is still a Jewish tradition to wash your hands, lift them up, as a surgeon does, and say the associated blessing. In some Jewish homes you may have noticed a beautiful two-handled ritual cup created for this hand-washing practice. It is a custom of ours to do *hiddur mitzvah*, "embroider a deed," or beautify a sacred act, in this case by selecting a specially designed cup reserved for the ritual. But if you don't have one, any cup will surely do. This practice is also meant to be done upon awakening, as a mini-*mikvah* immersion ritual for rebirthing yourself into every new day.

RECIPE #10:
Hand
Washing as a
Spiritual
Practice

- Look down at your own hands. What character and
  history do you see there? Imagine imbuing your
  hands with your strongest intentions to infuse holiness, healing, and caring into the world. Now elevate your hands, elbows bent, palms raised. Look
  up past your hands. Do this same motion again and
  reflect on the power within you to affect the world
  around you. Do the motion again and pray for your
  best intentions to be realized in your actions.
  Imagine doing this mind-shift before every meal.
  Would it affect your spiritual life?

When organizing a workshop for Jewish health professionals recently, I offered a similar experiment. Participants lifted up their hands after washing, which was nothing new for them. Then, each prayed in her own words—for courage, wisdom, for her hands to remain supple, to not miss anything she needed to feel during an examination, to be guided in her work, to no longer be called that pejorative term "health care provider," to reclaim his role as healer, to regain respect, to be forgiven for errors, and to be blessed with enough time and ability to create meaningful relationships with patients and family.

- Perhaps you are an artist, artisan, volunteer, writer, teacher, broker, parent, or lawyer. Whatever your holy work may be, look at your hands, lift them up. What blessing do you need for these hands of yours and their work in this world?
- When was the last time you washed and dried someone else's hands? Imagine you have filled a beautiful, large washing cup with warm water. A friend, a dear one, comes to perform this ritual with you. She removes any rings in order to be fully available to the power of the moment and holds hands outstretched as you pour the warm water over one side, then the next. Then your dear one holds his or her hands aloft and begins the blessing. Can you feel a gentle ripple in the fabric of creation because of *your* combined love and attention in this moment?
- Imagine drying the hands of this one for whom you care, gently, sweetly, attentively. If the person is

your life partner, replace the ring(s) on his fingers, meeting his eyes. Before restoring the ring(s), ask yourself: "Am I willing to recommit to this person?" Some couples repeat their actual vows to one another during this ritual. Just knowing that such a mutual moment of truth is approaching can lead to a process that makes for healing.

- Are you single? Be the high priest of your own life. This ritual does not require a partner. Go to the sink. Take off your rings, if you wear any. Take time to warm the water, to contemplate your hands, to focus your intentions. Fill a cup and then pour the water over each hand in turn. So unique and needed, or you wouldn't have been created, is your particular life. Lift up your warm, wet hands and the fabric of creation comes with you. Infuse the room, and by extension your world, with the quality of your intentions for living. Dry your hands lovingly.

- You have probably washed a child's hands at some point. Has a child ever washed your hands for you? Engaging in this process together, helping a young person to understand the power of intentions and blessings and the unique feeling of infusing life with holiness, is a way to engage in spiritual parenting.

- Add the power of a Hebrew blessing. With your hands held aloft, you can use the traditional opening for most blessings or a gender-neutral prayer opening.

Traditional beginning for a blessing:

baru<u>h</u> atah adonai	Blessed is *yud hey vav hey*
eloheynu mele<u>h</u> ha-olam	Our G*d, Organizing Principle of the Universe
asher kidshanu b'mitzvotav	that makes us holy through sacred acts of consciousness
v'tzivanu al n'tilaht yah-dah-yim	and guidance regarding the lifting up of hands.

ENGAGING THE POWER OF BLESSING

There are traditional blessings for acquiring new clothes, seeing a rainbow, witnessing a thunderstorm, eating a new fruit for the first time, before and after meals, for Torah reading, marriage, sitting in a *sukkah*, even a practice of putting your own handmade blessing sign over a limb of the first tree you see blossoming in the spring, and many more. Those who live in accordance with Jewish law actually make some one hundred blessings a day! Consciously watching for the blessings that flow through each day can bring needed light into inner darkness. Pausing to bless is a spiritual practice that helps the fullness of the moment to ripen.

There are three general categories of *bera<u>h</u>ot*, "blessings": *ha-na'ah*, for material pleasures, *hoda-ah*, for special times, and *al ha-mitzvot*, for engaging in mitzvot. Each blessing invites the thought—"How amazing it is that this is possible at all." For example, that we ever discovered that the seeds in a plant like wheat could be separated from the chaff and mixed with ingredients that turn what was in the earth into bread! The root of the word for blessing, *bera<u>h</u>ah*, includes the words for bend, knee, and pond, so, mystically, the opening formulation of a blessing can be understood as: "I bend my knee at the Pond of Blessings, the Threshold of Eternity ..." after which you add the particular ending for the blessing of the moment at hand—for example, for a meal with bread: *ha-motzi lehem min ha-aretz*, "that brings forth bread from the earth." To learn traditional blessing formulations, visit www.Reclaiming Judaism.org, and for a gender-free prayerbook reframing of the traditional liturgy seek out Marcia Falk's *The Book of Blessings*. For a highly accessible and deeper look, be sure to read Rabbi Marcia Prager's *The Path of Blessing: Experiencing the Energy and Abundance of the Divine* (Jewish Lights).

WHAT ABOUT THE NEED FOR CHANGE?

Judaism, as Rabbi Mordecai Kaplan so succinctly stated, is an "evolving civilization." Some prayers, such as the *shema* and the prayer for healing, the *ana el na*, are so ancient that they are found directly in the Bible. Kings David and Solomon commissioned many of the psalms and are also said to have composed many of them. As a matter of perspective, Abraham's time was somewhere between 2000 and 1400 BCE but the *l'hah dodi* and the Mourners' *kaddish* didn't enter the siddur until the thirteenth century, more than two thousand years later.

At one time the sacrificial system took the place of liturgy, but that system ended in the year 70 CE when the Temple and Jerusalem were conquered by the Romans, who then exiled our people. Since that time, prayers have continually been developed and incorporated into our tradition. Not only is adding to the liturgy a long-standing Jewish sacred art, but changes have been made over time to even the most basic of prayers. For example, in the evening service, the Talmud says a key prayer used to read: *oseh shalom u'vorei et ha-ra*, blessing the "Maker of peace and Creator of evil." Today, however, we find this prayer printed and prayed as: *oseh shalom u'vorei et ha-kol*, "Maker of peace and Creator of everything." The Shabbat *kiddush* blessing over the wine also seems to have changed since the Talmud describes it as having seventy words and now it does not.

More recently, female biblical ancestors are being added to prayers that used to invoke only patriarchs. Many congregations now expand the original ancestral lineage found in prayer as:

eloheynu v'elohey avoteynu	Our G*d and G*d of our fathers
elohey avraham, elohey hitzhak v'elohey yaacov.	G*d of Abraham, G*d of Isaac, and G*d of Jacob

either by changing the first line to:

v'elohey horeynu	G*d of our parents,

or by adding:

v'elohey imoteynu	and G*d of our mothers

and then:

v'elohey sarah, elohey rivkah,	and G*d of Sarah, G*d of Rebecca

v'elohey rahel v'leya	and G*d of Rachel and Leah

These additions led to the following curious exchange at my first pulpit:

"Rabbi, Rabbi! We went to a big synagogue in Cherry Hill for our cousin's bar mitzvah."

"Isn't that the first one you attended that wasn't here at our synagogue? How was it?"

"Really weird. Rabbi, they are so radical! Can you imagine? They took the *imahot* [matriarchs] out of the service!"

Most denominations have also expanded the prayer for peace, which concludes the *kaddish* and the *amidah*:

ya-ahseh shalom aleynu	Make peace for us
v'al kol yisrael	And for all Israel

and today we add:

v'al kol yoshvei teiveyl	And for all who dwell on this planet.

Go ahead; it's a good place to say it: Amen!

2

Reclaiming G*d with Integrity

When I see Your heaven,
the work of Your fingers,
moon and stars arrayed,
I wonder:
What is a human being
that You might remember us?
Of a child born to an earthling,
could You take notice?

—*Psalm 8:4*

Are you uncomfortable with the "G" word? I used to be. For me it conjured up obsolete, old-paradigm, fixed-Father images, prayers unfulfilled, and traumas that a caring G*d would surely have averted. Well, those were expectations embedded in Western culture and are not among the great messages that Judaism has to offer, though few of us were helped to realize this in religious school. In fact, the Jewish people stubbornly, even vehemently, refuse to put a wise old man, a resurrected young man, or any image at all above the caption for G*d in our hearts and our sacred texts. As a youth, Abraham learned this, and perhaps this is why he toppled the idols his father carved for a living. And, of course, one of the top ten instructions derived at Sinai is to worship "no graven images." Holding the mystery open and not imposing an image on it is such an important practice that even in English some of us write "G-d", "G!d," or, as I do, "G*d," to indicate that what is meant only points toward the most encompassing term for G*d in our tradition, *ayn sof*, "Without End," "the place to which no eye can penetrate, being most hidden and difficult to fathom" (Zohar 232b).

Instead of "image,"
a helpful term to use in a spiritual context
tends to be "experience."
Just as an orb of light radiates outward
in infinite directions, so too, humans can have
infinite varieties of G*d experience.
Because humans are complex beings,
we can hold opposing G*d ideas and experiences
as simultaneously meaningful.

Are there any moments in your life where you might say, "Yes, perhaps I too have experienced what humans might call 'G*d'"? Do any of the following reflect your view of the Divine?

RECIPE #11:
Your G*d
Experiences

Place a mark beside those that apply to you thus far in your life. It is fine to check contradictory experiences.

❑ For me, G*d expresses the Oneness of the evolving cosmos.

❑ G*d is that to which I cry out when I am in pain.

❑ G*d is a still, small voice within me.

❑ I do not believe there is a listening G*d.

❑ G*d is a direction for my awe and praise of the stunning fabric of creation of which we are a small part.

❑ Creation is a chaotic, random, emotion-free phenomenon. I experience no inherent Unified Field of Being.

❑ G*d is what you and I resemble in both our creative and destructive nature.

❑ G*d is creation evolving with an inherent curiosity and affinity for making connections, seeking all possibilities, becoming what it is becoming.

❑ As the head talks to the hand, the heart to the legs, as we have an inner intelligence that communicates with the whole, so too is there such an inner communication within all of life.

❑ G*d is the encoded consciousness of a unified cosmos that is innately aware of its needs, constantly deploying us as an important part of the present and future.

❑ G*d is the cosmos' ability to interact with us—our choices shifting its realities, its unfolding realities impacting on our choices.

❏ G*d is as vast and inconceivable as infinity and as
   intimate and familiar as love and death.
❏ G*d is our sensation of the deep structure of matter
   through which the words and the very letters of
   Torah, like a form of DNA, encode ways of
   achieving healing, connection, loving-kindness,
   and peace.
❏ Please add your own experiences/words.

Perhaps you will find refreshing the responses my colleagues
Rabbis Jane Litman and Marcia Prager have given to questions about whether they believe in G*d:

> When people ask if I *believe* in G*d,
> I say, "No."

> Then I surprise them by saying
> "Actually, I *experience* G*d."

Many who find the list above largely true may still feel
uncomfortable with the G word. As we will continue to see,
the term G*d is, indeed, sorely limiting in a way the Hebrew
language could never tolerate. Take a look at Figure 2.1, a
chart of terms for G*d. Do any of the terms call to you at this
point in your day, at this juncture in your life?

CALLING OUT

While many G*d experiences happen through synchronicity,
when we are engaged in acts of kindness or creativity, and

עליון *el elyon* Most High	אהיה *ehyeh* I Am Becoming, I Will Be	חי העולמים *hei ha-olamim* Life of All the Worlds	השם *ha-shem* The Name	מקור החיים *m'kor ha-hayyim* Source of Life
המקום *ha-makom* The Place	צור *tzur* Rock	שכינה *shehinah* Presence	מעוז חיי *maoz hayai* Fortress of My Life	שדי *shaddai* Breast / Hill, Nurturing One
אלהים *elohim* G*d of Creation	ריבונו של עולם *ribono shel olam* Master of Eternity	אין סוף *ayn sof* Infinite Without End	רחמנא *rahamana* Womb-like Compassionate One	אל ראי *el ro-ee* G*d Who Sees Me
הקדוש ברוך הוה *ha-kadosh baruh hu* The Holy One of Blessing	סתר לי *sehter li* My Hiding Place	עתיק יומין *atik yomin* Ancient of Days	אור מקיף *or makif* Surrounding Light	מעין רז *ma'yan raz* Well of Mystery
גלא רזין *galei rah-zin* Revealer of Mysteries	עזר לי *ozer li* My Help	אדוני *adonai* My Lord, Threshold, Connector	אור פנימי *or p'nimi* Light Within	מגן *magen* Shield
יוער *yotzer* Form Giver	תפארת *tiferet* Beauty	יסוד *yesod* Foundation	אלה *ayla* Power	שלום *shalom* Peace

Figure 2.1 Some of the many terms for G*d in Torah, Talmud, and Zohar.

through the power of nature, there are specific practices designed to increase our sense of spiritual connection. Here is a story that teaches the steps of how a practice called *hitbod-edut*, "making yourself alone," can transform isolation into spiritual intimacy.

Ten years is a long time to be alone, especially when you add another ten during which your marriage is dying. Friday afternoons were bad, particularly before holiday weekends. My patients and staff meant well: "Have a good Memorial Day weekend, Dr. Bub!" or "Are you spending Thanksgiving with your family, Dr. Bub?" However, their anticipation and good wishes only made my spirits sink lower as I thought of my empty-bedroom house in the woods. Gone were my wife, three children, and two dogs. My friends in the suburbs were mostly married and immersed in the busyness of family, community, and golf. They were rarely available on holidays.

When I found myself in a serious relationship, I would hang on long after the relationship was dead, because even a moribund relationship at least partially filled the emptiness I felt inside. When I was not in a relationship, I would drive sixty miles to Philadelphia to date. When not on a date, I squandered hours talking to single friends on the phone or chatting up prospective dates. In short, I did everything I could to keep from being alone; but talking to, or dating, other lonely people was not a cure for my loneliness.

By the time my friend Goldie invited me to spend New Year's Eve with her at Elat Chayyim, a Jewish Renewal retreat center in the Catskills, I had given up singles weekends completely. In this case, however, she explained that even though most of the participants would be single, the weekend had more to do with experiencing spirituality than finding a mate or simply partying. Spirituality was about the interconnectedness of all, and we would be expanding our spiritual awareness.

Huh? I didn't know what she was talking about, but I didn't want to spend New Year's Eve alone watching TV, nor did I want to hang out with the respiratory therapist I'd been dating. She had a good body, but what can you say about a respiratory therapist who smokes? So spirituality it was going to be. I packed my *kippah* and kept my expectations low.

That year, New Year's Eve fell on a Saturday night. We'd had a very relaxing day of prayer, text study and discussion, music and dance. As midnight approached, about twenty of us gravitated to the gazebo for a night of hot-tubbing by the light of the many candles that circled the tub. Under the influence of some kosher champagne, we soaked and sang chants, the words irreverently sabotaged by inserting "hot tub" in place of each *halleluyah*. The party ended at about 4:00 a.m. with some of us running into the snow to cool off and the rest of us heading off to bed.

If this was spirituality, I was all for it. But I still didn't understand it, and the next day I still had a nagging sense of aloneness despite having had the best New Year's in a long time. Talking to Goldie about it over breakfast helped me clarify the issues. In a few months, my daughter was going to have her first child. I was going to be a grandpa! And here I was, still living the single life. I had idolized my grandparents; they had been an ideal couple. There seemed no chance that I would be playing the role of grandfather in the way it had been modeled for me. In this wonderful supportive environment, with a caring friend, my desire for a meaningful serious relationship ironically felt more acute.

Goldie suggested I attend the afternoon session being led by her friend Rabbi Shefa Gold. I remember her words: "No one is ever disappointed by Shefa." I wanted to return to bed

(I'd only slept for three hours), but decided I could always nod off or slip away.

About thirty of us sat in a circle in a yurt—a very large, Mongolian-style, round tent located in a meadow. Shefa's instructions were simple. First we would chant a Hebrew phrase for about ten minutes while she played the drum, then we would quietly slip out and walk to a place where we could be alone. The one condition for this time alone was that we speak nonstop to G*d.

Speak to G*d?

Even if we didn't have anything specific to say, she continued, we were to keep talking without a break. We were to talk continuously and not worry if we didn't make much sense. And we were then to listen to what G*d said back to us. After a while, she would ring the bell for us to return and quietly resume our seats.

It was winter. The snow was halfway up to my knees when I found myself in front of a grove of trees talking to G*d. "I can't believe I'm doing this, G*d. This is such nonsense. What am I doing here, walking and talking in the cold to a three-letter word I don't believe in? I mean, what's the point? Do you even understand English? Mary had a little lamb, its fleece as white as snow and everywhere ... how is this accomplishing anything? I wonder if my absence will be noticed if I slink off to my room?"

Others had found their own spots in the woods and were earnestly talking to themselves or G*d. I watched them for a moment before continuing: "I'm alone. I feel so alone. G*d, even though there are people in the area, I feel it's just me and the trees. Yes, the trees—big tall ones, middle-sized young ones, and baby ones—little naked saplings bravely sticking out through the snow. Look at them struggling to survive. They don't have any leaves. I wonder if they feel the cold? The baby trees make me think of my future grandchild. He or she will be young and vulnerable. Ha, there are even dead old trees. They remind me of my father and grandfather. These are generations of trees. You know, G*d, they are no different from my family. My grandparents' generation, my parents' generation, mine, my daughter's, my future grandchild's—I'm connected to all these generations, five in all."

I took this in and wondered why I had never before thought of myself as being part of a lineage. Unlike the solitary figures muttering around me, the trees were clumped in a grove that stretched way out into the distance and across the horizon.

"G*d! Just like my family, living to the west in Seattle, north in Canada, east in Israel, and south in Australia and South Africa. It's not only about lineage. I am connected to a huge family that stretches across the world."

A voice entered my consciousness and began repeating: "You are not alone, you are not alone, you are not alone." No, I am not alone. Being alone is just an image I have of myself. Gently, then persistently, the bell intruded.

As I made my way back to the yurt, the "You are not alone" kept repeating.

Was that the voice of G*d she'd referred to? It's really a thought, not a voice, I told myself. Nothing mysterious … just some awareness. Still, I had been answered, even if the answer came from my own head.

I settled down in my spot in the circle. Shefa placed a bowl in the center. "Here are some slips of paper with quotes. You might each take one as we end this session."

I picked up one of the slips, not looking at it until I was outside. Then I read the words, written by Pablo Casals to his grandchild, which say in part: "When will we teach our children in school what they are? We should say to each of them:

Do you know what you are? You are a marvel. You are unique. In all of the world there is no other child exactly like you … And, when you grow up, can you then harm another who is, like you, a marvel?"

Now I was confused. To his grandchild. Is this just a coincidence? Guess I'll give this slip to my daughter. She can give it to my grandchild when he or she is old enough to appreciate it. No! Wait! I'll be this child's Grandpa. We'll have our own unique relationship: One day I'll give it to this grandchild myself. Gradually I experienced a glimmer of insight: I am not alone. I am connected not only to family and to the planet, but also to some Presence that can respond to my deepest private fears.

I never attended another singles retreat. Two years later Goldie and I were married. She travels internationally as a teacher; I go along sometimes, but I still spend a good deal of time on my own. Being alone does not necessarily mean feeling alone. The emptiness is gone.

This is a practice for allowing everything that needs to come up to arise and be released, so that you empty your vessel completely, making space for a renewed spirit to flow in. It requires no Hebrew; it is something every human can do.

RECIPE #12:
Hitbodedut

- This can be done on a mountaintop, in a desert, in your closet, an empty house, a car, or silently inside yourself anywhere.
- The process is to just start: speak, shout, sing, snap sticks, safely toss stones, do all it takes to empty yourself completely.

- When one wave of stuff you have to express comes to an end, make nonsense sounds until the next wave hits.
- When you are empty, listen, look, stay present and open to interpreting what comes into your range of awareness.

Can you imagine yourself taking the risk of spiritual adventuring that Dr. Bub did? Perhaps you have already. It's not a new technique; in fact, *hitbodedut*, "making yourself alone with G*d," is at least as old as Moses. He was always climbing a mountain to get away from it all, seeking and attaining new vision and wisdom. The Torah stories of his vision quests hold ideas and ideals that remain valuable to this day. Let's look in on one day when Moses poured out his greatest concern at a sacred site called *har ha-elohim*, "Mountain of the G*d," and heard one of the most profound answers in human history.

STEPPING OFF THE COMFORTABLE PATH

This pivotal biblical event begins when Moses, the adopted Israelite son of one of the pharaoh's daughters, seems assured of a lifelong position as an Egyptian prince. Suddenly—the Torah doesn't say why—Moses steps off the path of his comfortable life to "go out to his brothers and see their burdens" (Exodus 2:11). He then kills a taskmaster whom he finds beating an Israelite slave. Moses soon learns that he was seen committing this murder, and he has to flee because the pharaoh seeks his compensatory death.

Moses builds a whole new life in the nearby nation of Midian. He marries Tzipora, the daughter of a Midianite priest, and works for her family as a shepherd. But what of those he left behind? Does Moses ever think of going back? Does he wonder if his mother, brother, sister, foster mother, and perhaps friends from his days in the palace are still alive, and does he hope to see them again? How confusing is it for Moses, raised not in an Israelite home but an Egyptian palace, to have, at this point, a Midianite household, life, and wife? What is Moses' sense of identity? Does the plight of his enslaved family of origin gnaw at him? Is dramatic social change already on his mind? How much of an internship did he experience in the pharaoh's and his Midianite father-in-law's households? Back in Egypt he may yet have connections in government, especially among his peers. The anthropological record shows the death of the pharaoh at around this time. This would mean his foster grandfather is no longer the pharaoh. And the text itself (Exodus 4:19) confirms that: "Everyone has died who was seeking to kill you." So Moses' criminal act is likely to have been forgotten and it is probably safe to go back.

Perhaps this accounts for why Moses again steps off the now-customary pastoral path of his life one day when he is out grazing the flocks (Exodus 3:1). He takes them beyond the regular grazing area, all the way to the mountain with an Israelite G*d name, *har ha-elohim*, "Mountain of the G*d." Could it be that Moses is on a spiritual quest for insight and direction?

On *har ha-elohim* Moses sees the burning bush. A sign! Finding a sign in nature is an important part of a vision quest in many cultures. Where is the voice of G*d during an epiphany? Beyond or within? Take away the names and listen to the text: "I have seen the suffering of my people in Egypt and heard their cries ... I know their suffering. I will go down to rescue them from the Egyptians and bring them to a good and spacious land ..." and "Who am I to go to Pharaoh to free the Israelites from Egypt?" Did you know that Moses, *mosheh* in Hebrew *(mem shin hey)*, when held to a mirror spells *hashem* *(hey shin mem)*, "The Name"?

משה   השמ
השם

Figure 2.2 Moses/*hashem* as mirror images

The actual term *hashem* appears in the book of the Torah that is Moses' life review in Deuteronomy 28:58—*hashem ha-ni__h__bad v'ha-norah*, "The Name that is honored and awe-some/fearsome." What name? In the burning bush text, Moses confronts the question of how to put a name on this G*d experience that gives him the inspiration, support, and confidence to act. He puts his question out as part of his vision quest and receives the confusing answer: "*ehyeh ima__h__*—I will be with you." He then inquires again, perhaps thinking that a more specific question will elicit a more definitive response. "What name might I give to tell others with whom I have been speaking?"

Now, at that time, monotheism already existed in Egypt, having arisen during the reign of Akhenaten, who insisted that there was only one god, Aten, and that only Aten was to be worshiped. But the answer that comes to Moses is not a local household god name or a god quality common to the

times, like Neteret, Ra, or Amen. Instead Moses encounters a
no-label, radical brand of G*d awareness that requires a future-
form verb sequence to express it at all: *ehyeh asher ehyeh.* "I am
what I am," is the durative translation, but equally grammati-
cally accurate is "I am becoming what I am becoming," or, "I
will be what I will be."

> Moses discovers that G*d
> is the infinite force for change.
> The Totality that we can never back up
> far enough to fully comprehend
> is revealed as utterly dynamic.

> Moses learns The Name
> of what is literally the truth:

> *Ehyeh asher ehyeh,*
> "I am becoming what I am becoming"

> Injustice need not stand.
> All That Is and Will Be
> can and does change.

As it evolves, Judaism accepts this Power of Becoming as the
root of all hope, curiosity, creativity, and life force. We refer to
the Big Picture G*d, beyond the physical laws of our corner of
creation, as *ayn sof,* "Without Limit," and accept the stories in
the Torah as presenting many faces of G*d, a necessarily
stepped-down model of the Limitless to help each of us continue to hold ourselves open to also being able to say *ehyeh
asher ehyeh,* "I will be what I will be," because it is equally our

nature to change and develop. When we are humble enough to set aside seeing humanity as the crown of creation, we fulfill the mitzvah of being y'rei hashem—living in a state of awe-filled awareness of The Name that inspires revolutionary participation in creation. This awe helps us to remember that our filters of perception remove much of what is and let us see only what we can take in at this point in human development. As it says in Torah, "No one can see Me and live."

PRACTICES WITH THE NAME

In almost every blessing, this recognition of the infinite capacity for change is invoked by the presence of a unique, four-letter Hebrew name comprising all the third-person forms of the verb "to be." The letters are *yud hey vav hey*. The Torah explains that this name was spoken only on Yom Kippur by the high priest. Do you know which name I mean? Try to conceive a cartoon depicting Moses standing on the bank of the Red Sea and appealing to G*d for help. A nearby Israelite with a strong Texas accent looks at Moses, shrugs, takes out a bucket, and begins bailing, saying: "Okay, Aaaaa'll do it maaaah way and you do it yaaaah way." Well, Yahweh could never have been the pronunciation because there is no "w" sound in Hebrew. *Jehovah* arises as a preferred pronunciation form in sixteenth-century Christianity, but, of course, there is no "j" sound in Hebrew either. Passed on in secret through the generations from high priest to high priest, the pronunciation of *yud hey vav hey* has been lost, as far as we know. It is a long-standing Jewish spiritual practice not to utilize any possible or imagined pronunciations for the tetragrammaton, but to preserve the mystery and expansiveness of the whole G*d category in humble recognition that humans will never be able to back up far enough to comprehend the Big Picture. Accordingly, when the tetragrammaton appears in text or prayer and needs to be represented in speech, the term *adonai*, "My Lord," is substituted. This is a fascinating term, based, as previously mentioned, on the root *ehden*, "Threshold." The tetragrammaton letters are, however, considered important for contemplation by the kabbalists, who offer many meditation variations, including the following practice.

In Genesis 1:27 humans are depicted as created *b'tzelem elohim*, "in the image of G*d." Does this mean that G*d is in all of us; that, like Moses, we each mirror something about G*d? To experience this idea through a meditation, our mystics teach us to walk and breathe the *yud hey vav hey* name by correlating it with the four major sections of the human body (see Figure 2.3). You can do this sitting or walking. Imagine as follows:

RECIPE #13:
An Embodied
Meditation
on the Letters

> Your head is the comma-shaped
>   letter called the *yud*.
> Your upper body—shoulders and
>   two arms—are the first *hey*.
> Your trunk or spine is the straight
>   line of the *vav*.
> Your hips and legs—the final *hey*.

י
ה
ו
ה

Figure 2.3 In the image of God

- Walk along, moving each letter of your body in sequence, saying the sequence above aloud as a chant.
- If you do this outside in a park—sensing yourself as one of the infinite possible images of G*d—look around you. Every person is a *yud hey vav hey*. Each one of us is as precious as every other facet of being.
- After you have done this for quite some time, you might take your walking meditation a bit further, saying to yourself with each step: "I am becoming what I am becoming."
- What do you notice about yourself? About creation? About your experience of G*d?
- Begin to notice that these letters also appear in the shapes of branches, buildings, windows—everywhere. Take your time doing this; the experience unfolds in many ways during a lifetime.

RECIPE #14:
Breathing
the Name

Hityashvut means feeling settled, calm, possessed of equanimity, and is one of the goals of spiritual practice. I recently taught this entry-level technique at an American Medical Association national conference on physician health. Many of the people in the room had no history of spiritual practice, and yet the physical and awareness effects of this simple, ancient practice astonished them.

- Stand comfortably, with your head aligned to the heavens and your feet grounded on earth.

- Find an image for breathing that works for you—
  perhaps that of filling yourself with an energizing or
  purifying color of light or air.
- As in Figure 2.3, envision your head as the first
  letter, *yud*.
- With your arms outstretched in front of you, palms
  up, draw into your head a breath full of energy, life,
  or light, according to your preference. Allow your
  arms to come toward your body as you do this.
- Your shoulders and two arms form a *hey*. As you
  exhale to release this light, energy, life breath that
  filled your *yud*, release it through a flowing release
  of your arms outward and down, forming your *hey*.
- Your torso, from the pelvis upward, is your letter *vav*.
- Relax your upper *hey*, shoulders and arms.
- Open your legs slightly and draw the image of
  energy, air, breath of life up through your pelvis,
  through your organs, and into your heart.
- Your hips and legs form the final *hey* in The Name.
  Release the breath of air, light, life through your
  heart, organs, pelvis into your legs, and reground it
  in the earth.
- Practice this sacred cycle until you can do it
  without reading the instructions and are just
  praying/breathing in *yud*, exhaling *hey*, inhaling
  vav, exhaling *hey*, breathing naturally with an
  awareness of being filled with the Source of Life
  and Light.

This can be silently practiced almost anywhere—between
classes, patients, during services, while stuck in traffic. Derived

from medieval mystical sources, it also fits well with the verse in the morning prayer service: *elohai neshamah shenatata bi tehorah hee*, "G*d, the breath you have placed in me, pure is She."

COMPASSIONATE PRESENCE

During much of early post-exilic Jewish civilization, the Torah was read not only in Hebrew but also via *targumim*, "translations," into Aramaic, the lingua franca of rabbinic times, because most of the people couldn't understand a word of Hebrew. These *targumim* often prove to be more than translations, however, because the words they use to translate and the phrases they insert to explain meaning within these "translations" give insight into what the people of the time believed.

In these *targumim*, the term *shehinah* is used when the presence of G*d is felt to come down—as a cloud on the tabernacle, on a mountain, into or in front of the camp of the Israelites. In the book of Lamentations, G*d is described as weeping along with the traumatized remnant of our people being sent into exile, and the G*d name commentators associate with this weeping One is *shehinah*, One Who Dwells—within, among, between all of us. This quality of G*d experience is so precious as to inform a verse of traditional prayer and meditation—*shviti shehinah l'negdi tamid*, "I set the *shehinah* in my foreground, "always," *shviti*, "dwelling," *l'negdi*, "across from me." *Shehinah* is a feminine noun, and requires feminine verbs and feminine descriptor suffixes. Later, in the Zohar and other Jewish mystical sources, *shehinah*, also called *shabbat*, the "Sabbath," takes on feminine cultural and sexual characteristics such as receptivity and the capacity to be present in human acts of kindness, compassion, and connection, in contrast to *meleh*, another familiar name for G*d, which has strong masculine associations from its literal root meaning "king" and its mystical sense of being the law, structure, and ordering of the universe. You can find more on *shehinah* and *meleh* in *Reclaiming Judaism as a Spiritual Practice: Holy Days and Shabbat* (Jewish Lights).

SHVITI MEDITATION

On the walls of Jewish homes you can sometimes find a work of art called a *shviti*, from our study verse, *shviti shehinah*. Many symbols and shapes are traditional for *shviti* designs, particularly a menorah and a Star of David, but the sacred letters *yud hey vav hey* are essential to any *shviti* because, in whatever form, it is a meditation tool and it is those letters and the many ways "The Name" comes to hold meaning for you over time that are the primary focus of the meditation. Often a *shviti* will visually incorporate verses from Torah, especially psalms (in Hebrew or your native language). By making a regular practice of gazing at a *shviti* to see which words, letters, or images draw your attention on any particular day, new awareness and often a centered feeling of connection and greater well-being will emerge. You could enlarge the stacked image of the letters in Figure 2.3 to use for such a purpose and then add your own decorative touches and frame, or check Judaica shops for some of the many beautiful versions available.

A *shviti* could be viewed as a Jewish mirror, except that instead of seeing your corporeal self, the letters invite you to bring forth your higher self. In the Torah, when a person's name is called twice, it is a divine calling. There is a time when Moses himself engages in such a calling (Exodus 34:6–7). When he descends from the mountain to find that the people have forged a golden calf to use in their worship, he drops the first set of mitzvot engraved on two stones, and they shatter. How can *hashem* and Moses get back that loving feeling for each other and the people? Moses' strategy is to reconnect with the qualities of higher self by invoking G*d's name twice and calling out numerous positive attributes of G*d. Similarly, after calling G*d by name twice, a set of Thirteen Attributes derived from Moses' experience are also read out intensively seven times during the closing service of Yom Kippur:

adonai	adonai
adonai	adonai
el	G*d
ra<u>h</u>um	compassionate
v'hanun	and gracefully giving
ere<u>h</u> apayim	slow to anger
v'rav <u>h</u>esed	and abundant in lovingkindness
v'emet	and truthful
notzair <u>h</u>esed la-ah-lah-fim	bestowing abundance to thousands of generations [before and after us]
noseh avon	forgiving distortions
va'feshah	and misdeeds
v'hah-tah	and missed marks
v'nah-keh	and so [all is] clean/cleared.

While on the one hand, Moses' invocation could be seen as a prayer of petition or "sucking up to what is projected as G*d's good side," it is Moses who has to reconcile with the people and mentor them beyond this period of doubt and trauma. So what Moses called out may well have been the very qualities he most needed to reconnect with in himself in order to begin to heal the anger he felt at the people's betrayal. Rabbi Moshe Cordevero, an important kabbalist known as the Ramak (1522–1570), taught in his work *Tomer Devorah* that reciting the Thirteen Attributes is not enough for us either; they are crafted with the intent that we will emulate them. Meditatively chanting these Thirteen Attributes to experience them as your own is a practice many do each day. You can find a chant audio file for this at www.ReclaimingJudaism.org.

shviti shehinah l'negdi tamid   I will set the presence of God across from me always

The Talmud tells of a sage who had a disfigured person walk along with him whenever he went out. "Why do you do this?" many inquired. "To see the presence of G*d in another; this is *shviti shehinah l'negdi tamid*." Perhaps he did more than that; maybe the recipient of his *shehinah* attention experienced the unique fulfillment of feeling honored and dignified. Tzeitl Locher of Groenekan, the Netherlands, teaches how to give this gift of holy wholeness to yourself or another, and her work is adapted below.

RECIPE #15:
Shviti
Practice

- Find a willing partner, someone upon whom you are going to visualize the *yud hey vav hey*.
- Begin to see a glowing *yud* upon your partner's forehead.
- See the light of the *yud* filling this person's mind.
- Visualize the *hey* of your partner's shoulders, arms, and fingers filling with Presence, with *shehinah* energy.
- Now visualize the top part of the *vav* touching and opening your partner's heart and then filling the spine downwards.
- Visualize the *hey* of your partner's hips and legs filling with Presence, the *shehinah* energy flowing down to his or her toes.
- Continue chanting until your partner is filled in this way a second time.
- Now have your partner chant this full sequence to you.
- Then simultaneously start to chant to each other.

This is a way to fulfill the mitzvah found in Deuteronomy 6:5, "to love G*d with all your heart, your soul, and all your ability."

This can also be done alone, imagining someone you are concerned about who is far away, or you can focus upon your own body.

PRACTICING SAFE SPIRITUALITY

In every generation, humanity has its share of "meshuganosis," a social condition that makes pious fools of otherwise intelligent people. These people take the loudest voices in their heads to be the word of G*d and then inflict horrific damage on themselves and others in G*d's name. In Jewish practice, it is the still, small voice underneath the loud voices of ego and indoctrination that is identified as a G*d experience.

Rav Avraham Kook taught that the soul is always trying to be fully realized, that it strives to link with every aspect of the life of the universe, and that a sudden spiritual clarity *can* come to every person. First, however, you have to create an inner clearing by removing what he termed "toxic stones," the heaviness of heart that accrues after years of not listening within.

So each of us is a sanctuary, a sacred space that needs special care. Moses is told to have the people *asu li mikdash v'shahanti b'tokham*, "Make a sanctuary for me, so that I can dwell within them" (Exodus 25:8). Even a prophet had to learn this.

The prophet Elijah is described in the First Book of Kings as being existentially confronted by God:

"Why are you here, Elijah?"

"I am moved by zeal—the Israelites have forsaken Your covenant, torn down Your altars, and put Your prophets to the sword. I alone am left, and they are out to take my life."

What a challenging situation—fear combined with the dangerous energy of the zealot. G*d immediately sends Elijah out on a vision quest that distinguishes acts of nature—tornado, earthquake, fire—from the subtle Voice that comes during stillness within.

> Elijah! Go out
> and stand on the mountain
> in the face of
> G*d.

G*d passed by,
and a great and strong wind
tore the mountains
and broke in pieces the rocks
before G*d.

But G*d was not in the wind;
and after the wind an earthquake
But G*d was not in the earthquake;
and after the earthquake a fire;
but G*d was not in the fire;

and after the fire?
a subtle still voice.

—*1 Kings 19:11–13*

Do you, like Elijah, have a whirlwind response voice that gives you guidance, or an earthquake or raging fiery voice within you? Do you know how to become still so that the subtle, wise, higher-self Voice gets a chance to be heard? In the Hasidic source *Eitz Ha-Z'man*, "The Tree of Time," this Voice is described as an echo of the great wisdoms embedded in creation, which can be "polluted" away by the louder voices.

RECIPE #16:
Focusing
Within

The following practice differs from meditation because you are not transcending all to enter the tranquility of the void but going toward equanimity by deeply listening for something new. This is one approach loosely based on a spiritual-health technique called *focusing* that was developed by Dr. Gene Gendlin.

- Sit comfortably with your eyelids lowered but not shut tight. Notice your breath and follow its flow for several breaths. Now put your attention in your heart, your chest, the whole middle of your body. Sit comfortably with eyes softly focused, asking, "How am I?"

- If anything comes up, imagine placing it tenderly on your outstretched palms and promise you will get back to it, but you are going to do something special now that will make you a better partner to this response when you return to it. Create a shelf of honor in your imagination.

- Place each awareness that arises onto this shelf respectfully; you will come back to it later, refreshed and better able to deal with it. After one thing comes and you place it onto the shelf of honor, return to see what else arises. Don't investigate each thing; just let a full inner inventory happen.

- Happy or challenging items may come up. If the feeling is about something difficult, beware of senses or voices within that carry guilt, shame, or say "should" and "if only." Without giving these voices extra weight, let them take their place on the shelf along with the stiller, softer voices. Remember, Ezekiel says the voice of G*d is not in the whirl-wind, the fire, or an earthquake, it is in the stillness, where you can hear a small, soft, subtle voice.

- When you feel empty of life matters to be placed on the shelf of your life during this exercise, sit quietly. Be with yourself. Your body will speak to you, maybe via a glow of happiness, or you could feel like dancing or purring, or sense a tugging, hurt or turmoil somewhere inside. Pick one sense—it might be murky, unclear right now—and rather than thinking about it, feel its effect on your body and spirit. Gently sit with the sensation and where it is within you. Now gradually become curious about it.

- Is there one word, sense, or image that comes up about this matter? What quality helps this place to be better described? Go back and forth between it and the word or sense you have about it until you have a way to describe it. You may want to do this a number of times so that a larger unfolding within is possible than with just one inquiry.

- When you have a good sense of what "this whole thing" is, you can ask this feeling what it needs. Perhaps it is a good feeling that will come out as a prayer of gratitude for life. Or if it is a trouble, ask it what should happen. Ask it what it wants from you. Ask it what's in the way of it becoming OK.

- If you feel stuck, try inviting strength and support from the great dynamic flow of all possibilities in creation to help you. Stay for awhile in this slowish place where new knowings are born. See what comes in there.

- Focusing amplifies and eases the way into engaged spirituality. For example, in the morning blessings, we read a blessing of gratitude for "freeing those who are bound." Focusing can help open up this prayer by asking within, "Where am I currently 'bound?' Hmm. This prayer implies that I could be free—ah … *there* is my longing to be free. What would it be like to be free? Can I 'taste' it? It would be right for me to be free. It says here that G*d—or whatever All That might be called—could free me. How can I relate to this promise of no longer being so bound? Hmm. Some possibilities are coming to mind…."

- Even five minutes of focusing before religious services as a silent way of connecting your needs and longings to your davening experience can make a great difference. Visit www.focusing.org to learn more.

ANGRY WITH G*D

There are some huge blockages to connection for some of us, experiences of an absent or abusing G*d in particular. It is perfectly kosher to get angry with G*d, to express this sense fully and out loud. Even if nothing shifts "out there," doing this can be important for "within." In Mishnah Taanit 3:8, during a drought, the folk character Honi draws a line in the sand before G*d. Well, actually he draws a circle, stands within it, and says, "I will not move from here until You have mercy upon Your children." Then the rain begins to fall lightly. Honi thereupon exclaims, "It is not for this that I have prayed but for rain to fill cisterns, ditches, and caves." And the rain starts to come down with great force. Whereupon Honi exclaims,

"Not for this but for rain of benevolence, blessing, and bounty I pray." And the rain falls in a normal way.

This accusatory precedent matures with time into the diatribe known as the *kaddish* of Rabbi Levi Yitzhak of Berditchev, who lived from 1740 to 1810, and was keenly attuned to the ravages of anti-Semitism in his time.

Good morning to You, Lord, Master of the Universe.
I, Levi Yitzhak, son of Sarah of Berditchev,
I come to You with a judgment from Your people Israel.

What do You want of Your people Israel?
What have You demanded of Your people Israel?

Everywhere I look it says, "Say to the children of Israel,"
And every other verse says, "Speak to the children of Israel,"
And over and over, "Command the children of Israel."

Father, Sweet Father in the Heavens,
How many nations are there in the world?!
Persians, Babylonians, those from Edom …
The Russians, what do they say?
That their czar is the only ruler.
The Prussians, what do they say?
That their kaiser is supreme.
And the English, what do they say?
That George III is the sovereign.

And I, Levi Yitzhak, son of Sarah of Berditchev, say,
"Yisgadal v'yiskadash sh'may rabbah—
Evolving and holy is Your Name."

And I, Levi Yitz<u>h</u>ak, son of Sarah of Berditchev, say,
"From my stand I will not waver,
And from my place I shall not move
Until there be an end to all this."
Yisgadal v'yiskadash sh'may rabbah—
Evolving and Holy is Your Name.

The Torah does not project a perfect G*d. Surprised?
Disappointed? Relieved? Want proof? The Torah projects a
G*d that can be mistaken, forgets, gets surprised, and acts out.
Remember the flood? G*d's first symbol of promise for better
behavior is the rainbow, because there are design flaws in our
very essence as is noted in Genesis 20:8, where G*d is
depicted as doing *teshuvah*, a "turnaround" of awareness and
intention: "I will no longer curse the earth because of the
human, for the imagination of a person's heart is evil from
youth." The rainbow becomes documentation of a cosmic
"oops," as the Creator realizes the creation is equally flawed
and it's not the creation's fault, so to speak.

Like humanity, G*d, in Torah, doesn't stop acting out for
very long. Genesis 16:11 tells part of the story of Hagar, the
mother of Abraham's son Ishmael. Hagar experiences an
annunciation, a *mala<u>h</u> adonai*, "a messenger of G*d," that
informs her G*d will favor her son to father many nations and
that her son Ishmael (*ish*, "man," *mae el*, "from G*d") will be
a "wild ass of a man, his hand against every man, and every
man's hand against him." Might this be a recurrence of the
persona G*d vowed to revoke after the flood? Is that
unbounded aggression reappearing in the form of Ishmael and
his descendents? Can you almost see a warning rainbow

flashing? A few verses later, G*d catches G*d's self at it again and makes a different covenant with the domesticated civilization son model, Isaac.

Hasidic tradition teaches that every character and image in the Torah is a face of G*d. That's right, Pharaoh, Sarah, Ishmael, everyone, every word, and every deed. This helps us understand how Ishmael-like consciousness will become the force of slavery in the Egypt story. And how, when the Israelites cry out, G*d is again depicted as waking up and recovenanting, rewriting the therapy contract if you will, cultivating a new consciousness that comes through as Moses' awareness of a better plan, a new ethical form of civilization created through mitzvot, the living process of Torah.

The healthy exercise of power is so challenging that the sages of the Talmud speak about a G*d that prays and cite as G*d's prayer:

> May it be My will that My mercy should overcome My anger and that My mercy dominate My attributes. May I act with My children with the attribute of mercy, and go beyond the requirements of judgment.
>
> —Berahot 7a

FACING THE ABUSING OR ABSENT G*D

As a rebbe on the road, I love attending or facilitating Jewish women's monthly Rosh Hodesh gatherings, which are held around the time of the new moon throughout the world. These are almost universally openhearted spaces of welcoming and deeply sharing the current challenges and delights in each woman's life. This time, the invitation to attend and help guide a discussion for a gathering in Amsterdam comes only a few days in advance. Old and young, there are a few dozen Dutch Jews and a half-dozen expatriate Americans present. So when the organizer asks, "Rabbi, how long will your talk be?" I feel a little panic. Talk? A talk takes lots of preparation. A small sea of expectant faces is turned my way. How to handle this? Who's here? What's needed? Be quiet all inner thinking, and let my soul become transparent; trust that intuition will dawn.

After the formal introduction, opening song, and learning the names of those present, I make a suggestion: "Instead of a talk, I'd like to offer an option here—for you to witness or participate in a Gestalt-like experiment. It is important to never fully give up your power to a spiritual teacher. Even the most well-intentioned among us can't see all that well into our own shadow-sides, and so you must take responsibility for deciding your own limits. If at any time you feel unsafe or unsure, sit out all or part of this experience, because it is essential to engage in self-care. Also, it is not my intent for us to deal with issues of sexual abuse today, so if this is in your history, please reach for a different order of memories as our experience unfolds."

We begin. "Would everyone please form two lines, face each other, and find a partner across the way with your eyes.

"Now, without receiving an answer, will each of the women in the line on my left please call out to the woman opposite you: 'Where were you?'

"Good. Now, please call out 'Where were you?' seven times, varying your voice each time to try out the feeling of these different tones. Then pause and wait for another instruction.

"Did you notice that sometimes a person from your past seemed to be superimposed on the person receiving in front of you? That's normal. Please take whatever you noticed during this experience and put it into your memory chest.

"Now, the row of women who were the receivers, please do the same; ask the women opposite you seven times in varied voices with a pause between each, 'Where were you?'

"Again, honor what you have noticed by placing it gently into your memory chest. We will continue in the same pattern. After each set of seven, I will give you a different phrase to try out.

"These are the phrases:

" 'Where were you?'
" 'I missed you.'
" 'Don't ever do that to me again.'
" 'That was great. Let's do it again.'
" 'I forgive you.'
" 'I love you.'

"Now, please everyone in the two lines turn your backs to one another and face outward…. We will be repeating the same phrases, out loud, to G*d."

There is an audible gasp. Bomb shelters and World War II memories are still on or very close to the surface of European lands and souls. Some in the room have experienced a long period of chilling silence in their relationship with G*d. While seeking the comfort of synagogues in order to be among their own in a place where familiar melodies and words are recited, it has, nevertheless, been very lonely in G*d's house. Their relationship to G*d has been much like one you might have with a relative you've cut off and with whom you find it harder and harder to reconnect over time.

In this room the wall of silence falls away suddenly as, palpable and surprising, words that have been dammed up are allowed to be voiced.

Many arms are upraised in the instinctive movement of beseeching. One of the Americans races over to me, loudly indicating those arms, demanding that I abort the activity. Distracted from the trance of leading, I feel a rational wave of anxiety—of course, several of the upraised arms reveal the tattooed numbers of concentration camp survivors. I waver in my conviction; intuition is an opportunity, not a directive.

Then, a very elderly survivor turns toward me and the loud American. "Do not dare get in the way of my having a conversation with G*d," she says slowly, with great emphasis, in heavily accented English. "It is long since time, and don't you worry, we survivors know how to take care of ourselves better than you ever will." As the others nod vigorously in agreement, the American looks relieved and goes back to her row. One person leaves, two sit down and remain as witnesses as we continue.

At the end, each woman decides whether to share what this experience of reclaiming G*d has been for her. Many recall with precision when their anger and disillusionment were born and are happy and intrigued at the new sensations aroused by what just happened. When a woman bursts into song, we all join her.

MESSY MESSIANISM

Oy. Messianism is an idea that gets quickly out of hand. Humans are so susceptible to playing "swallow the leader," to accepting the notion that someone may have been or will be anointed with more G*d spark than the next person—that is, be *the* messiah who rescues us from ourselves. This kind of messiah is a post–Five Books of Moses idea; the first five have no ideas about "messiah," *mashiah*, *moshiah*, or afterlife— that's all a later effect of our contact with surrounding cultures.

By 132 CE Rabbi Akiva believed that Bar Kochba ("son of a star"), the leader of the Jewish military revolt against the Romans, was the *mashiah*, "anointed one," the destined next king of Israel. What are the criteria for declaring someone *mashiah*? In 2 Samuel 7:12–13, the details are spelled out: a military leader. One who would return the Jewish people to sovereignty over the lands described in Torah as given to Jacob, end the brutality of life under the Roman Empire, and continue to serve as king in a region that would be idyllically at peace.

Well, Rabbi Akiba lived in turbulent times, and Bar Kochba did, in fact, fight against the Roman Empire and, amazingly, did retake Jerusalem. Born under the "right star," he restored the sacrificial system at the site of the Temple and made plans to rebuild; established a provisional government and began to issue coins in its name. Bar Kochba appeared to fit the expectations of the *mashiah*: a designated military leader from the line of David through his son Solomon who could get "Rome, the lion" to lie down with the inherently disempowered lamb, a.k.a. the Jewish people, to restore our remnant from the four corners of the world to sovereignty in Israel (Isaiah 11:12), which would result in the fulfillment of the vision of Micah: "They shall beat their swords into plowshares, and their spears into pruning hooks; nation shall not lift up sword against nation, neither shall they learn war anymore" (Micah 4:3).

Anthropomorphic messianism has been, well, messy. Even for those who prefer a deliverance model of spirituality that requires the arrival of a G*d-sent individual who will be "The Messiah," it has proved foolish and dangerous to anoint messiahs based on early election returns. The effects of the Bar Kochba rebellion were promising but short-lived. Numerous young men and their followers have bethought themselves messiahs over the years. It seems to be a condition particularly common among charismatic, mystically inclined, relatively young males. As it turned out, Jesus, like Bar Kochba and many after, was also unable to revitalize the Temple, an accomplishment considered one of the messianic criteria. In fact, the Temple was completely destroyed, the Jews were further exiled, and world peace remains a world hope. Another large-scale example comes in the 1600s when a rabbi named Shabbatai Tzvi came along in what was thought to be an auspicious messianic year. Jews by the hundreds of thousands believed him to be "it," sold their businesses and packed up, ready to move to Israel. However, the sultan of the Ottoman Empire was not amused at the socioeconomic disruption of his reign, and Shabbatai Tzvi ended up converting to Islam and living out a life of small-time, ongoing deceptions.

Alas, this anthropomorphic messianism evolved into dogma in some circles. The "have to accept the messiah to pass go and get into heaven" trap fueled horrors like the Crusades and the Spanish Inquisition, as well as a rather inert Vatican response to the Holocaust. It may also have been part of the unspoken, perhaps subconscious rationale of those who turned in or shoveled Jews* into ovens during the Holocaust.

In the twelfth century, even the now-acclaimed, then-controversial physician and community leader Maimonides, in his commentary on Sanhedrin 10:1, lists a set of what he wanted to be seen as the core principles of our faith. These were set into a hymn called the *yigdal* that is found in most every siddur to this day. His list includes *yishlah l'keytz ha-yamin m'sheeheynu,* "He will send our messiah at the end of days." Many of Maimonides' rabbinic peers were appalled and decried his dogmatic approach to Judaism.

Despite the hymn's persistence in the prayer book, Judaism was and remains a nondogmatic tradition in which each person's choice of action and lifestyle reveals his or her sense of "G*d."

Perhaps it's time to concede that the anthropomorphic messiah idea hasn't panned out. It's an emperor of hope with no clothes, and it's decidedly counterproductive in the long term for us to project our societal challenges onto someone else. But, before assigning it the label *anachronism* and consigning the role of messiah to the bygone times of kings and prophets, can *mashiah* be redeemed for contemporary spiritual practice through one of its *penimiut,* "inner meanings"? Reb Nahum of Chernobyl pointed out that the word *messiah* in Hebrew can be understood as *mae-siah,* "from dialogue." As compassionate listening methods and projects continue to multiply, perhaps there will come an end to times as we've known them and the potential for enduring peace. To make this happen, each of us needs to become a *mashiah*—a redeeming presence—in our own lives.

EQUANIMITY PRACTICE

While we have touched on quite a number of practices as portals to G*d experience, I have intentionally sidestepped much in the way of formal theology. The goal of *Meaning and*

Mitzvah is to facilitate spiritual health—for you and for the greater good. What gets learned through the regular embodiment of a practice quickly exceeds anything simply read or learned in a lecture.

And, speaking of repetition, if you have had periods of attending services at synagogue in your life, you are sure to recall the typical closing hymn, *adon olam*. Hidden behind the infinitude of melodies to which this majestic prayer can be sung is a stunning theology that builds on the Hebrew vocabulary you have already encountered. *Adon olam* can be translated as "Threshold of Eternity" and was composed by the eleventh-century mystic Rabbi Shlomo Ibn Gabirol (1021–1058). Ibn Gabirol was treated as a heretic by the Jewish establishment of his time because of his emphasis on secular philosophy and his significant role in introducing Neoplatonism to Europe. His liturgical works have nonetheless long taken center stage in Jewish life and for good reason: *adon olam* offers a possible vantage point from which to achieve an experience of *mohin d'gadlut*, "expanded consciousness," so great that the respectful distance of living the mitzvah of *yirat hashem*, fear/awe of G*d's words and ways, dissolves into a deep and joyful sense of equanimity.

Adon Olam

adon olam	Threshold of Eternity
asher malah	That was the Organizing Principle
b'terem kol y'tzir nivrah	Before everything's form was created,
l'eyt nah-sah	Which was made at a time
b'heftzo kol	Of complete desire.

azai mele<u>h</u>	What a Governing Principle! [King!]
sh'mo nikrah	Let Its Name be called.
v'a<u>h</u>arei ki<u>h</u>-lote ha-kol	And after the end of everything
l'vado	On Its own
yimlo<u>h</u> norah	It will awe/fearsomely reign
v'hu haya	It was
v'hu hoveh	It is
v'hu yih-yeh	It is becoming
b'tifarah	Ever magnificent.
v'hu e<u>h</u>ad	It is a singularity
v'eyn sheyni	There is no second
l'hamshil lo	For analogy
l'ha<u>h</u>birah	To this Composition
b'li reysheet	Without beginning
b'li ta<u>h</u>leet	Without substance
v'lo ha-oze	All force
v'hamisrah	And domination.
v'hu eyli	This is my G*d
v'<u>h</u>ai go-ah-li	The Life that redeems me
v'tzur <u>h</u>evli	The Rock, my umbilical tether
b'eyt tzarah	During times of affliction.
v'hu nissi	It is Miraculous
u'manoce li	My Refuge
m'nat kosi	My Cup's Content
b'yom ekrah	On the day I call out.

b'yado	Into G*d's keeping
afkeed ru<u>h</u>i	I will appoint my soul.
b'eyt ishan	When it's time to enter sleep
v'ah-ee-rah	And upon awakening
v'eem ru<u>h</u>i g'vee-yati	By means of my spirit and my body
adonai li	G*d is there for me
v'loe ee-rah	and so I will not fear.

3

Taking Torah Personally

The Torah is not what it seems.

Much more than a collection of Bible stories,
Torah is the foundational text of Judaism,
one of the most ancient of wisdom traditions.

The sacred meeting place of the generations,
Torah is where we dialogue, dance, wrestle
with our ancestors' visions and formulate our own.

Yes, Torah is a place to find and make meaning.

The meaning is often hidden,
buried inside the text
and inside of you.

Torah technically refers to the scroll that contains the first
five books of the Bible, which in book form is called a _humash_,

from the Hebrew word for "five." Jews do not appreciate the term *Old* Testament and consider it derogatory; we prefer the word *torah,* from a Hebrew archery term meaning "giving direction."

In addition, however, Torah can refer to the entire Jewish Bible, which is also called by the acronym *TaNaKh.* T= *torah,* N= *neviim* (prophets), K= *ketuvim* (writings), and it includes books such as Job, Ruth, Ecclesiastes, Proverbs, Psalms, and many more. Moreover, those who engage in Torah study often use the term *TaNaKh* to refer to the entire ever-growing body of works concerning Jewish law and lore: Talmud, Mishnah, Midrash, Codes, Responsa, Zohar, Tanya, and so on.

Books of the *Tanakh*		
Torah	Prophets, *Nevee-im*	Writings, *Ketuvim*
Genesis, *Bereishit*	Joshua, *Yehoshua*	Psalms, *Tehillim*
Exodus, *Shemot*	Judges, *Shoftim*	Proverbs, *Mishlei*
Leviticus, *Vayikra*	Samuel I & II, *Shmuel*	Job, *Iyov*
Numbers, *Bamidbar*	Kings I & II, *Malahim*	Song of Songs, *Shir ha-Shirim*
Deuteronomy, *Devarim*	Isaiah, *Yeshaiahu*	Ruth, *Rute*
	Jeremiah, *Yirmiyahu*	Lamentations, *Eihah*
	Ezekiel, *Yehezkel*	Ecclesiastes, *Kohelet*
	Hosea, *Hoshaya*	Esther, *Estehr*
	Joel, *Yoel*	Daniel, *Dani-el*
	Amos, *Ahmos*	Ezra-Nehemiah, *Ezrah v' Nehemiah*
	Obadiah, *Ovadiah*	Chronicles, *Divrei ha-Yamim*
	Jonah, *Yona*	
	Micah, *Mihah*	
	Nahum, *Nahum*	
	Habakkuk, *Habakuk*	
	Zephaniah, *Zefaniah*	
	Haggai, *Haggai*	
	Zechariah, *Zehariah*	
	Malachi, *Malahai*	

Torah is valuable far beyond the endlessly intriguing matters of intellectual, anthropological, and historical interest that are involved in the development of such a clever, profound, and intricate document. The study of religion, while fascinating, is not the same as experiencing the effects of it. Torah is brought to life by experiencing it.

To get a better idea of what this means, think about velvet. It's probably interesting to know such things about a piece of velvet as: Who was the manufacturer? When was it made? How was it dyed? What is the technical process by which it is made? You could know all that and never have touched velvet, never have slept on velvet, never have held a velveteen-stuffed animal and talked to it, danced with it, projected feelings onto it, and loved it. In other words, you might never have actually experienced velvet and yet you know a great deal about it.

So, too, you could know a lot about the construction of the Torah:

- It is written on the hide of a kosher animal with special durable yet nonindelible ink.
- Quills, usually turkey quills, are used for writing Ashkenazi-style scrolls and reed pens for writing Sephardi-style scrolls.
- A Torah is written in painstaking calligraphy by a pious person.
- The *sofer*, "scribe," will have a ritual bath each day before writing passages that contain the tetragrammaton, the YHVH G*d name, and a scribe prays before starting, "I am writing this Torah for the sake of the holiness of the Torah."

- Before writing the name of G*d, the *sofer* repeats, "I am writing the name of G*d for the holiness of [G*d's] name."
- A new Torah might command a price of at least $40,000 if written in Israel and $65,000–$70,000 if written in the United States.
- The garments worn by the Torah are distilled from the high priest's head ornament, breastplate, sash, and embroidered garment. Even the bells on the crown of the Torah reflect those described in the Torah as appearing on the hem of the high priest's robe.
- The *aron kodesh*, "holy housing," for the Torah, symbolizes the Holy of Holies, the inner sanctum of the ancient Temple in Jerusalem.
- The wooden staves upon which the scroll is mounted are called the *atzei ḥayyim*, trees of life. Sephardi Torahs generally have a hard decorative casing, and Ashkenazi Torahs have a finely woven cover.
- There is a story about a tree of life in the Torah scroll itself, in Eden.
- And, you may recall that the prayer used during services for returning the Torah to its cabinet (ark) opens with the verse:

eitz ḥayyim hee	She* is a tree of life
la maḥazeekem bah	for those who hold fast to her.

When you touch velvet, you know you are having a unique experience for which it is difficult to find adequate words; no

*Torah is a feminine noun.

amount of knowledge about velvet is equal to the experience of it. The same is true of Torah.

How can such a curious thing as a scroll full of ancient stories become known as a "tree of life," something life-giving? There have been times in our history—during the reign of the Syrio-Greeks, during the Spanish Inquisition, or in the USSR during the dominion of communism—when any contact with Torah or any Jewish text at all was deemed treason against the state. In the second century CE, Hananiah ben Teradyon was burned to death wrapped in the Torah for the crime of teaching it, and from 1240 to 1757 mass burnings of Jewish sacred texts were ordered by the popes and held in public squares. What could be so powerful that it would lead whole empires to restrict our access to it? Why did staff members of the Inquisition studiously examine verse after verse of Jewish sacred text looking for the dangerous and subversive? Is the great power suspected of Torah evident to you?

Do you believe the entire Torah was given by G*d
in one experience at Mt. Sinai?

Or are you certain
that the Torah is a set of myths
collected and compiled over time?

No matter.

Torah gives life meaning
when your journey and your questions
pass through the prism of the text.

In Genesis 24, the second-generation patriarch and matri-arch, *yitzhak*, "Isaac," and *rivkah*, "Rebecca," meet for the first time.

va-yeitzei yitzhak lasuah	Isaac goes out into the field
ba-sa-deh leef'note ah-rev,	to meditate toward evening
va-yisah eynav	he looks up and
va-yahr v'heenay g'malim	he sees camels coming.
ba-im.	
va-teesa rivkah et eynehah	Rebecca looks up
va-teyreh et yitzhak	and she sees Isaac
va-teepole mae al ha-gamal	and she falls off her camel!

If you don't remember the story reading exactly this way, it might be because only recently do translations offer the simple meaning of *va-teepole*, "she falls." Previously, because scholars didn't want a future matriarch of the Jewish people to look undignified, they had offered the words "alights" or "descends from the camel." So if you study Torah in translation, be sure to have a few different versions available. As you will learn in chapter 4, "Hebrew Is a Spiritual Practice," the beauty of the language is how diversely each word can be understood.

Have you ever "fallen off your camel" over someone? In the Introduction a question is raised regarding this text: What advice would you give a young person about the difference between *growing* in love and *falling* in love? Let's move out into your life with this question. Make a list of some four

individuals or groups of people with whom it might be important to study these two questions that have emerged from the
text. My list would include my two college-age sons, my
women's group, my husband, and a single adult bat mitzvah
student who is studying privately with me.

Imagine studying this text in a dorm with other students,
with a grandparent, with a Hebrew high school class, with a
beloved. Much wisdom can be stimulated by accessing even a
brief vignette of Torah!

CONTEXT MATTERS

While even a single verse can yield important insights, a
meta-story is also happening in the Torah; like a luscious layer
cake, there are many dimensions available for study. In regard
to the text above, did you know that Isaac was set up? In the
Torah's story sequence we last see Isaac in the famous *akedah*
scene, the "binding of Isaac"—a coming-of-age ritual, child
abuse, or an act of faith, depending on your perspective—
when he was being held under the knife by his father. After
the ritual, Abraham descends the mountain alone, and Isaac
goes another way, toward his adult destiny. We don't even
know when he learns that his mother, Sarah, has died.

His father, however, remains quietly involved in his son's
life and organizes a *shidduh*, a "match," behind his back.
Abraham sends a servant to visit his brother's children in
search of a fine young woman for Isaac. In the scene just
before the one cited in Recipe #17, the servant has found one
of Abraham's brother's granddaughters, Rebecca, and secured
her willingness to be matched with Isaac. So, as fate or the
servant's careful planning would have it, she comes upon him

alone in the fields, and we await the results of that first meeting with baited breath. Good, she falls off her camel for him. And what about Isaac? Will this match work for him?

va-y'sapayr ha-eved l'yitzhak et kol ha-devarim asher ahsah	The servant tells Isaac everything he has done.
va-y'vee-eh-ha yitzhak ha-oh-heh-lah sarah eemo	And Isaac brings her to his mother Sarah's [now empty] tent
va-yee-kah et rivkah	And he takes Rebecca [euphemism for consummating physically]
va-t'hee-lo l'eeshah	and she becomes a wife for him
va-yeh-eh-hah-veh-hah	and he loves her
va-yee-nah-heym yitzhak aharei eemo	and Isaac is comforted on account of his mother['s death].

Now let's see how the text above reveals the pathway from falling in love to growing in love. Isaac listens to the servant, learns the plan, and agrees to the arrangement. Unlike Jacob, who has to labor many years for his father-in-law in order to attain his beloved Rachel, Isaac weds the unknown Rebecca immediately. Will it work out? Will they have a good life, or will he later regret not taking more time to find a mate? In one sentence the text reveals all. Rebecca becomes more than the next matriarch to occupy Sarah's tent, more than a sex partner. The text says that she also "becomes" an *eeshah*, a "woman." And, what is more, the text says that "he loves her," which is not always the case in arranged marriages.

Perhaps as you explored the recipe above, friends or family observed that sustainable love can take a long time to arrive, even in a good marriage, and is the most precious experience a couple can have. Dr. Harville Hendrix talks about an "imago relationship," one in which both the positive and challenging qualities of your parents are present in your mate, as holding the greatest potential for a healthy marriage. And indeed, our study text appears to conclude that Isaac was comforted for the loss of his mother when the fullness of partnership was found. May we all be so blessed!

BRANCHES OF THE TREE

When Isaac meets Rebecca, the text says that he is "meditating," *lasuah*, out in the fields as evening approaches. Scholars cite this verse as providing the basis for *minhah*, "afternoon" prayer practice. The importance of precious pausing for reflection is central to Judaism; on the Jewish path you strive to do this three times each day. If you look at Judaism as a living tree with roots deep in antiquity and branches that come through each period of history carrying vital nutrients for the human soul stream right up to our times, you will understand that each practice is rooted by the sages in a verse of Torah. For example:

- Morning prayer, *shaharit*, has its verse origin in Genesis 19:27 when Abraham "hurries early in the morning to the place where he has stood before G*d."
- And evening prayer, *ma'ariv*, is derived from the Genesis 28 scene of Jacob's ladder, where we read

that, even though Jacob is in the wilderness and alone, it has become dark and he must take time for sleep. *Vayifga b-makom*, "he comes upon a certain place." *Vayifga*, however, can also mean "he entreats," and *makom*, "place," is viewed by the sages as one of the names for G*d. So evening is, indeed, another of the special places to pause, to go beyond work and duties, to reflect, connect, and release the flow of desires, concerns, and gratitude that we humans tend to have so steadily arising within us.

This is the nature of Torah study. The more we learn, the more our mind functions, as did the minds of our sages, like a giant hard drive on which key word and episode searches reveal opportunities for expanded meanings. Abraham, Jacob, and Isaac each engage in a prayerful pausing that changes the course of his life—finding G*d, finding a vision for his future, finding a life partner.

THE ORIGINAL HYPERTEXT

Over time, many sages have left their findings for us. Their profound notes function like hypertext, but they can't say and know all that is to be experienced through Torah, because they each lived in a different time. Like the many layers of geological strata here on earth, so too the sages' commentaries reflect varying local conditions. Their roots, however, all go back to the beginning, and the branches continue to reach those of us who are the flowering and fruiting of Torah in our times.

Major Commentators Over the Ages

2nd century	Onkelos, Israel
1040–1105	Rashi—Shlomo ben Yitzhak, France
1085–1174	Rashbam Shmuel ben Meir (Rashi's grandson), France
1092–1167	Abraham Ibn Ezra, Spain
1135–1204	Rambam—Moses ben Maimon (Maimonides), Spain
1160–1235	RaDaK—David Kimchi, France
13th century	Da'at Zkeinim Mi'Baalei Ha-Tosafot: Commentaries by students of Rashi
1194–1270	Ramban—Moses ben Nahman (Nachmanides), Spain
1275–1340	Yaakov Baal HaTurim, Germany/Spain
1288–1344	RaLBaG—Levi ben Gershon, France
1437–1508	Isaac Abravanel, Spain
1475–1550	Ovadia Sforno, Italy
1550–1619	Kli Yakar—Shlomo Ephraim ben Aharon Lunschitz, Poland
1565–1630	Hashelah HaKadosh—Isaiah ben Abraham HaLevi Horowitz
1641–1718	Siftei Hahamim—Shabtai Bass, Poland
1696–1743	Ohr HaHayim—Chaim Ibn Attar, Morocco
1746–1813	Rabbi David of Levov, Poland
1762–1839	Chatam Sofer—Moshe Schreiber, Germany/Bratislava
1765–1827	Simcha Bunem of Przysucha, Poland
1800–1854	Mordechai Yosef of Isbitza, Poland
1800–1865	ShaDaL—Shmuel David Luzzato, Italy

1809–1879	MaLBiM—Meir Lev ben Yechiel Michael, Poland/Rumania
1847–1905	Sefat Emet—Yehudah Aryeh Leib of Ger, Poland
1838–1933	Chafetz Chayyim—Israel Meir HaCohen Kagan, Poland
1865–1935	Abraham Isaac Kook, Latvia/Israel
1902–1994	Menachem Mendel Schneerson, Brooklyn
1903–1994	Yeshayahu Leibowitz, Riga/Israel
1905–1997	Nechama Leibowitz, Riga/Israel
1930–1989	Pinchas HaCohen Peli, Israel
1930–2001	Chaim Stern, USA
b. 1922	W. Gunther Plaut, Germany/USA/Canada
b. 1937	Adin Steinsaltz, Israel
b. 1944	Avivah Gottlieb Zornberg, England/Israel

Let's take a minute to get used to how the sages comment on a word. The Rashbam in the twelfth century notes that *lasuah* can have as its root *siah*, meaning "plant." He is positioning Isaac out in the field as involved in the planting. However, Rashi, his grandfather, prefers to derive the word from *siha*, "speech," or "dialogue." And Rebbe Nachman of Breslov understands this to be a meditation in nature, supported by the life energy of growing things. Rav Kook, who teaches that "The soul is always praying," will understand this as a time for Isaac to recharge his spirit after the traumatic events he has been through. For Rav Kook contemplative prayer in nature is when "The soul flowers with new strength; branching out naturally with inner emotions." So if the soul is always praying, why do we have three specific periods of prayerful pausing as a daily practice? My answer would be the importance of CPR—to intentionally look, listen, and feel, within, between, and beyond. It is at just such a time that Isaac is open to a shift in his destiny, the arrival of Rebecca. Perhaps this is even what he is praying for.

What wisdom have you gained in your life about the importance of creating and sustaining such prayerful intervals? What would you teach your students, children, and grandchildren about how to see what's on the horizon of life?

HOW TO GO WITH THE FLOW

One *parsha,* "portion," of the Torah is read each week, in sequence, and we read the whole scroll through in one year, then start anew. You will find infinite new meanings during Torah study sessions. Why? Because times change and we change. Your vantage point, the accrued life wisdom you can bring to bear on the issues in the text, the questions that you hope will shed new light on your life—all these shift steadily. And you can steadily advance your skills, begin to pick out nuances in the Hebrew, start to learn the backgrounds of the commentators and understand points they are making in the context of their times. You can also learn the numerical value of the letters and see fascinating correspondences so that you become aware that words aren't just what they mean on the page; they can be metaphors. You will discover hermeneutics—traditional agreements about how to use verses to reshape laws given in Torah to serve later generations—and you will begin to see how and why particular practices (like the practice of thrice-daily prayers) stem from certain passages.

You will read and create your own midrash, "inquiry" or "story," to amplify the white spaces where words seem to be missing, or where the grammar or topic invites further explanation. There are a great many more vantage points from which to study, and there is no rush; you have at least this lifetime!

Whatever you discover from contact with the text is your personal religious discovery, more technically called a revelation. A revelation might arise within your intellect or spirit, strike you when someone is teaching, or be found through the traditional partner study process called ḥevruta, "friendship," which is one of the great joys of life.

THE TORAH OF FRIENDSHIP

Our sages said, "Take yourself a friend; go and study." Let's open our inquiry by listening in on a ḥevruta session that is taking place between Dennis, a physician, and his friend Benjamin, in a beit midrash, "house of inquiry" or "house of study." Often found in schools and synagogues, a beit midrash can also be created in your own home. Choose a place with good lighting and proper seating (although some prefer to stand facing each other across the study table). Pile your table with helpful resources—dictionaries, commentaries, a laptop with a searchable media containing of all major texts in Hebrew and translation, a bookstand to put your text at a comfortable angle and the proper distance from your eyes and body. Bring in a pot of tea and a nosh, if you wish.

REB GOLDIE: Today we are going to focus our learning on a subset of verses from the weekly parsha that deals with the sacrificial system. That's right, the part that seems very hard to make relevant and meaningful in our times. I think you will be very surprised by what you find. Dennis, why don't you read first. Read the whole text out loud dramatically so that both you and Benjamin have a sense of the full section. Here's the text:

Leviticus Chapter 4

22 If a leader [of Israel] is off the mark and unintentionally commits one of all the commandments of the Lord, which may not be committed [for example, thou shalt not steal, or thou shalt not murder], incurring guilt;

23 if his mistake that he has committed is made known to him, then he shall bring his offering: an unblemished male goat.

24 And he shall lean his hand [forcefully] upon the goat's head and slaughter it in the place where he slaughters burnt offerings, before the Lord. It is a sin offering.

25 And the priest shall take some of the blood of the sin offering with his finger, and place [it] on the horns of the altar [used] for burnt offerings. And then he shall pour its blood onto the base of the altar [used] for burnt offerings.

26 And he shall cause all its fat to [go up in] smoke on the altar, just like the fat of the peace offering. Thus the priest shall make atonement for his [the errant leader's] sin, and he will be forgiven.

REB GOLDIE: That's great, but let's not comment yet. Now, Ben, please read just the first sentence again, aloud. Then Dennis gets to comment on it.

BEN: "If a leader [of Israel] is off the mark and unintentionally commits one of all the commandments of the Lord, which may not be committed [for example, thou shalt not steal, or thou shalt not murder], incurring guilt;"

DENNIS: I wonder if as a doctor I'd be considered a leader in this context? What about a teacher, too?

BEN: How about the head of a corporation? This society is so unforgiving; if you make a mistake you are maligned and sued. Dennis, you always look so exhausted, the stress of being a doctor, with lives in your hands, it must be so intense.

DENNIS: For me the hard part is bearing the guilt, because on rare occasions significant mistakes do happen, especially the way they overbook us in the HMO. It's very rare—I'm so careful— but I'm also not a machine. I'm only human, and there's no way to ever forget. Even if the public doesn't notice, I know.

BEN: You can't hit the mark every time. Read on a bit, shall we?

DENNIS: "If his mistake that he has committed is made known to him, then he shall bring his offering: an unblemished male goat."

BEN: That's important, the first part. What if you don't know you've made the error? It was unintentional, you help someone in the emergency room who comes from another state; they go on home and you'd never know something went wrong unless they told you.

DENNIS: Or what if you're a parent and you make a mistake and that "oh no" voice inside wakes you up. Parenting mistakes lead to so much guilt, too.

BEN: I see you have to give up something that's in really good shape, an "unblemished" animal. In college in comparative religion we learned that the priests didn't draw a salary, so all these sacrifices were primarily used to feed their families. It was actually the least usable parts that got burnt.

DENNIS: That's very interesting. It never made any sense to me that they'd kill all those animals just for the ritual of it all. But I also like that there is somewhere safe to go with your guilt, with the knowledge that you made a significant mistake.

BEN: "And he shall lean his hand [forcefully] upon the goat's head and slaughter it in the place where he slaughters burnt offerings, before the Lord. It is a sin offering."

DENNIS: Ugh. That word *sin* can't be right, how can a mistake be a sin?

BEN: Let's ask the *beit midrash* teacher. Reb Goldie, why does the translation say "sin"?

REB GOLDIE: The English word is problematic. <u>H</u>eyt in Hebrew, which is so often translated as "sin," derives from an archery term that means "missed mark," just as Torah derives from an archery term for "giving direction." In our tradition, humans are not expected to be perfect or mistake-free. Our tradition understands that no matter how much we try to line up our lives with desirable ethical targets, we will tire, err, and miss some of the marks that the Torah encourages us to attain. So in our tradition, the goal is to keep realigning ourselves so that, as much as possible, we end up with a mitzvah instead of a miss. Judaism is very clear that humans need to invest effort in order to continually develop into our highest selves, and there has to be a way to get past mistakes and move on. For example, you two have been speaking about the practice of medicine, and without risk-taking how can science ever advance? But that doesn't mean it isn't difficult to accept our own errors in judgment.

DENNIS: So the ritual helps you forgive yourself and realign by admitting to yourself that you made the mistake and stepping into a public space to acknowledge it.

REB GOLDIE: Exactly. Ben, you're a therapist, do you see any value in the placing of hands onto the goat?

BEN: Well, only that I'm stubborn as a goat; it would take a lot of pain for me to step up to the plate to do this.

REB GOLDIE: You're learning beautifully on many levels. Is there a mistake you made that still hangs around your consciousness? Now there's something called a heat sink in many electronic items that takes the excess heat away from the appliance so it can keep working. In Temple times, for humans, that heat sink is the goat. You lay your hands on it, remember the error that has sunk into your spirit, and transfer that toxic energy symbolically to the goat. Now, please continue on your own.

DENNIS: "And the priest shall take some of the blood of the sin offering with his finger, and place [it] on the horns of the altar [used] for burnt offerings."

BEN: Blood is life in Judaism, that's why we use salt to draw it out of our meat, and in the rules of keeping kosher Jews can't have blood in our food.

DENNIS: There was this young girl with whom I made a medication mistake. I drew from the wrong vial. I'd have shed my own blood if I could to bring her back. Could that be what's happening here? Something about the effect of breaking a mitzvah can be like shedding blood? Wouldn't that be something, for someone to value us enough to let us get past our mistakes instead of treating us like criminals?

I looked up *blood* in this book of midrash. It's very interesting. This says one who reddens the face of a person is as though he shed their blood. I accidentally humiliated a pharmaceutical salesperson this week who came to talk about a new product for blood pressure. He went from red in the face to worse, pale like death. There ought to be a way to own up publicly without being afraid people will see me as weak. Actually, what synchronicity, at services last week the rabbi mentioned a rabbinic text about whitening the face. He said the sages describe political situations where that happened, even in the house of study and the Sanhedrin, and they liken it to killing someone as well; I guess they mean killing someone's spirit.

BEN: Listen to this: "And then he shall pour its blood onto the base of the altar [used] for burnt offerings. And he shall cause all its fat to [go up in] smoke on the altar, just like the fat of the peace offering."

DENNIS: We ought to study that peace offering on another day. Why is it included here? When do they do that one?

BEN: I don't know, but you'll never believe this—there's only ten minutes left before it's time to go home! Let's forge on so we finish: "Thus the priest shall make atonement for his [the errant leader's] sin, and he will be forgiven."

DENNIS: Imagine if President Clinton could have immediately admitted his inappropriate sexual liaison with a student intern and there was some sort of ritual to reintegrate him as an honored leader as this text does. The people would know he knew he was off the mark so they could trust that he'd try to recalibrate.

REB GOLDIE: There are commentators throughout the ages who have left us the equivalent of Cliffs Notes. I gave you texts that have the *meforshim*, the interpretations of early commentators, under each line. Dennis, why don't you read what the French sage Rashi says about our study text. Rashi generally tries to underline the most potent immediate meaning of the text.

DENNIS: *Asher nah-see yeh-heh-tah*, "when a prince [leader] sins."

BEN: Misses the mark.

DENNIS: Right, but wait. Rashi says *asher*, a term that usually means "that" or which might be viewed here as an expression of *ashrei*, happiness or good fortune. "Fortunate is the generation that has as its prince [leader] one who gives his heart to bring an atonement for his inadvertent mistake, all the more so would he regret his intentional ones."

REB GOLDIE: Rashi is fascinated by the *asher,* not just because of this wordplay, but because the verses for all the other unintentional mistake categories start with *im,* "if." But here, the text starts with "when," indicating that it's a foregone conclusion that leaders will err. So what I believe Dennis in essence has said is that it is a very special and fortunate case when a country's leader can publicly acknowledge a mistake; that is very holy! I'm sure we are all aware of missed marks in our own lives. My blessing for you is to create your own ritual or process for atonement, or, one might say, the restoration of at-one-ment with yourself and those affected.

Okay. We're about out of time. During *hevruta* one tends to fall into a kind of study trance as awareness unfolds and time stands still. I see you nodding affirmatively. I understand! Now, please thank your study partner for today's insights and the gift of shared learning.

It is a Jewish tradition to speak words of Torah whenever Jews gather. Indeed, when Torah serves as a catalyst to put us in touch with the core issues of life, our conversations are enriched. Sharing life's wisdom among grandparents, children, friends—this is one of the joys of cultivating a relationship with the Torah and the cycle of Jewish time.

Notice what *you* feel
and realize from reading the text.
What comes up for you is *your* revelation.

The torah of *your* life. Share it.
Torah sharing can be a great source of
intimacy and meaning.

These are some of the principles and important ground rules for *hevruta*.

RECIPE #18:
The Ingredients of Healthy *Hevruta*

THE "AND" METHOD. This kind of study is collaborative, additive, and noncompetitive. Each person's insights are honored, supported, and treasured by the other. You are going on a spiritual adventure together. When your friend offers an insight, first empathize with what she said and then say "AND what this part of the text makes me particularly aware of is …"

TAKE TURNS READING AND RESPONDING. First, read your piece of study text aloud. Next, your study partner reads just the first sentence again, aloud. You get to comment on it first. Then your partner summarizes/empathizes with what you've noticed and adds his own views. Continue to explore the verse, or have your study partner read the next one aloud. The process continues until you finish the piece, or, more likely, run out of time.

ETERNITITIS. There is a world of spiritual intimacy that opens up during a mutual exploration of meaning through Jewish text. My rabbinical school study partner, Rabbi Brian Nevins-Goldman, and I called this feeling "eternititis," losing all sense of time and place while making rich, deep, and amazing learning discoveries together. Because of this delightful side effect, if you have a scheduled appointment following your _hevruta_, it's a good idea to set a timer before you begin your session.

THE RACE GOES TO THE DEEPEST. Success in Torah study goes against the tenets of Western academic training. Being the first to finish analyzing a text for meaning rarely indicates that you will have the most profound insights to share. In _hevruta_, you go slowly, even word by word, wondering at the author's choice of terms, juxtaposition of ideas, turns of phrase. Take your time; the journey is everything.

SHARE THE TORAH OF YOUR LIFE. Life experiences and resources such as poems or articles that relate to the ideas you develop during your text study should be brought into your study process, too.

PICK SOMEONE WITH HEALTHY BOUNDARIES. It is important to select a safe study partner, someone with good boundaries who can keep confidences. Sharing the intersection of the torah of your life with the Torah text is very holy and very personal.

USE SCHOLARLY RESOURCES ON THE SECOND ROUND. Once you have arrived at a first level of understanding of the text with your partner, you might want to return to it in the company of the thoughts of commentators throughout the ages. Often, they will have noticed different things than you have, for they have viewed it through a different sociocultural and historical lens. And they are also experts in the grammar and drenched in the full scope of Torah, including the _midrash aggadah_, which explores ethical ideas, biblical characters, or interesting moments or gaps in the narrative, and *midrash hala<u>h</u>ah*, which deals with practical matters of Jewish law and behavior.

ADD *YOUR* VOICE TO THE DIALOGUE OF THE GENERATIONS. Your thoughts, intuitions, and research into the text may be quite original, and certainly the lens of your generation and life is unique. Be sure to write up your own best insights on Torah as commentary and share them.

PRACTICE SAFE SPIRITUALITY. In addition to revelation and other forms of insight and amazement, what arises in this process is a feeling of closeness, respect, and love for your study partner. Sometimes this can become such a passionate dynamic that it is easily confused with romantic love or lust. Anything that surfaces resembling sexual energy or romantic love needs to be plowed back into study, as a sacrifice to the holy project in which you are engaged.

Often, meaningful *<u>h</u>evruta* relationships endure long after the actual opportunities to meet have passed. You and your partner have shared the torah of your lives while encountering the sacred text. In an age where it is hard to get past the superficial, *<u>h</u>evruta* is Judaism's special gift of spiritual intimacy. When properly executed, this recipe is guilt- and calorie-free. Enjoy it!

ENHANCING YOUR EXPERIENCE OF TORAH READING AT SERVICES

Do the people clustering around the Torah during Saturday morning services

seem to be members
of some kind of special club
with its own code, signals, and duties?

Are seven people each given an *aliyah,*
a chance to "go up" to the Torah,
say a blessing, and be honored witnesses
to the week's rapidly mumbled
yet somehow interminable reading?

What are the rest of us supposed
to be doing during that time?

As we've already learned, the Torah is read section by section, sequentially throughout the year. Each of these *parshiot,* "portions," is given a name based on a key phrase from the text. For the purpose of our discussion, let's look at Exodus 18, the *parsha* known in Hebrew as *yitro,* and often oddly rendered in translations as "Jethro." (There is no "j" sound in Hebrew.)

In *parshat yitro* we find Moses struggling to be an effective CEO for the Jewish people. Although he trained in the palace of the pharaoh, the business of supervising without the context of slavery is proving terribly difficult. The Israelites' communal enterprise does not yet have an infrastructure. Fortunately, Moses' father-in-law, Yitro, who also happens to be an experienced leader—a Midianite priest—visits the encampment, and Moses uses this occasion to have a heart-to-heart talk with him. Yitro, taking note of how difficult Moses is finding the task of leadership and, particularly, how overwhelming it is to have all the people coming directly to him to settle their interpersonal disputes, commences to give

Moses one of civilization's earliest recorded management consultations, including instructions on how to set up a seventy-member transition and governance team.

At Torah reading time, during Saturday morning services, arrange for the person leading the service for *parshat yitro* to invite those wrestling with leadership issues in some aspect of their lives to either: incline their hearts to the issue of leadership during the reading of these verses; or come up to the Torah to be part of a "group" *aliyah*; or rise at the end of the *aliyah* for a blessing about leadership issues in their lives.

RECIPE #19:
The Art of
Meaningful
Aliyot

Meaning-making innovations are perfectly legitimate within Judaism. Could this approach work in your community? Here's how it might play out.

- Perhaps you are struggling with leadership issues in your life, so you join the surprisingly large stream of people heading up to the Torah. How is it helpful to you to take this option of participating in a group *aliyah*?
- This is a moment to honor the place that leadership issues occupy in your life, to realize how human that is.
- Perhaps you also reflect on how you are a leader for those in your life or what you might find timely to ask an elder mentor like Yitro.
- What advice might a Yitro-type person offer to *you*?
- Are you feeling successful about a recent act of

your own leadership? Let this *aliyah* be your way of celebrating your courage and clarity.

- Notice who else has chosen to come up for this *aliyah*. These might be important dialogue partners later, perhaps during refreshments after services. (Engage with such individuals gently. Matters of the soul can be very tender. Please show understanding should someone prefer privacy.)
- If you were to receive a blessing to gain the support you need as a leader, what might that blessing sound like?

The service leaders often give a blessing for those who come up for an *aliyah*. In the case of our example above, you might want to be blessed to receive the insight, kindness, strength, cooperation, and courage you need to be effective, or you might want a blessing to be able to find a mentor, to recognize the wealth of capable consultants hidden in your midst.

RECIPE #20:
Utilizing
Themed
Aliyot

The person leading the Torah service must study the *parsha* carefully. Take note of those verses that jump out with meaning for you, the leader. Is there a way of understanding those verses that will speak in a particularly meaningful way to a common aspect of the human experience? If so, you have arrived at a possible theme for one *aliyah*.

Personalized *aliyot*, during which one or more persons come up to the Torah, are already a tradition. For example, there is the *ufruf* ritual of honoring a couple about to enter a committed relationship with an *aliyah*, or one for new parents with a baby to name, your own personal bar or bat mitzvah *aliyah*, the taking of a Jewish name, or *bensching gomel*, saying a prayer of gratitude for having narrowly escaped death (such as following a car accident, after major surgery, or upon the lifting of life-threatening depression). One *aliyah* is often reserved for those needing healing or wishing to honor a deceased loved one. Sometimes the number of *aliyot* is expanded to allow for other special needs such as honoring community leaders.

Most communities utilizing this approach have three such themed *aliyot* rather than seven, because it takes longer for a whole group to come up and sit back down than it does for one person to do the witnessing.

It is helpful to briefly summarize what the three themes will be before the first group is called up. This lets people prepare emotionally and choose which themes call to them. Most leaders emphasize that people can come up, or rise for a blessing, during one, two, or all three, depending on what speaks to their spiritual condition.

Witnessing the Torah reading is a covenantal act for those who have formally become Jewish, so the person who technically represents the formal witnessing of the *aliyah* needs to be Jewish. The Bible, however, is for all people who feel touched by its words, so it is one of our people's sacred tasks to put into action the message of the Torah service and keep words of Torah at the center of our religious civilization.

After the themes are announced, the first group is called up. The reader indicates the place where the *aliyah* begins in the scroll, so that those who want to can touch that place with a fringe from their *tallit* (prayer shawl).

Next, everyone who came up for this *aliyah* chants an

opening blessing together. There are several forms of this blessing now in use, from the very traditional to those that are more inclusive and gender-balanced. Some communities prefer to designate one Jewish person to say or lead the blessing since *aliyah* is a covenantal obligation.

In communities where few people understand Hebrew, instead of a lengthy *leyning*, the traditional "chanting" of all the words of each portion, the service leader will first give a summary of the portion. The reader will then chant the verses that most apply to the theme of the *aliyah*. Traditionally every word of the portion is chanted quite carefully with *gabbai* (a layperson who is thoroughly versed in the Torah and the Torah readings) nearby to check for accuracy and make corrections.

The closing blessing is chanted, and then the Torah service leader or a designated helper will offer a blessing that is both termed and invokes the *mi sheh-beirah*, "One who blessed" the ancestors, and is specifically formulated to empower the healing, awareness, or action implied by the theme of the *aliyah*. Empathy is required to make a blessing that will be absorbed deeply into the souls of those who come up and will also be received by those who did not come up but who still felt connected to the theme.

All the people who came up for this *aliyah* then return to their seats. The theme of the next *aliyah* is described and those who chose it come up to the Torah. Even if you came up for the first *aliyah*, it is important for you to return to your seat with what you learned and then decide whether to go up for another, as well as to recite the blessings again.

What if it's a bar or bat mitzvah? It is a wonderful option to use group *aliyot* at such events. B-mitzvah students can be encouraged and assisted in developing their own themes from the weekly portion. Learn more about this and find a full guide to how to prepare *divrei torah* in my book *Make Your Own Bar/Bat Mitzvah: A Personal Guide to a Meaningful Rite of Passage*. Alternatively, sometimes it works well to invite family members and friends to come up to the Torah in affinity groups. For example, "Would all my aunts and uncles please come up for this *aliyah*," or "I invite my grandparents up for the first *aliyah*," or "Would everyone who goes to school with me who has already had a bar/bat mitzvah please come up for the last *aliyah*," or "Would my parents' friends please come up for this *aliyah*; I would like to honor your important place in the life of our family."

Even with desired change there is loss. Losses to consider in adopting this group approach might include missing out on that special feeling of having your own solo *aliyah*—a pride in your own skills and presence as you chant the blessings for all to hear—and letting go of the order of calling up Jews by the ancient Temple categories of Cohen (priest), Levite (Temple worker), Israelite (regular folk). Some religious communities have been inadvertently preserving these categories out of habit; others hope to reinstate the sacrificial system someday and are thus deliberately preserving a record of the men whose family origins may bear such a history.

One particularly helpful method of Torah study and teaching has been made accessible to our generation by one of my teachers, Rabbi Zalman Schachter-Shalomi, who has extracted the key principles of some very remarkable Hasidic practices and trained many of us who live outside that system in their

RECIPE #21:
An Easy Guide to Torah Study in the Four Worlds

application. In this recipe I have further modified his methodology in order to offer an introductory model useful for helping mainstream readers, teachers, and communities to find meaning and spiritual connection during Torah study. This approach can be applied to any part of the Torah you wish to take to a richer level of meaning. The order given below is traditional, but all of these dimensions coexist simultaneously, so go with the order of inquiry that works best for you.

THE *ASSIYAH* DIMENSION. Focuses on the facts, the characters, the setting, the action. In Yiddish we call this the level of *ta<u>h</u>lis*, "substance." The key question to explore here is: What is the actual text?

Often memories from popular culture intrude and you may be surprised at what the Torah actually says. For example, the Torah does not say that it was an apple Eve gave to Adam. What was it? You'll find the answer in Genesis.

In *assiyah*, first read the text out loud in the language that works for you. Then take notes: What is happening in the *p'shat*, the "simple" story level of the text? Who is speaking? What do the characters say and do?

Is some of the language difficult? Highlight new or difficult words, place names, concepts. This is a good time to look up Hebrew terms; create a list of definitions beside your text.

THE *YETZIRAH* DIMENSION. Focuses on emotions. In Yiddish this level is called *kishkes*, "gut feelings." The key question to explore here is: Whose voices, issues, and experiences in the text could be mine, and what do I learn by entering into the voices, issues, and experiences of the people in the text?

Reread the text with drama in your voice; envision the setting—the sky, the time of day, the staff in your hand, the heaviness of the stone covering the well, and more.

Use a colored highlighter to emphasize the words of a character who touches your heart, memory, or sensibilities.

Become that character. Become the text by empathetically taking on the voice of one of the characters or symbols; create a little monologue as your character or symbol of choice, or write a letter to the symbol or character you feel drawn to—enter the text.

Now, let your character enter into dialogue with another of the characters or symbols in Torah. Notice important relationships and characters (G*d, for example) that may not be present or speaking in this particular section of text; invite them into the story. Become their many perspectives and voices. It is a Hasidic practice to view every character in Torah—even Pharaoh—as a face of G*d. How does this affect your understanding of the text?

Notice if there is a particular word, phrase, or concept to which you feel a response in your body.

Now express out loud the strongest emotion the text brings up for you. You might use facial expressions, voice, body, and hand motions to express yourself.

Stay with what your body senses underneath the strong emotions. Are there softer voices, memories, and guidance coming through the intersection of Torah with your life?

THE BERIYAH DIMENSION. Emphasis here is on thought and the intellect. This is the dimension of the *yiddishe kup*, "Jewish creative intelligence." The key question to explore here is:

What knowledge or information can be brought to bear upon this text?

What do the sages point out in their commentaries?

Is there a connection to mythology or regional history (Egyptian, Mesopotamian, and the like) that might illuminate this text?

What opportunities within the nuances of Hebrew translation are there to expand the range of possible meanings?

Investigate the significance of the names of places and persons; they almost always symbolize more than is immediately apparent.

What issues are being raised that relate to present times?

What are the relationships between places and persons from other parts of Torah that shed light on the place and persons in this part of the text?

Now, what questions could you ask of this text, these characters, and the author(s)?

Ask them of the characters and answer in their roles. What is revealed through the answers that arise from you and your study partners when you imagine yourselves in the roles of characters in the text?

What principles for living would you want to teach based on your encounter with this section of Torah?

THE *ATZILUT* DIMENSION. This is where you become the text by entering the level of unification with the Source, a timeless experience called *yehidut*. A key question to ask here is: How do I now set aside my thinking, my understanding, my feeling, to dissolve into connection with G*d the silent, as well as G*d the speaking?

In this dimension, the whole scroll unravels and flows like a river of light within you—you are one with the entire Torah, not just the page we are on.

This is where the faces, the characters, the symbols dissolve before your eyes, the letters dance, the wordplays emerge and recede, the white spaces between the letters expand; it is where, like Moses, you are in the cleft of the rock on top of the mountain, all study and understanding are behind you, and suddenly you are seeing through G*d's eyes. It may be impossible to explain or share what you experience in *yehidut*, but when it happens you will never forget being there.

PRODUCT LABEL WARNING

Exploring the Fourth Dimension is a very delicate enterprise and best done with an experienced teacher who can open up the more mystical realms with you. You will find Torah study retreats listed at www.ReclaimingJudaism.org.

THE TORAH OF HONEST AWARENESS

The Torah is full of stories of dysfunctional family relationships.

Torah confronts us with parallels to our own actions and reveals the complexity of issues and outcomes.

Samson sleeps with Delilah.
Eve and Adam disobey G*d.
Jacob steals his brother's birthright.
The Israelites build an idol, a golden calf.

Rebecca sets up the plot to deceive Isaac.
G*d floods earth, murdering almost all living things.
Abraham lies to Pharaoh, saying that Sarah is his sister.
Yehudah secures the services of Tamar as a prostitute.
King David sends a man to die so he can have the man's wife.
Elijah reports Israelites have killed most of the prophets.
Moses disobeys G*d by hitting a rock in a display of anger.

Yet all these folks and many more
get top billing in the biblical hall of fame.

What's going on?

The sages get it.

Torah
inspires our people
to become study groups
on how to evolve
into our highest selves.

OUCH! SOMETIMES WHAT THE TORAH SAYS HURTS OR IS VERY DISTURBING!

There are episodes in the Torah to which you may react with anything from anger to compassion, distress to joy. In Numbers 12 Moses' siblings, Miriam and Aaron, express concern about Moses' relationship with a Cushite woman. The commentators wonder whether this refers to Moses' wife Tzipora, whether he has taken a new wife, or whether, G*d forbid, he is having a relationship on the side. We can't tell.

G*d enters this scene suddenly, saying in no uncertain terms that only Moses receives revelation from G*d; Miriam and Aaron's level of understanding comes only through dreams. Previously, they had thought of themselves as a leadership triumvirate. Now, however, it is made dramatically clear that there is, in fact, a hierarchy. The text reports that Miriam's reaction is to become *k'sheleg*, "like snow," a skin reaction the Torah terms *tza-ra'at*, which is often mistranslated as leprosy. (See pages 162–163 for details of this mistranslation.) What is happening to Miriam? Her emotional response is being given physical expression.

Seeing that Miriam has become ill, Aaron seems to attribute this to retribution from Moses. He begs Moses not to punish her, and Moses then prays to G*d for her healing. Rashi and other sages use this text to teach against gossip, and although Miriam was speaking with Aaron, they blame her for "speaking about Moses and the Cushite woman," and note that G*d describes her condition as humiliation, and makes the following analogy: "If her father had spit in her face, would she not have been in disgrace for seven days? Seclude her outside the camp for seven days and after that she can be reintegrated."

G*d orders Miriam to be sent off on the ancient version of a retreat. There, as she gets some perspective on the political situation with which she has been struggling, her skin problem resolves itself, and seven days later she is indeed able to reenter the community, which clearly values her. "The people did not move on until she was added in" (Numbers 12:15). In the next chapter Aaron is appointed high priest. Although he too questioned Moses' behavior, he is promoted.

Hmm. Aaron is promoted while Miriam is humiliated and banished from the camp. Do you note a certain gender bias here? This episode has often been cited as divine confirmation of the proper place of women. Ouch! The text is our people's record of a woman smacking up against the stained-glass ceiling.

Miriam's body responded to stress with a skin problem.
How does your body respond to stress?
What do you do to get healing from a difficult situation?
How do you get perspective on your life?

What wisdom do you have for a young person
who experiences a setback in life as Miriam did?

You can be an important spiritual mentor!
During Torah study,
share what you know about navigating life.

I believe it was Rabbi Pam Wachs who told me of a story she'd heard about a little girl who was playing beside the ocean and finding herself constantly knocked over by the waves. She went to her father and asked: "Does this have to keep happening?! It's not fun. I don't want to be knocked around by the sea any longer. Isn't there another way?" And her father answered: "There is another way. I can teach you how to dive in, to go deeper, beneath the surface. Are you willing to learn? It will be a very different experience."

So it is with Torah: When the text grates, it is a signal to go deeper. It's like being in therapy: When you feel afraid to talk about something, or you are hiding a memory of deep humiliation, or raging in anger, that is the most important place in yourself to explore for growth and healing. That is the kind of fear and anger that heralds a new level of consciousness. It usually means an important revelation is ready to emerge. When these moments happen during Torah study, they can signal a great change coming in your life, your community, or even in the role you will take in society.

WHEN YOU FEEL ANGRY IN RESPONSE TO THE TORAH'S MESSAGE

Let's apply this analogy of going deeper to our experience of Miriam's losing her bid for equal leadership with the men in her family. Just as the decay of ancient life forms has resulted in the fossil fuel we use to power much of our civilization, so too the decay of a paradigm can yield the emotional fuel necessary to power motivation for major change. The fundamental motif of the Torah, which has provided universal inspiration, has been that of liberation—the liberation from slavery modeled in the great Exodus epic. This part of Miriam's story teaches us that inspiration can also be drawn from what troubles us in the Bible. Recent generations have felt called to liberate not only slaves but also women. And indeed, while many alive today know women who were not given a Jewish education because it was deemed important only for their brothers, that is no longer the case. Women study beside men across the spectrum, and, for the first time in Jewish history, there are *yeshivot*, places for sacred study for women around the world.

This paradigm change occurs, like many others, in tandem with organic changes in nature. As population surges on the planet, women are being widely redeployed from responsibility for reproduction into leadership roles. Women leaders draw on our skills at sharing and empowering others to create a planet where coexistence rather than conquering is the paradigm. The text was hurtful, we got angry, energized, organized, and today there are increasing numbers of "Miriams" in positions of leadership. We are providing a style that is complementary to that of men. Both men and women are stretching, learning from each other's styles. All are growing and changing in necessary ways.

The trick to dealing with the text
when it is hitting you in the face
is to stay in relationship with it,
to go deeper.

Growing pains lead to knowing gains.
Even when the text makes you angry,
it is valuable.
Trust your reactions to Torah;
they are holiness fueling the future.

MAKE YOUR OWN KIND OF MIDRASH

In the late 1990s I was at Reconstructionist Family Camp, a trial program of the National Havurah Institute, a gathering of individuals and families seeking a more intimate Jewish experience. Each adult was partnered with a child as our *hevruta* study partner. Each pair would ultimately do a presentation to the group of what we had studied together. A precocious and bright nine-year-old girl, Ronya Geller, picked me as her partner.

"I want to study with you, Reb Goldie!"

"What would you like to study?" I ask.

"Girls," she answers.

"In the Torah?"

"Yes, silly, we're supposed to study *Torah*."

"Okay, which girls should we study?"

We both fall silent. There are no stories of girls in the Torah. Ouch.

"Okay," she says. "How about mothers." (Oh, no, I think to myself, there is not one mother-daughter dialogue in the whole of the Torah. This is going to be very disappointing for her.)

"Which mothers?" I ask.

"How about Abraham's mother?" (Oy vey, she is never mentioned.)

"What about Abraham's mother would you like to know?"

"Well, I was thinking he must have been such a difficult child to raise. Always questioning the value of things, mocking his father's idols, wrecking them. Probably she gave him a lot of time-outs!"

"Sure sounds that way. And how did she feel about him speaking out loud to a G*d she'd never heard of and couldn't see!"

"I bet she told her friends he was a gifted child who would discover and invent things *they* couldn't even imagine! But, Rabbi, don't you think it was terrible that he ran away from home? Wasn't his mommy very sad? Do they ever see each other again? What does the Torah say?"

"Abraham's mother isn't mentioned in the Torah. I think you have done a great mitzvah, bringing her back to life. We should write down our ideas about her story."

"No one remembers Abraham's mother's name!?"

"Amathalia the daughter of Karnebo is the name given for

her later, in the Talmud Baba Batra 91a."

"Reb Goldie."

"Yes."

"What about Noah's wife? She worked so hard, and they had children. There must have been daughters. Does anyone remember her name?

"Well, Ronya, many years later a midrash suggests her name was Naamah."

"What about Lot's wife? Is that the only name she got?"

"In the Torah, yes. Later on, in commentary called *midrash*, the Rabbis give her the name *Idit*, 'witness.'"

"It says she was turned into a pillar of salt because she looked back."

"Ronya, what do you think that means? Why was it bad to look back?"

"Reb Goldie, I know why the Torah says Lot's wife turned into a pillar of salt. She didn't really die, you see, she looked back like grandmothers did during the Holocaust and she couldn't stop crying because of what she saw. She looked back to make sure all of her family was keeping up with her and she couldn't find one of the children, so she went back to check. Where she stood, she left this huge pile of salt from her tears. And maybe she really is out there somewhere in the world still looking for one of her daughters. Because that's what a Jewish mother would do. And if it was my mother, I would still be waiting for her, every day."

(Long pause ensues.)

"Rabbi, I'm so sad. Why doesn't the Torah remember the name of mothers? Why don't we read about mothers talking with their daughters?"

"I have an idea."

"What, Reb Goldie?"

"Let's write down our dialogue; that way someday there will

be a record of what women rabbis and girls talked about. It is a good place to start, a dialogue about remembering the mothers."

"Let's do it!!"

The method we just used is a type of commentary called *midrash*, from a root meaning "to search out." There are countless volumes of midrash written by our *man*cestors as well as several published by women in the last thirty years. Midrash is very important to the evolution of Judaism; it is a traditional method of renewing what we have inherited. In response to the cultures within which we lived and the changing societies of human history (nomadic, agricultural, feudal, republican, socialist, democratic, and such) our ancestors began to see different meanings in the text and to import new values for the health of our "evolving civilization," as Rabbi Mordecai Kaplan has defined Judaism. You'll find a Jewish Women's Torah Commentary online at www.ReclaimingJudaism.org and links to commentary sites and midrashim throughout the web.

And, midrash is something you can write too! Find the missing voices in the text and give them your voice. Your revelation will come through. Write it down, dance it, film it, sing it, and share it. The Torah has been passed to you as a sacred trust.

SACRED TEXT AND THE ART OF CHANGE

Talmud and the traditional commentaries are rivers of wisdom and change.

Although people love to disagree, at least at first, there is, in fact, no such thing as a Jewish biblical fundamentalist. The art of interpretation is central to rabbinic Judaism; our sages took and take little or nothing at face value. In the words of Barry Holtz in *Back to the Sources*, "All the Rabbis would subscribe to a doctrine of the eternal interpretability of the Torah and we might say that if there is any one dogma of rabbinic Judaism it is that everything is contained therein."

How does this work? Much like young Ronya's ideas expressed in the dialogue above, the sages saw a verse and read into it with spiritual imagination. Whether needed at that moment or seized upon by later generations, the reflections of the sages became the shoulders on which we have stood to justify a new approach to something in the text. Finding a precedent in the midrash is a very useful tool for Jewish social change.

ACTIVIST TEXT STUDY

Many sages left extensive commentaries, which are now glorious opportunities to discover—through the ways they responded to, interpreted, and applied Torah in their lives and with their communities—what issues they faced in their own generations. Let's take *bar mitzvah* as an example. It is not mentioned in the Torah at all, and the age of majority is set at twenty years of age in Numbers 14:29. Yet bar mitzvah has become as real and authoritative to us as any of the commandments. Here's a taste of the rabbinic imagination at work making midrash:

"And the boys grew."—Genesis 25:27 (Re: Jacob and Esau)
Rav Pinḥas said in the name of *Rav Levi*: "They were like a myrtle and a wild rose bush growing side by side; when they

reached maturity, one yielded its fragrance and the other its thorns. So for thirteen years both went to school and came home from school. After this age, one went to the house of study and the other to the shrines for idols."

Rav Elazar, the son of Rav Shimon, said: "A man is responsible for his son until the age of thirteen; thereafter he must say: 'Blessed is the One who has now freed me from the responsibility for this one."

Note again that the only contribution the Torah made to this work, which is often quoted as formative in leading to the establishment of bar mitzvah, was "And the boys grew."

Living with the Torah takes a very creative group of people. It contains, for example, a whole chunk of the Code of Hammurabi, which declares you must remove "an eye for an eye and a tooth for a tooth." This is a far cry from the ethics for justice to which Judaism subscribes today.

The Torah allows polygamy, right? How did that get changed, you might wonder. And for the woman suspected of infidelity, there was the *sotah* ritual, which required her to drink ashes from the altar that included some torn-up sacred text. If she lived she would be deemed innocent. This and many other challenging instructions were midrashed away out of practical necessity. Let's look at a prime example.

A fascinating example of change at work occurs in Deuteronomy 21:18–21, where we are clearly told to stone a rebellious son to death:

RECIPE #22:
Activist
Talmud Study

If a man has a stubborn and rebellious son, who doesn't listen to the voice of his father, or the voice of his mother, and though they discipline him, he doesn't listen to them, his father and his mother ought to grasp hold of him and bring him out to the elders of his city, to the gate of his place and then they say to the elders: "This, our son, is stubborn and rebellious. He does not listen to our voice. He is a glutton and a drunkard." [Now] all the men of his city will stone him with stones, so that he dies. This is so you will purge the evil from your midst and all Israel shall hear and fear.

Seems quite straightforward, doesn't it? But the Mishnah, a postbiblical text that is the foundational part of the Talmud and hence the source of many major Jewish laws and traditions, takes this Torah regulation apart, and nullifies it almost completely. This is an example of activist text study, an authoritative method of change in Judaism.

If [the boy accused of being a stubborn and rebellious son] stole his father's [meat and wine] and ate [them] in his father's domain [he is not considered a stubborn and rebellious son].

If [the son accused of being a stubborn and rebellious son] stole the [meat and wine] of others and ate [them] in their domain [he is not considered a stubborn and rebellious son].

Until [the son accused of being stubborn and rebellious] stole his father's [meat and wine] and ate [them] in another's domain, he is not considered a stubborn and rebellious son.

Rabbi Yose bar Rabbi Yehuda says, "[He is not considered a stubborn and rebellious son] until he steals from [both] his father and his mother."

—*Mishnah Sanhedrin 8:3*

Can you almost see the generations looking at each other across the table, pointing, and saying in a singsong style, "What if he stole from only his father and not his mother?" "What iiiiiffff the stealing is from others, not the family?" Every effort is being made to loosen the stricture.

This is not done capriciously, nor is it done without deep respect for and study of all the related decisions that came before. It is done when it really matters to the health and evolution of our people. At times Moses even added to G*d's commands right in the Torah text itself, and so this process is also sometimes used to tighten guidelines, when that is what is called for. And the talmudic commentators, known as *Tosafotists*, state that at times the everyday people's customary practices had a role in shifting a law or tradition. This shows how important it is to speak up, lobby, and help Judaism reflect our changing norms!

A good example of new thinking is provided by Rabbi Judith Abrams, author of *The Talmud for Beginners*, who taught me to see something new in the rebellious son text. She noticed that the son is called a stubborn drunk who does not listen, who steals from his parents, and she reads this as being about addiction in an age when there was no effective treatment. Imagine adding a column to the Talmud page that includes the values, vision, and views of a society that sees this condition so differently from the way the ancients ever could.

- What guidance would you give to the parents?
- What would you say to the son?
- How would you add your voice to this text when seeing it from the point of view of how to create

societal guidelines for dealing with addiction in the case of a minor?

- How might a Jewish community handle this problem today?
- What values, traditions, and texts might you draw on to frame your response?
- Rather than stoning, what measures to care for this youth and family would you want to see in a new column of Jewish commentary on the Talmud page of the future?

See how quickly you become a part of the dialogue and process of the generations! A very healthy, holy, and important part of being Jewish is feeling empowered to contribute to the process of evolving our tradition.

I hope you are feeling empowered, strengthened, and enriched.

In your spiritual imagination
walk up in front of those leading the Torah service.
Clap your hands and attract their attention.
They are turning to look at you.
Tell them anything you need to say about what is going on
    there.
Express your feelings, hopes, frustrations, and desires.

Now, walk over to the Torah,
touch the wooden staves.
Remember, they are called the *atzei hayyim,* "Trees of Life."
What does it feel like to touch this part of the Torah?

Now, walk around to the center of the Torah reading table.
Look with your own eyes into the open Torah scroll.

What do you feel?
What do you hear?
What do you see?

Can you say, *"hineini"*?

Hineini—"Here I am." All Jewish souls are reunited when we
recall ourselves standing at Sinai. This is what happens when
we use ourselves as a prism through which the Torah text is
refracted and live from that place of being what the mystics
called *m'kuballim*, "receivers," transducers of the sacred into
daily life.

4

Hebrew Is a Spiritual Practice

The ball is in the air, coming toward you.
It has been set up to come to you,
right where you are;
up at the net of your life.

Who set this up?
Are there instructions?
Go ahead, open the manual.
Whoa! Why is it mostly in Hebrew?

Happily, you don't need to be fluent in Hebrew to enjoy engaging with it as a practice that opens up the highest gates of meaning within Judaism. Each letter, new word, and phrase learned is an actual portal for emotional, intellectual, and spiritual expansion. So, while learning a few key principles that will empower your studies, let's look into a few of the linguistic gems of spirit to be found within Jewish texts and tradition.

HAVE YOU HEARD ABOUT THE VOWEL MOVEMENT?

The Hebrew language played a huge role in making possible the easy exchange of written information for all time and throughout the world. To understand this, let's take a very brief look at the way writing developed. Roughly twenty thousand years ago written language started out as pictographs—single, simple images like a heart, a stick figure, or a house, whose meaning was plain to everyone.

Researchers date to 3500 BCE the Sumerian clay tablets found in southern Iraq that reveal how writing begins to shift from pictographs to icons. Icons are symbols that don't look identical to what they represent but do convey a commonly accepted meaning. An example of a contemporary icon would be the "don't" symbol in our culture, a thick circle with an equally thick diagonal line through it that connects fully with the perimeter. It takes thousands of icons to represent a whole language. In antiquity, any significant amount of writing, as well as the interpretation of written materials, was limited to a very small group of trained political leaders, priests, and scribes.

The next development around 4000–3500 BCE is in Sumerian and Akkadian (northern Iraq) writing. Here symbols called logographs represent syllables, which means they can be arranged in sound-based sequences to represent different words or meanings—more efficient than icons since fewer symbols are required, but still a substantial and tedious process.

Then, around 3100 BCE some consonants are developed within Egyptian hieroglyphics and added to the logographs. And by 1800 BCE, in the region of Canaan (Israel, Lebanon, and Syria), evidence of an alphabet, termed proto-Canaanite by scholars, begins to emerge. Here words are written by using strings of consonants based on some thirty symbols. From that beginning, written language continues to simplify to the point where, around 1000 BCE, a formal abecedary (see Glossary) of twenty-two consonants proliferates in the region and becomes the basis of early Hebrew. In Figure 4.1, you can see the phases of development from proto-Semitic pictographs to Hebrew script, calligraphy, and a printer's text font.

A radical transformation with dramatic effects on civilization begins in the ninth century BCE with the invention of vowels within Hebrew and Aramaen civilizations. To illustrate the importance of vowels, consider the consonantal way things would have worked; let's take G-L-D in English—this could

Cannanite Pictograph 1500 BCE	Symbolizes	Text Calligraphy Script	Name of Hebrew Letter	Modern Hebrew Word for Image
⊔	Front teeth	שׁ ‎ שׂ ‎ e	shin	שֵׁן ‎ shein ‎ tooth
∿	Water	מ ‎ מ ‎ N	mem	מים ‎ mayyim ‎ water
⌂	Human head	ר ‎ ר ‎ ר	reish	ראש ‎ rosh ‎ head

Figure 4.1 The phases of Hebrew development.

signify guild, gold, glued, glide, or even glad. The development of written vowels made it possible for the first time to
sound out a word with relative accuracy. By the eighth century
BCE, our Hebrew ancestors have discovered how to represent
vowel sounds, which has a profound impact on the future of
humanity. From Hebrew and Aramaic, both with newfound
vowels, will be derived the majority of the world's languages,
starting with Greek, Latin, Arabic, and Sanskrit.

> The discovery of vowels tapped into
> a revolutionary force for human liberation,
> making it possible for the first time in history
> for the masses to be able to read and write.

> What are the vowels the Hebrews established?
> Letters that double as consonants: *yud, hey,* and *vav.*

> The very letters that form
> the most sacred sequence in Torah,
> the letters of *hashem,* "The Name"
> of G*d:
> *yud hey vav hey,*
> giving the power of reading and writing;
> advancing the capacity for shared learning.

MULTIPLE MEANINGS IN MANY WORDS

Because it is composed of root words—two or three consonants without any vowels—whose meanings are modified by
the addition of one or more vowels, it is in the structural
nature of Hebrew for each word to carry multiple meanings.

This is one reason why Hebrew sacred texts have remained relevant for thousands of years, up to this very day.

Frequently, the original Hebrew sacred texts have no vocalization marks (vowels). This makes many combinations and, hence, interpretations possible. Scholars have discovered that between 600 and 800 CE at least three research teams, called Masoretes, collected traditions about the meaning and pronunciation of biblical texts and created a system of markings to convey the meanings they believed to be most accurate across the generations. To do this, they used dots and dashes placed above and below the root to serve as vowels or musical notations, called trope.

In the Introduction, we saw that a root word of "Lord," *adonai*, is *ehden*, "threshold" or "sill." This hypertext-like experience of meaning is not possible within most languages. An excellent explanation of how this works is offered in the thirteenth-century text *Shaarei Orah*, by Rabbi Joseph Gikatilla, a Spanish kabbalist who uses as his example one of the most common words in any Jewish service.

The word that opens virtually every blessing is:

bless   *baru͟h*   בָּרוּךְ

Baru͟h has a three-consonant root:

ברך

Variations in word meanings come from the vowels, prefixes, and other marks that can occur around roots such as the one above. Here are some of the possibilities for the root letters of *baru͟h*.

Bless	baru*h*	בָּרוּךְ
Kneel	bara*h*	בָּרַךְ
Knee	bere*h*	בֶּרֶךְ
Pool	b'rei*h*ah	בְּרֵכָה
Blessing	b'ra*h*ah	בְּרָכָה

The dot you see inside the first letter of our sample word above is called a *dagesh* and can appear in other letters to affect their sound and meaning as well. So, for example, the first letter of the word *baruh* now has a "buh" sound, whereas without the dot it would have a "vuh" sound and could signal an entirely different word or word context.

Do you see the extra letter *hey* at the end of the last two words above? This converts our three-letter root into a feminine noun form.

Several Hebrew letters have a different shape when appearing at the end of a word. That is why the third letter of our root, *haf* ךְ, has a long tail when at the end of a word but appears as כ when it is within a word or begins one.

So, linguistically bundled into "bless" is the sense of living near a pool of blessings.

With this explanation, Rabbi Gikatilla helps us to amplify blessing practice, to not simply recite a traditional blessing formulation, but to pause in awareness of a moment of feeling blessed, as though we were kneeling beside this pool.

THE POWER OF TRANSLATION AND INTERPRETATION

A popular joke revolves around a telegram sent from Lenin to Stalin: "You were right. I was wrong. This is communism." Beaming, Stalin reads the telegram to a group in his office. A Jewish man steps forward and asks, "May I reread that for you?" Delighted to hear it again, Stalin passes him the letter. The man reads it aloud, changing only the inflection: "*You* were right? *I* was wrong? *This* is communism!?"

As the joke illustrates, the meaning of the written word is often as heavily dependent on the reader's perspective as the writer's. In Hebrew, given the flexibility of interpretation to which root words are subject, this is even more the case than in other languages. Jewish mystics and scholars of every generation draw on this flexibility to keep generating new interpretations for new times. Some have proved to be quite enduring, as, for example, these three possibilities that draw on the lack of punctuation in the Torah scroll as their source of permission to set the period according to their own insight about the first sentence of the Torah:

> **Standard version:**
> *b'reishit bara elohim et ha-shamayim v'et ha-aretz*
> "In the beginning G*d created the heavens and the earth."
> **Version of Rabbi Dov Baer, the Maggid of Mezrich:**
> *b'reishit bara elohim et*
> "In the beginning *elohim* created *et*."
> **Version found in Zohar [1:15a]:**
> *b'reishit bara elohim*
> "By means of wisdom x created *elohim*."

Intriguing? Let's strive to understand. The *maggid* describes his approach, putting a period after the *et*, as uncovering one of the mysteries of the Torah. Although *et* is usually a conjunction that shows the direction of the verb action, he suggests that its use here, since it is composed of the first (*aleph*) and last (*taf*) letters of the Hebrew alphabet, indicates that the alphabet itself and all its potential combinations were created "in the beginning." This is a central part of how Torah describes creation: that the world is spoken into being—the words precede the event, the letters precede each word, and each letter can enter into combinations that make whole worlds of meaning. Indeed, even on our own microcosmic level, many of us have spoken words that created new worlds for those around us.

Now, many religious seekers are looking for "the truth," and many religions claim to offer "the truth." But again, Judaism—and the Hebrew language itself—doesn't allow for simplistic, dogmatic responses. The Hebrew word for truth is *emet: aleph—mem—taf*—precisely the first, the middle, and the last letters of the Hebrew alphabet. Our mystical tradition accords *aleph* the status of representing your past, *mem* your present, and *taf* your future. So truth is created in the very beginning of time, from *aleph* through *taf*, *et*, and comprises what was, what is, and what will be.

The Zohar places the period even earlier in our sentence. (You can skip over this section if your mind is already spinning; there is much that is technical about Kabbalah.) Still with me? Let's begin to decode a radical bit of Zohar.

The "b'" at the beginning of the sentence in question doesn't have to mean "in." The authors of the Zohar know of a midrash that understands "b" to mean "by means of." So, according to Zohar teacher Rabbi Jonathan Omer-Man, this piece of Zohar is based on the midrash, "By means of *reishit* Elohim created the heavens and the earth." This midrash utilizes the nuances of *reishit* as meaning "first" and its related root *rosh*, "head." Much of traditional midrash was written while the Jewish people were under the influence of Greek philosophy, so *reishit* then is Sophia, "wisdom," termed *hohmah* in both Yiddish and Kabbalah. Not human-style wisdom, however; we're talking here about Ultimate Integrative Wisdom beyond our individual comprehension and attainment. Now our verse means, "By means of wisdom *elohim* created the heavens and the earth."

But something even more radical is afoot here. The kabbalists aren't working with an anthropomorphic G*d model. They intuit the Big Bang in their theories and understand creation as we know it to have emanated from that. By putting the period after *elohim*, the author of this part of the Zohar, building on the midrash, is saying that *reishit* represents Supernal Wisdom, and *elohim* represents supernal understanding, *binah*. And so our verse now reads: "By means of wisdom x created understanding."

So what is "x" in this verse?! *Ayn sof*. *Ayn sof*, the Limitlessness that precedes the creation of our plane of being and exists beyond it, the place where we opened our inquiry in chapter 2, "Reclaiming G*d with Integrity," "the place to which no eye can penetrate, being most hidden and difficult to fathom" (Zohar 232b).

The kabbalists postulate *ayn sof*, that which is beyond the physics of our universe, and they also have *elohim*, how G*d manifests within our physical universe. This opening verse is the foundation of the kabbalists' *eitz hayyim*, "tree of life," model whereby the world is emanated into being by *ayn sof* and we are holographically constituted of this Source's same ten components, or *sephirot*, of which wisdom, *hohmah*, and understanding, *binah*, are two. Helpful works to continue with this line of study are listed in the bibliography.

THE POWER OF THE *HEY*

Stepping away from the kabbalists' interpretive mode, *elohim* in Torah is most often the facet of G*d that is the power of nature. It is not until chapter 2 of Genesis, once a human is created, that the tetragrammaton, the four-letter *yud hey vav hey*, appears as The Name for G*d. The *yud hey vav hey* is the name of G*d that signifies a sense of relationship, the "I was, I am, I will be" power within, between, and beyond us that makes transformation possible. It is the name Moses uses when he calls out for compassion, grace, and patience.

After the seven days of creation are narrated in the Torah, a summary appears as an introduction to the story of the Garden of Eden. In this summary (Genesis 2:5–7), *yud hey vav hey* (spoken as *adonai*) is paired together with *elohim* as one name: "No bush of the field was yet on earth, and no grasses of the field had yet sprung up, because *yud hey vav hey elohim* had not sent rain upon the earth, and there was no human being to till the soil." There is neither dualism nor polytheism in Judaism; the names are paired in the text, perhaps by a later editor, after the creation narrative that associates *elohim* with the days before the creation of a human precisely to make that clear—all is one. Now, since *el* is a generic regional term for a god used in Hebrew, Ugaritic, and Phoenician, and for the Canannites *el* is the name of the god that fathered their primary regional deity, Baal, and *im* is a masculine plural ending, *elim* means "gods." Could *elohim*, therefore, also mean "gods" and not G*d?

mi<u>h</u>a mo<u>h</u>a ba-elim yud hey vav hey
Who is like You among the gods, *adonai?*
— *Exodus 15:11*

Notice the consonantal difference between *elim* and *elohim*. It is the letter *hey*, the very same letter that gets added to Abraham and Sarah's original names in Torah when they experience G*d and their consciousness shifts. *Avram* becomes *avraham* (Abraham is the anglicized pronunciation), *sarai* becomes *sarah*, just as *elim*, "gods," becomes *elohim*. All are recognizable as Israelite naming practices because of the *hey*, one of the four famous vowels. And it is those vowels that will supplant even one of the names of G*d: In Moses' encounter at the burning bush, even G*d describes a shift in naming—with a double *hey!* "I am *yud hey vav hey*. I appeared to Abraham, Isaac, and Jacob as *el shaddai*, but I did not make Myself known to them by My name *yud hey vav hey*" (Exodus 6:3).

TAKING A SACRED NAME

Over time not all sacred names have a *hey* inserted, and many Hebrew names have come to carry sacred significance. And, with the death of so many of our recent relatives in the Holocaust, Yiddish names are increasingly used as sacred names in Jewish rituals and documents as well. Taking a Jewish sacred name is a precious and powerful spiritual practice, whether it is reserved as a name for Jewish ritual or taken as your regular name, as I took mine when I changed it from Gail to the Yiddish name of my courageous great-grandmother Goldie, who would hide her two children behind the boards of a widened central wall in their home while she sat with a bottle of vodka and fresh glasses to await the arrival of the Cossacks—both herself and the drink serving as decoys to keep them from harming her girls. During a time in my life when I needed the courage to stick to my plans for making a major change, the legend of great-grandmother Goldie would often arise in my thoughts as an inspiration. One day I realized that my soul needed to take on and so honor her name, and amazingly my parents and friends quite instantly agreed.

If you have a Jewish name—whether it is Hebrew or Yiddish—that you don't appreciate, you can change it easily by being called to the Torah with your new name and receiving a blessing that includes mention of the taking of this name. Or, if there's a family story behind your name and it would be super "sensitive" to change it, you might decide to make it a middle Hebrew name and put your preferred one in front of it. And, if you don't have a Jewish name yet, check in with yourself—are you ready to consider finding just the right one? But, first, let's look at one particular name quest:

"Reb Goldie, how do I get a Jewish name?"

Irina's parents had served time in Siberia for holding a secret Shabbat service in their apartment before the Cold War ended. Irina's passport no longer bears *Yevreiska*, "Jew," on the identification page, and now she wants a Jewish name.

"Irina, why do you want a Jewish name?"

"Reb Goldishkeh, a name is part of belonging to our people, like you taught. And for me, Torah brings the color back to life, helps me believe times will continue to change. My life as a single parent is very hard and my name is tired of its life. I love the idea of a G*d called 'I am becoming what I am becoming.' I need this faith in the future. I want a name that shows I am part of this people."

So we began a process of finding the name that would fit her, that was perhaps the name of her soul before her body ever formed. She walked and wondered and dreamed and tried on several names and then came and asked: "Reb Goldie, is Talya a Jewish name?"

"Oh yes. *Tal-ya* means dew of G*d."

"Dew? Like soft tears that moisten the heart and let love arise again like tender new plants?" Her own tears are now falling. Her name has been found.

RECIPE #23:
Finding or
Changing
Your Jewish
Name

Jewish sacred names are most often given at birth, and are sometimes changed or expanded in adulthood. Changing your name if you are ill or struggling to encourage desired change or to sidestep persistent misfortunes is a long-standing Jewish custom. The qualities of a name affect how you think about yourself and what others may associate with you. A name with many points of connection within Torah and tradition will yield many moments for exploration and deepening over the course of a lifetime. I named one of my sons Ari, "lion," because, while he would appreciate the association with the popular animal as a child, as a man he could discover the Ari, Rabbi Yitzhak ben Shlomo Luria, a great kabbalist (1534–1572) whose life and teachings would be a rich source of inspiration for him.

CATEGORIES OF JEWISH NAMES

- Characters or symbols from the Torah or Talmud such as Tzipora (songbird), Evan (stone), Rina (joy), Bezalel (artist for the Temple whose name means "in the shadow of G*d"), Yonatan (Jonathan—gift of G*d).
- Desired qualities such as Bahirah (clarity), Tikva (hope), Simcha (happiness).
- Names from nature like Shoshana (lily, or some say rose), Ari (lion); Yona (Jonah, dove), Aviva (spring), Meira (illumination), Ori (my light).
- It's also helpful to know that while Sephardi Jews traditionally consider it an honor to take on the Jewish name of a living member of the family, Ashkenazi Jews carefully reserve this as an act of memorial. If a memorial name that was given to you has never felt quite right, a respectful strategy is to move that name to become a Hebrew middle name, and add a new sacred first name that really lights up your soul.

HOW TO FIND YOUR NAME

- Don't rush. Imagine being called this name by your friends. Even go so far as to ask a few people in your life to try calling you by the name that provisionally feels like "the one" for a few hours to see how it feels.
- Write yourself a letter addressed in your new name and mail it. When the envelope arrives, see if this feels as if it's really for you.
- Check out a name's usage in Judaism. In what verses of Torah and prayer does it appear? A

keyword search online or on a Torah disk can prove fascinating and sometimes sobering. There may be an important message embedded in that verse for you, or the name might have connections you don't want.

- Drop by a Jewish library, where dictionaries and books of Hebrew names will be on hand to help with your search.

- When it's right, you and those who understand you well will feel that the name resonates with your soul. Then go for it—organize a ritual to formally take on your name, and then let positive change in the world become quickly associated with your new name; make a donation to a good cause in honor of this special step you've taken.

BUTTERFLIES TO WISDOM

Hebrew letters also represent numerical values, as do letters in the languages derived from Hebrew. Beside the number 1 in Figure 4.2, you will see an *aleph*, the first letter of the Hebrew alphabet. Continue to read down the first column: The second letter of the Hebrew alphabet is called *bet* and has the value of two, the *gimel* three, and so on. *Aleph*, *bet*, *gimel* in Hebrew, "one, two, three," appear later as *alpha*, *beta*, *gamma* in Greek. And, of course, the word "alphabet" originates in the letters *aleph*, *bet*, later know as *alpha*, *beta*. The Hebrew letters' values follow the order of their appearance in the abecedary. By jotting down the numerical value for every letter in a word and adding them up, you will arrive at a total numerical value for that word.

ק	100		י	10		א	1
ר	200		ך כ	20		ב	2
ש	300		ל	30		ג	3
ת	400		ם מ	40		ד	4
			ן נ	50		ה	5
			ס	60		ו	6
			ע	70		ז	7
			ף פ	80		ח	8
			ץ צ	90		ט	9

Figure 4.2 Hebrew letters and their numerical values.

Gematria—the numerological system by which hidden meanings of words can be discovered through various ways of figuring out and comparing or utilizing their numerical values—was not viewed as a game by the sages, who used it to determine some aspects of Jewish law and recognized the right of anyone to create *gematria*-based interpretations that uphold Jewish sacred practices. Many of them loved to explore the correlations between the values of words, and they created many permutations of the Hebrew letters through their numeric values. *Parparot l'hohmah*, "butterflies to wisdom," is the affectionate expression used for this practice, perhaps because a fluttering of new awareness shimmers as the mind does calculations and notices correlations that "take wing" as the human spirit connects with possible depths of meaning in Torah.

The famed eleventh-century Torah commentator Rabbi Abraham Ibn Ezra wrote three treatises on numbers that brought Muslim numeric principles, including the concept of zero, to Europe. He also noted in his commentary on Genesis that a person can design *gematriot* (plural) to teach good or evil. As with any other spiritual practice, the value of *gematria* rests in the ethical condition and degree of awareness of the practitioner.

Let's experiment with learning a few words and principles of Judaism by using aspects of *gematria* as our system of study.

THE LETTER *MEM*

To start simply we will look at one letter, *mem*, מ, which has the numerical value forty, a number with a great deal of significance in Judaism. As the Torah recounts:

- Forty days and forty nights of rain turned the earth into a womb of new life and new possibilities.
- Moses' mountaintop retreats are for forty days, during which time Torah, a new vision of civilization, will be birthed.
- After the breaking of the waters of the Red Sea, the Israelites wander forty years in the wilderness, discovering what it takes to become a free people.

And, it's important to recall:

- A normal human pregnancy has forty weeks of gestation.
- A pool for ritual immersion, symbolizing the Cosmic Womb and a place of spiritual cleansing

and rebirth, must have forty *seah*, "units" of water,
to be kosher.

So whenever the number forty comes into play, a major transformation at the level of soul is likely to take place.

The letter *mem* has two forms,
one closed:

מ

traditionally symbolizing pregnancy—incubation
of a child, a concept, an idea, a new possibility—

and one open:

מ

symbolizing birth
of the child, the concept, an original creation,
or a new level of awareness.

Now that many associations with the *mem* as a symbol of transformation have been established, let's move on to a whole word,
מים, *mayyim*, which means "water" and utilizes both forms of
the *mem*. The practice of immersing yourself for spiritual purification, called *mikvah*, is being reclaimed in a variety of ways
across the full spectrum of Jewish practice—as part of the
healing ritual for rape victims, cancer patients entering or com-
pleting courses of chemotherapy, and in other health situations;
prior to rabbinic ordination; following a troubling experience,
such as a visit to Auschwitz; and more traditionally to prepare
the body and spirit of brides and grooms or of those readying
themselves at the level of soul for Shabbat or a holiday.

The *mikvah* must include *mayyim <u>h</u>ayyim*, "living waters,"
such as rainwater or ocean or river water. It recalls every

human's womb-time, as well as the waters of Eden, the birthing place of expanded consciousness. Going under water as a purification process returns you to the closed *mem*, the place of new beginnings, and as you emerge, the second *mem* of *mayyim* opens, releasing you slightly changed and ready for a step forward in your life.

RECIPE #24:
A *Mem*
Practice

Whatever your reason for contemplating a ritual immersion, preparation is key to the experience. Be sure to select a place that is private. Find out whether there are affordable and attractive local *mikvah* facilities, or determine a time when the tide of a local river, lake, or ocean is high enough and you are likely to be undisturbed. In a pinch, some have been known to simply add rainwater along with fresh tap water to a large hot tub. It is customary to wear nothing during immersion—to be like you were at birth. Every hair is meant to go under, so having a friend along to watch over you is a precious partnership to forge. *Mikvah* facilities provide someone to do this, but you might want to ask someone who understands your life and who can be a support to you. In Sephardi families the women often hold a *mikvah* party for a bride. Now, here is a creative approach to preparing yourself:

- Lacing your fingers together, allow your body to take the shape of a *mem sofit*, the closed *mem* of incubation. What are you holding that you wish to release during your immersion? Let yourself become clear about this; form your awareness into words.

- Open your arms and contemplate what you want to be able to take into the spaciousness you are creating. If you are leaving the workweek for Shabbat, what qualities do you wish your home to attract? If you are entering a challenging personal process of some kind, what qualities do you want strengthened in yourself? Formulate your questions and your responses as you prepare.
- In the *mikvah* itself, you might form a *mem* again with your arms and recall what you wish to release, then immerse.
- Create a closed *mem* and open it to welcome the qualities you wish to support, and immerse again.
- Immerse one last time and just purely enjoy the experience of being a human be-ing. The first breath you take as you emerge from this Cosmic Womb experience is like the first breath of life, or as Genesis 1:2 describes it, *ruah elohim m'rahefet al p'nai ha-mayyim*, "the breath of *elohim* flutters on the surface of the water."

Once your partner confirms that all your immersions are full and kosher, complete your ritual by reciting the blessing for immersion:

> *Baruh* [you know what this means!] *atah* are You *adonai* [and you know what this means] *eloheynu* [our *elohim*, you know what this means] *meleh* [king, or as you saw in chapter 2, "Reclaiming G*d with Integrity," a more mystical version is, Governing or Organizing Principle] *ha-olam* of the world [*olam* also means eternity and universe; you can sense all three here] *asher kidshanu* [that makes us holy] *b'mitzvotav* [through

mitzvot, sacred acts done with consciousness] *v'tzivanu* [and commanded us; that is, it's in the user's manual] *al ha-t'vila* [regarding the immersion].

See *Reclaiming Judaism as a Spiritual Practice: Holy Days and Shabbat* for a creative *mikvah* blessing and additional ideas and background on the practice, and visit www.Reclaiming Judaism.org for more traditional sources.

RECIPE #25:
Try Your
Hand at
Gematria

Figure out the total numerical value of מים *mayyim*, "water," by looking up the numerical value of each Hebrew letter in Figure 4.2 (see p. 155).

Now what is the value for לבבנו *levahveynu*, "our hearts"?

Both should have come out to be the same value. If not, redo your calculations.

Now, using a concordance, a book that lists where in the Bible every word appears, or doing a keyword search on a Torah CD or website, you will find that *levahveynu* occurs in Deuteronomy 1:28, where Moses is recounting the fantastic journey he and the people have made together, saying that because they were so fearful, some of the challenges they faced seemed like giants to them. The phrase Moses uses to describe how they were affected by the mighty challenges they faced is *heymaso levahveynu*, "they melted our hearts," meaning their courage or determination melted away. Their love for freedom, for the whole idea of *yud hey vav hey*—the capacity to be in love with life, to have *ahavat hashem*, to "love G*d"— melted in the face of fear.

In the Introduction the concept of *penimiut*, the "inside"

meanings of Torah, was introduced. This often means discovering that the *p'shat*, "simple," or face value of a verse, is virtually the opposite of its more profound meanings. This will prove to be the case with our verse.

If you do a keyword search in Torah on "heart," you will find among the options both heart and water in the same section: "I will sprinkle pure water upon you and you will be pure from all your errors and all your idols. I will purify you. I will give you a new heart and I will give within you a new spirit and I will remove the heart of stone from your flesh and I will give you a heart of flesh. I will put my breath/spirit within you so that you will walk in my statutes" (Ezekiel 36:25–26).

Water in Torah is always a symbol of the presence of G*d. Melting a stone-cold heart and being able to move forward require reconnection with *yud hey vav hey* awareness, which is when the greatest fear of change arises; this is the place of greatest opportunity for freedom and growth. It is a mitzvah articulated in Friday night *kiddush* to remember *yitziyat mitzrayim*, "leaving Egypt," as a way to stay connected to the Power that Makes for Transformation.

Now you have seen how just one small formulation of *gematria* can work. Links at www.ReclaimingJudaism.org will help you travel further if this fusion of Hebrew, numerology, and Torah study appeals to you.

THE POLITICS OF SACRED LANGUAGE

Every Shabbat we are all reading and discussing the same chapter of the same book, the Torah, and yet coming up with many rich and helpful new insights and interpretations in every generation. There is a caution to be noted: It is important to work with as many different commentators' works as are accessible to you, and, since we are not all talented in Hebrew, it is important to read with the awareness that translations have allowed for some serious moral manipulation of the text by sages and interpreters. The majority of translations, for example, perpetuate a major error in the translation of the word *tza-ra'at*, which is found twenty-one times in the Torah. Scholars both greater and lesser offer "leprosy" as the translation for this word, but it can't mean that, because epidemiological research has found no evidence of leprosy in any skeletal remains until long after biblical times. In addition, none of the symptoms of Hansen's disease, "leprosy," correlate with those given for *tza-ra'at*. And, finally, *tza-ra'at* occurs most often as a psychospiritual reaction to a toxic event, as, for example, we discussed in depth in chapter 3, "Taking Torah Personally." There Miriam challenges Moses' relationship with a Cushite woman, is then severely chastised by G*d, and her anger and humiliation are manifested in a skin eruption or scaling called *tza-ra'at*.

How did such an egregious mistranslation occur? When the Torah was translated from Hebrew into Greek in the year 250 BCE, *lepra*, the generic Greek term for any skin disorder, was used. Then, when the Greek was translated into English, the term was viewed as a transliteration, and "leprosy" was picked up as the intended meaning. Since leprosy had emerged as a significant new disease by the time the Christian Scriptures were written, it didn't occur to anyone to question the translation. Since the 1800s, however, starting with a British monk who first identified the error, scholars have from time to time taken note of the problem. But few translations have corrected the error, in part because a theology of punishment by G*d is heavily keyed to this interpretation. The use

of leprosy as the translation for *tza-ra'at* has allowed funda-
mentalists to declare that people with leprosy were being pun-
ished by "G*d," which has, in turn, allowed others to justify
treating lepers and women seeking leadership roles as less than
human. And this same rationale is now being brutally applied
in fundamentalist religious circles to those with AIDS.

SO CLAIM YOUR POWER

Consider the word *arum*. In the Garden of Eden story the snake
is called *arum*, and this is usually translated as "cunning." Then,
when Adam and Eve eat of the forbidden fruit they realize that
they are *arum(im)*, generally translated as "naked." During a
Shabbat afternoon Torah study, my husband, Barry, then new to
the in-depth study of Torah and Hebrew, noticed the likely
common root *aleph—reish—mem*, and asked whether you could
read the passage to mean that the snake was naked and Adam
and Eve were cunning. After all, this story is full of scapegoating
(scapesnaking?). Adam takes the Eve-made-me-do-it approach,
and Eve has the-snake-made-me-do-it defense.

The answer is that many linguists and some commentators
see *arum* and *arumim* as coming from different root families, so
that one means "uncover" or "lay bare" and the other means
"clever." But since all the stories were transmitted in oral form
before the Torah was written, likely the long ago listener
would also have heard and appreciated this interpretation.

Many have faulted Eve and termed this interval the "original sin." But what if this were seen as a coming-of-age story?
While I was teaching in Russia, a group of Jewish women who
had never before been exposed to the story saw Eden as symbolic of a womb incubating humanity and the animals, and

they believed that Eve's curiosity was essential to the birthing of the fullness of creation. Is bringing forth children with pain, as the Torah describes Eve's plight, a punishment or a really good description of the learning process in the story—that growing pains lead to knowing gains?

These unique interpretations are examples of how the power of even a little Hebrew can send you through a new and intriguing doorway of consciousness.

THE VALUE OF TRANSLATIONS

As your fluency in Hebrew increases, multiple meanings will begin to sing out for your consideration. Take, for example, the scene at Sinai, just before the giving of Torah. G*d tells Moses to prepare the people for three days, and indicates that their preparation should include washing their clothes. Moses issues instructions for spiritual preparation that include: "Wash your clothes, bathe, and [he adds of his own accord] for three days do not go near a woman." Excuse me! Surely there's another possibility here? And there is. The scene is full of volcanic imagery, lightning, and fire, which allow for another interpretation—one our *man*cestors did not notice. The Hebrew text is *al tigshoo el eeshah*. Could this verse be read instead, using the same Hebrew letters, as "Don't go near *eish-ah*, 'Her fire?'"

But why "Her," you might ask? First, *eishah* would be a feminine verb form, and second, as you learned in chapter 2, in the *targumim*, the Aramaic Torah translations that were read aloud when we lived under the Greek Empire and few knew Hebrew, the feminine noun *shehinah* is used when the presence of God is felt to come down—as a cloud on the tabernacle, on a mountain, into or in front of the camp of the Israelites. The mountain is pouring out fire; a boundary has been set that the people may not cross "lest you die." While our *mancestors'* translations and commentaries, regardless of the language in which they were writing, consistently sustained the interpretation "Don't go near a woman," I see "Don't go near Her fire." How about you?

Just as in this chapter's study of water, we could go on to look at the word *eish*, "fire," and find more interpretive options that would yield worthwhile insights. Indeed, you are accumulating a range of interpretive methods for working with a Hebrew word: studying words from the same root, looking at other usages in our sacred texts, accessing commentary by the ancestors, figuring out the *gematria* for a word or phrase and looking up words and phrases with the same values, fact-checking assumptions about a word's meaning, and using your *seyhel* (Yiddish for innate sense).

> Every translation is really
> someone's interpretation,
> based on politics,
> life experience,
> assumptions,
> values.

> Judaism invites your voice.
> We're a free people, with a saying:
> Two Jews, three opinions.

> Go for it, fly direct.
> Find your own meaning
> through the lens of the
> original Hebrew text.
> Your interpretations are holy, too.

5

Living a Mitzvah-Centered Life

Living a mitzvah-centered life
is the primary form of
Jewish spiritual practice.

Mitzvot
are concentrated legacies;
cues for where to enter the
infinite potential
for meaningful transformation.

Imagine walking in the world as if all those you encountered
were your guests—folks on the bus, in line at the supermarket,
in class, around the table at home, and so on. This is an
example of living in a mitzvah-centered state of consciousness; it is perhaps the opposite of living with consumer consciousness, where you are watching carefully to make sure you
receive all allotted entitlements. One of Judaism's 613
mitzvot, "guidelines for living," *is hahnassat orhim,* "letting in

guests"—that is, living with the flaps of the tent of your life up and open, being aware and receptive. Based on its root, *tzav*, "command," *mitzvah* (singular) is typically translated as "commandment." The mitzvot originate in the Torah as a template for the transition of those acculturated to systems of enslavement into the capacity to live as a *goy kadosh*, a "holy nation."

Taken together the mitzvot create a blueprint for conscious living that is in a continuous state of v.o.s., "verify on site," because they require study and reflection in order to ensure meaningful application to the times in which we live. There are two major types of mitzvot:

- 365 *mitzvot lo-taaseh*, "not to do" behaviors from which to refrain, such as killing, lying, polluting, seeking revenge.
- 248 *mitzvot aseh*, behaviors "to do," such as the pursuit of peace and justice, studying, caring for the poor and elderly, seeking happiness.

Every chapter of this book and its companion volume is concerned with mitzvot, because they are the foundational units of Jewish life. This chapter will reveal an even wider array of life-enhancing mitzvot. To begin, let's look in as a group of young Jewish Ukrainian students attending a Project Kesher seminar encounter a group of children suffering from the after-effects of the Chernobyl nuclear disaster. Project Kesher is a grassroots organization that partners Western women with Jewish women in the independent states of the former Soviet Union (FSU). Project Kesher provides a process, an infrastructure, and resources to help the FSU women define and address their own needs in their own communities, and its priorities have proved to be renewing Jewish life, empowering women financially, and securing women's health and safety. So, let's join that group of women.

Oy. Where are those feathers? It is time for the closing ritual of the Ukraine-based mother-daughter retreat on meaningful living through the lens of Jewish practice. I'd set a packet of brightly colored feathers in the craft supply cabinet with the intention of blessing and decorating the girls with them to symbolize how each is expressing *shehinah*—G*d as Sheltering Presence—through the qualities of her actions each day. Hmm. Maybe I forgot and left the feathers in the kitchen storage area?

We are sharing the retreat center, a former tuberculosis sanatorium, with several hundred children who have contracted fatal illnesses and are slowly dying from the radiation spewed into the atmosphere by the Chernobyl nuclear plant disaster. The children are on a state-sponsored retreat and, although we see each other across the dining room at every meal, the sanatorium administration has declared them off-limits to our group. The staff have also taken down the mirrors in the main program rooms, declaring that the children are better off not seeing the fullness of their sorry physical appearance while on vacation.

My feather hunt leads me to the dining room. What a scene! The girls from our Project Kesher retreat are gaily running amidst the children of Chernobyl, decorating them with feathers and showing them how beautiful they look in the tiny compact mirrors these newly-exposed-to-makeup, post–communist era Ukrainian girls all seem to carry. The children of Chernobyl are preening and giggling—the first happiness seen from them in a week.

The sanitarium staff rush over to me, gesticulating forcefully, clearly intending in the absence of a translator for me to get the girls to close those mirrors and leave, at once! Behind them looms a now-antique mural of a woman who seems to be the Arm and Hammer Baking Soda box lady. She is glaring down at us in equal disapproval. What to do with such a conflict of policy and happiness?

The Project Kesher students notice my presence and begin to look concerned. One runs out and returns with a translator in tow. Soon all the girls surround me, eagerly speaking in cacophonous excitement.

When she feels that she's heard enough to interpret, the translator enters the fray: "Reb Goldishkeh—these girls, they hope you are happy with them. They say to tell you that they have just made their first mitzvah!"

RECIPE #26:
Mitzvah
Cards

- Gather three highlighter pens, each a different color.
- Read over the mitzvah cards that appear in the Appendix (see pp. 237–241). Linger with each one before moving on. With one color, highlight those that are already active cornerstones of your daily life. (It is especially nice to photocopy these pages and cut out each card so that you have a deck. You might also create a batch of blanks—although the deck may feel full, it's only a subset of the many mitzvot available for activation in your life.)

- Now, review the cards that remain unhighlighted. With a different color, highlight those mitzvot that do *not* speak to you at all or that you doubt you ever will have an interest in fulfilling.
- With the last color in hand, read all the remaining unmarked cards and highlight those mitzvot that pique your curiosity and draw your attention.
- Now consider this last group of mitzvot. Which ones create a shift you sense in your body, not just in your active thoughts? Stay with those. Which one of these seems most appropriate for your life course right now?
- Make a plan to try out this particular mitzvah, to learn more about its full expression. You might journal on what you notice as you prepare for it, engage in it, and how you feel afterwards. Courses on mitzvot tend to be widely available in local communities. If you seek and don't find one whose orientation suits you as a learner, drop by www.ReclaimingJudaism.org, where from time to time classes and retreats are offered on mitzvah study and implementation, and where you can also arrange for a private tutorial. Each mitzvah you learn is likely to open into a lifetime of spiritual adventures.
- Now go for it! Pick up your markers and see what highlights you might select to enter into the story of your life!

Note: The sixteenth-century sage and chief rabbi of Prague, Rabbi Yehudah Loew, known as the Maharal, taught that

unless we align our actions with the mitzvot, the very existence of the world is jeopardized. Revisit the mitzvah cards
with this concern in mind. Could he be right?

PREPARING FOR A MITZVAH

It is customary to prepare for a nonemergency mitzvah with
a sacred phrase called a *kavannah*, "intention," based on the
root *kav*, "line," indicating focus. The *kavannah* for a *mitzvah*
begins with one of two very similar words—*hareini* or *hineini*,
"Here I am." This is the response given by those who feel
called. In the Torah such callings involve a name being
called twice—"Abraham. Abraham!!" "Moses. Moses!"
"Samuel. Samuel!" As you become accustomed to mitzvah
practice, opportunities may well begin to tug at you, once,
twice—

hineini [or *hareini*]	Here I am
muhan u'm'zuman	ready and invited
l'kayem mitzvat	to carry out the guidance
bo-ree	of my Creator
_____	[here add the name of the mitzvah.]

Or, you might put this into a more personalized formulation:

Hineini, present in this moment, I am here to undertake
the mitzvah of ... supporting someone in need ... as you
write a check, offer a meal, provide shelter, and so on.

... watching over my body as sacred space ... as you
take in proper nutrition and exercise, go for a checkup,
and do all that is necessary to protect your health.

... experiencing the holiness of time ... as you make Shabbat, fast for Yom Kippur, take meals in your *sukkah*, and so on.

... or as you refrain from acts that can do damage:

Hineini, here I am

... tempted to advertise a product by touting virtues it doesn't have, I take on the mitzvah of not engaging in g'*nivat da'at*, "theft of awareness," and will hold back.

... about to speak ill of a colleague, I take on the mitzvah of refraining from gossip, *lashon hara*, "evil speech."

Your custom-made *kavannah* might become a chant that helps you to keep your intentions aligned with your actions. Those who start young are blessed with moments like this one experienced by my grandson, age three:

"*Tatte*. Daddy!"

"Yes, Binyamin Zev?"

"Kids were saying mean things about me at school today."

"Let's go together to tell your teacher about this and she'll speak to those boys."

"*Tatte?*"

"Yes, son?"

"But I can't tell you their names: That would be *lashon ha-ra*."

Lashon hara—speaking ill of someone, even when it's true, unless there's a serious duty to warn, is a great example of one of the 365 *mitzvot lo-taaseh*, guidelines for "what not to do."

> All depends on the *kavannah,*
> "focus" of the heart.
> —*Megillah 20a*

INCREASING MEANING FOR LIVING

Ivan, a historian and sometime guide during my first teaching assignment in Ukraine, insists that I must visit Shargorad, a *shtetl*, "tiny town." Though no Jews live there now, he describes it as a town frozen in time, the 1500s to be specific. "Why don't Jews live in Shargorad?" I inquire through my ever-present translator, Tonya.

"Shot by the Stalinists," he explains, "buried in the depths of the forest."

Shargorad does indeed provide a pure *shtetl* scene: donkey-drawn carts; women carrying buckets of well water over their shoulders; cobblers in leather aprons working in stone grottos; narrow, winding, cobbled streets; and at the front of the town an Ottoman-style synagogue, now a winery. We turn down a noncommercial street and soon Ivan stops to point at the porch of an abandoned house. "This was a Jewish house," he announces with apparent satisfaction at finding something Jewish to show us.

"How do you know that?"

"The Jews loved porches. On Shabbat afternoon they would sit out with sweets and take turns strolling along the streets visiting friends, sharing a leisurely afternoon."

We step up onto the porch of the house to check for the shadow of a mezuzah on the doorway, except that my first step crashes through the ancient floorboards. Oops. I mutter a "Sorry" under my breath to the former tenants.

Suddenly, the door flies open and an elderly woman emerges screaming at us in indignant Russian. When she slows down a bit, Ivan explains that he is showing a *genchena ravveen*, a "woman rabbi," the history of the area. Without missing a beat the woman begins to shout at us in Yiddish, finally ending hoarsely with what translates to: "Don't pee down my back and tell me it's raining! There's no such thing as a woman rabbi, and if there were, she'd have more respect for private property!" And she is incredulous to learn that we believed Jews no longer live in Shagorad.

"Of course Jews live in Shargorad! Where don't Jews live? Not that we would let the world know we're here. It's not exactly a good idea to be known as Jewish. Don't you know history? Do you want to meet the Jews of Shargorad? It's Sunday. I can bring them here to you."

She eases her way down the broken steps and heads off. We wait. Soon the alley beside her house begins to fill with Jews of all ages. In the thigh-high snow of a Ukrainian "spring," I envy them their tall fur hats. They are talking among themselves, I understand only a bit: *"Ravveen! Ravveen?!"* " Rabbi! Rabbi?!" Then an older man shouts out quite angrily. I turn to my translator, Tonya. She appears not to have noticed.

"What did he say?" I ask.

"Who?" Tonya asks.

"That man over there."

"… Him? Oh, nothing."

"What did he say? I need to know."

"It's not important," she replies.

"What did he say?!" I ask more insistently. "Look, I am paying you to translate for me. What did he say?"

She sighs and shrugs, as though to say, What can I do with such an obstinate person?

"He said that Judaism is nothing but magic and superstition; that Jews put amulets on their doorways to keep away evil spirits and no wonder Jews helped to invent communism."

Another man shouts. "What did he say?" I ask.

"He said that if there really is such a thing as a woman rabbi, you would teach some Torah."

Oh, G*d. What a challenge. I had just been to the grave of the Baal Shem Tov, the founding rebbe of Ḥasidism. (Yes, another fascinating story, for another day.) Although I usually "pray direct," standing there before an array of unexpected Jews, a spontaneous plea arose within me: "Please, Baal Shem Tov, this is your neighborhood. You know how to work this crowd. Please help me! What could be the right words of Torah to teach, right here, right now?"

The sea of people disappears from my awareness. Something or somewhere is opening inside. Like a gift from Beyond, or perhaps from the Baal Shem Tov himself, a completely new teaching comes through, one not found in books.

"When we Jews come to the door of our homes, we aren't meant to run right in and spill the *shmutz* of the day out onto those inside. Instead we are taught to pause before entering our homes and to notice that little box on the doorpost that is called a mezuzah. Inside that little box is a tiny scroll with a section of Torah written upon it. It is from *devarim*,

'Deuteronomy,' and includes the message *shema v'ahavtah*, 'Listen so that you can love.'

"The mezuzah is actually a Jewish consciousness-shifting tool, reminding you to pause at the doorways of your homes, to pause and remember to enter *shema v'ahavtah*, listening so that you can love."

Emerging from the trance-like state that had allowed the Torah-telling to travel through me, I notice a few people have tears sliding down their cold-reddened faces. I hear the Russian word *m'leetvah*, "prayer," whispered alternately with "*Torah?*" The same man calls out again. He sounds soft and dignified this time. Tonya translates his words as: "Thank you, Rabbi. Perhaps you could stay on? It seems this town may still need a rabbi."

RECIPE #27:
Preventing
Blood on
Your
Doorposts

Pause in your religious imagination and listen at the doorposts of your home. What do you hear?

Walk through your home. Is there a particular room that most needs to be renewed spiritually?

Consider taking this walk with other occupants, including children of all ages, and listen to what they recall without becoming defensive. Listen so that all can love.

RECIPE #28:
Holding a
Hanging Party

Ritual energizes transformation. A mezuzah-placing ritual can be held for numerous reasons. Here are just a few:

- Dedication of a new home or place of residence.
- Has an elderly parent come to live with you? Would it be meaningful for family to gather and join in a welcoming dedication of her room with a new mezuzah?
- Are there rooms you noted in Recipe #27 where perhaps unkind words were exchanged and a re-dedication is appropriate?
- Perhaps a new baby has arrived or a child has become bar or bat mitzvah and a mezuzah-placing seems timely. Is the mezuzah case in place now too child-like for a young person returning from college? Again, a great opportunity for a mezuzah-placing ritual.
- Recently a family spoke of bringing a mezuzah to hang on the doorpost of a loved one's hospice room. The doctor also asked to attend the ritual and described the experience as deeply moving and meaningful for him as well.
- Someone heading off to college? The doorpost of a dorm room will also benefit from a visible mezuzah.
- There are many more—what will you add to this list of mezuzah-hanging moments?

While hanging a mezuzah is meant to be done when you move into your home, it can also be done at any time other than on Shabbat or a holy day, when you would abstain from labor. There is also a tradition of doing mezuzah-hangings on Hanukkah, the holiday of "rededication" of the Temple. _Hanukkat ha-bayit_, "dedication of the home," the name for the mezuzah-hanging ritual, shares a root with Hanukkah, _hee-_

nuh—"education, dedication, enlightenment, upbringing, consecration," which makes <u>H</u>anukkah an especially appropriate time for giving and hanging a mezuzah.

- For your mezuzah ritual, you will need a kosher mezuzah scroll and a case. These are available from Jewish gift shops and online. To be kosher the scroll is handwritten with "focused intention," *kavannah*, and precision, by a *sofer*, "scribe," with special ink on special paper. The paper then gets rolled up and tucked into the mezuzah case. If you already have a mezuzah on every doorway, you might change to a more beautiful casing as part of your ritual.
- Before the day of your ritual, open the case and check the scroll to make sure it isn't a photocopy and, if it is authentic, check to see if it has aged due to indoor high or low humidity or outdoor weather conditions and visiting insects. A scroll should be replaced if it has holes, even tiny ones, or has faded.
- Check your doorpost(s) to see if they are metal or wood. Double-sided tape will be needed for the former and tiny screws for the latter. Screws are better than nails because you'll be less likely to break the case when you want to remove it from the doorpost to open it and check the scroll at some later date.
- Choose a popular melody or verse from Torah to gather the energy of your community of friends and/or new neighbors. You might simply chant a

verse from Psalms such as *ashrei yoshvei veite̲ha*,
"happy are those who dwell in Your house," or one
of the names of G*d, perhaps *ha-makom*, "the
Place." If you hold the silence at the end of such a
chant, it is likely to be a warm, rich silence, full of
the holiness that is filling your new room/home.
Visit www.ReclaimingJudaism.org to listen to some
chant options

- Now, the home/apartment/office/room's primary
  occupant(s) might speak about what this space
  means to them.

- While they do pass the mezuzah around to all the
  guests. As it makes the rounds, each person can
  hold it between his or her hands and infuse the
  mezuzah with a customized from-the-heart blessing
  for your new home. For example, "May this home
  be full of joyful gatherings of friends and family."
  Or, "May feelings revealed be received with understanding and kindness in this sacred place." You
  might invite participants to offer their blessings out
  loud, but also give them the opportunity to demur
  by simply passing the mezuzah on to the next
  person.

- A bit more chanting, then hold the mezuzah in
  place, about one-third of the way down the right
  side of the doorway as you enter, and set it comfortably at about shoulder height. Let the intentions of
  your heart for your home pour into the doorpost
  while you are holding the mezuzah in the place you
  will affix it. If others share your home, invite them
  to help hold and join in affixing the mezuzah.

- Attach the mezuzah and recite the traditional beginning of a blessing, *baruh atah adonai eloheynu meleh ha-olam asher kidshanu b'mitzvotav v'tzivanu,* and conclude with the *hatimah,* "seal" or "ending" of a blessing, which, in this case, is:

leekboa mezuzah   to affix a mezuzah.

If this is the first time you have ever put up a mezuzah, or the first time you have a place of your own, or the first time you've owned your own home, a *sheheheyanu* blessing for first times and special occasions is in order as well. The *sheheheyanu* has the same beginning, but instead of *leekboa mezuzah*, you say: *sheheheyanu* (that gives us life) *v'kimanu* (and sustains us) *v'higeeyanu* (and brings us near) *la-z'man ha-zeh* (this [special] time.)

Guests can now call out *siman tov* and *mazel tov*, which are astrologically based Hebrew blessings, retained in songs for joyful occasions. *Siman tov*—may this be happening under a good sign for you—and *mazel tov*, under a "good star," may its blaze bring good fortune. Today, *mazel* has come to mean *luck*—good luck for you in your new home. Now singing, socializing, noshing, and even dancing are in order!

WHAT ABOUT *HALAHAH?* CAN JEWISH LAW CHANGE?

Halahah technically refers to the full body of majority and minority reflections and decisions over the ages on how to implement and cultivate the foundational principles of Jewish living. The word *halahah* (most often spelled *halachah*) contains the nuances "walk," "way," "path," and "law." As the software of Jewish life, *halahah* sometimes requires a major upgrade, the primary example being when the Temple was destroyed and the sacrificial system was transformed into a model for personal and communal prayer at home and in synagogue. At other times, just a line of text needs to be added for the programming to run well in changing times. A good example of a line change is to take note of how most of the patriarchs in the Torah married multiple wives and legally sired children with concubines. Even so, in the tenth century a sage known as Rabbeinu Gershom began to issue rulings that eventually led to the institution of a *takannah*, a legal "repair" requiring monogamy within Ashkenazi Judaism. (While polygamy is still technically permitted in Sephardi Judaism, the State of Israel has ruled it to be illegal.)

Orthodox and some Conservative Jews follow a halahic chain of thinking within their daily life and will seek out the assistance of their rabbi when the decision-making pathway for a personal situation isn't clear to them. For unusual ethical dilemmas there are *poskim*, scholars who specialize in responding to challenging new areas of Jewish ethics and law—for example, cloning, genetically engineered crops or children, or the need for reducing the number of fetuses in a pregnancy so that some can survive. In Reconstructionism scholars and leaders will prepare study materials to help communities decide on local practices or major ethical issues. And all branches of Judaism have a process for reaching consensus and forming national positions. For example, the Reform, Reconstructionist, and Jewish Renewal movements have all agreed on the importance of full recognition and Jewish ritual for gay and lesbian marriages, an issue still under consideration by the Conservative Movement's Committee on Jewish Law and Standards.

Halahah evolves steadily.
Once negated as too risky
to donor and recipient,
today becoming an organ donor is a mitzvah.

Have you signed your card
so that one day you can fulfill
the mitzvah of *pikuah nefesh*,
"saving a living soul"?

Change is a Jewish tradition.
Some changes are rapid,
Others transpire at glacial pace.
All, once adopted, seem
always to have been the case.

YOU DECIDE THE PATH OF THE TRADITION, TOO!

Decisions are not always made by rabbis, scholars, or religious courts. The Talmud shows that a consensus of behavior emerging from within the Jewish people can also sometimes change the way a practice or tradition is applied. For example, across most of the Jewish spectrum, advances in the status of women are a direct result of activism. You, therefore, have an important role to play in the formulation of the Judaism of the future. Deep thinking from the past, however, figures just as prominently in the legacy you've been handed. Let's look at the intersection of mitzvah and modernity and talk about food.

CONSCIOUS CONSUMPTION

The regular kosher way is about the dishes that mustn't be contaminated and so on. If I pick a cup to have coffee, Styrofoam would be the best thing to have. It hasn't been used before, and after I drink from it, I'll throw it away and nobody else will use it. From the usual kosher place that's the direction to go ... but in comparison to what will happen to the planet by my drinking from Styrofoam, I'd much rather make the other choice ... eco-kosher.

—*Rabbi Zalman Schachter-Shalomi*

Conscious eating practices and the ethical considerations behind them are a major Jewish spiritual practice. At least six mitzvot will synergize for you intellectually when you contemplate what "eco-kosher" could mean as a Jewish software upgrade:

- *Bal tash-hit*—Tolerate no wanton destruction of the planet (Deuteronomy 20:19–20).

  Is the environment protected by the packaging and planting practices of the companies from which you buy?
- *Tzaar baalei hayyim*—Allow no unnecessary pain to sentient beings (Exodus 23:5).

  Is the veal milk-fed? Was a baby animal confined in a tiny cell for your eating pleasure? Were dolphin-safe fishing practices utilized by the tuna fishing firms? How were the laborers involved in the production, transportation, and packaging of your food treated in terms of wages, benefits, hours, and working conditions?

- *Shmirat ha-guf*—Care for your body as it is a precious gift (Deuteronomy 4:9).

  Do you want bovine growth hormone in the milk your children drink? What about certain pesticides? Are you on a calorie-restricted diet? If you are to prepare a meal with your own health considerations in mind, what criteria need to be added to this list?

- *Lifnei iveyr lo teeteyn mikshol*—Put no stumbling block before the blind (Leviticus 19:14).

  What are the dietary needs of those at your table: Is someone a diabetic? A heart patient? An alcoholic? It takes thought to prepare a meal that will bring pleasure to all while not tripping up those with serious health considerations.

- *Hahnassat orhim*—Ensuring your guests feel truly welcome (Genesis 18:1–8).

  While not all guests have medical problems, they may well have important dietary preferences, such as a vegetarian lifestyle; or they may observe the more technical practices of keeping kosher. Often accommodating such dining differences is not as complex as it may sound—just ask your guests what would work for them.

- *Kashrut*—Pay attention to what you choose to eat and how it is prepared (Leviticus 9:1–11:47).

  Jewish tradition teaches the importance of making distinctions through conscious eating. This vast system of separating milk from meat foods, dishes, utensils, and more stems in many ways from a verse in Exodus 23:19: "Do not seethe a kid in its mother's milk." Milk is the gift of life. Meat is life taken away.

It is part of the mitzvah of keeping kosher, *kashrut*, to remember the gift and the sacrifice of the animal's life by keeping that which is dead separate from that which gives life. Does this idea touch you in any way? Free-range kosher products are becoming increasingly available and these multiply many times the mitzvah of *kashrut*. The more of us who participate, the more affordable for all and the more kindness to animals, planet, workers, and self will prevail. *Kashrut* is a system with many aspects; you can learn more at the www.ReclaimingJudaism.org website.

The mitzvot that connect to eating invite you to create your own running commentary when you go marketing, to keep asking yourself, "Is this product ethically kosher?" Try an experiment:

RECIPE #29: Developing an Ethical Eating Practice

- Head to the kitchen cabinets or refrigerator and take out some processed foods. Something made with milk products would be good, canned fish as a second item, and also something meat as a third choice, if you have meat in your home.
- Holding each one in your hand, and recalling the principles above, consider these items in relationship to the ethical aspects of Jewish sacred eating practice.
- Write down your own principles for ethical eating and consider carrying them on your next trip to the market.

CARING FOR YOUR BODY

What goes into your body is a subset of the mitzvah system called *shmirat ha-guf,* "watching over the body." In Judaism your body is meant to be treated far better than a rental apartment for which you hope to get the return of your security deposit. It is, indeed, the instrument on which you play your life. While I was sharing this principle during a Judaism and women's health workshop in Russia, the seed of a mitzvah awareness took off with remarkable power and poignancy.

My translator, Tonya, looked at me in that ashen way she had when I've made a huge mistake. "In Russian culture, you can't talk about your body and touch your breasts in public. Besides, you are a rabbi!" I was connecting the mitzvah of immersion, *mikvah,* upon monthly completion of a woman's menstrual cycle with another regular (w)holy healthy prac-tice, breast self-exam.

"Tonya, let's not jump to conclusions. Ask them what they think and feel about this idea." A dear friend had just died tragically young of cancer. A little embarrassment didn't seem like a big sacrifice if I could encourage good health care through Jewish spiritual practice.

Tonya interpreted my intent and a hand went up. A woman physician from a rural region asked, "Reb Goldie, do you mean to say that in the West there is a method for the early detection of breast cancer?"

Tears were falling as she spoke. I realized it was important to go around the room and invite people to share what they were feeling and why. Many described a legacy of losing beloved family and friends to breast cancer. The problem was worse there than in the West because of the lack of treatment and the absence of health education, pollution controls, and early detection mechanisms in most regions.

That connection—the leap from the spiritual practices honoring a woman's reproductive cycle, called *niddah*, to breast self-exam—triggered a huge project. A call to the United Nations and also the World Bank health departments led to one staff person responding angrily because I had introduced a concept for which there are few resources for treatment. "You will increase women's suffering if they know sooner that they have cancer!" The other organization was thrilled. "This will encourage women there to organize, lobby for social change, demand a shift in priorities in that country's gynocidal health policies."

As it turned out, the daughter of a Project Kesher supporter works at Planned Parenthood. When she related this story, her daughter secured Planned Parenthood support for the production of Russian-language cards teaching self-exam for breast and testicular health. The women in our seminars helped to distribute the cards, reaching out with the vital health information to church groups, too. Now Western volunteers are bringing over mammography equipment and technicians. The power of seeing life through the mitzvot was again realized in a positive, life-enhancing way, all triggered by what had appeared to be a side trip on the path of life.

MITZVAH OR CUSTOM?

While wearing a *kippah*, "skullcap," is a strongly held Jewish custom, the specially fringed *tallit* is an actual mitzvah *d'oraita*, which is Aramaic for "from the Torah."

And God told Moses:
"Speak to the children of Israel,
and guide them throughout their generations
to make fringes on the corners of their garments."
                                    —*Numbers 15:37–40*

Tallit eventually became associated with men. Today, however, many women, upon learning the words of Rabbi Yehudah found in the Talmud—"All must observe the law of *tzitzit*, Cohanim, Levites, and Israelites, converts, women and slaves" (*Menachot 43b*)—have again taken up the powerful and beautiful—and for women ever-so-natural—practice of wearing a prayer shawl.

Wherever you may be in the world, your *tallit* (*tallis* is the Ashkenazi pronunciation) is a portable personal sacred space made up of a shawl or a smaller undergarment (called a *tallit katan*, "small *tallit*") with specially knotted fringes on the corners. Once primarily blue and white or black and white, in our times a full rainbow of *tallit* colors and textures prevail. The *tzitzit*, "fringes," on each corner of a *tallit* are a reminder of how the fringes of all our lives are interconnected and symbolize Torah's 613 mitzvot, "sacred states of connected consciousness." While in Ezekiel, the prophet uses the word *tzitzit* to literally mean "strands," in the Song of Songs (2:9) the "Lover" in this magnificent epic work is described as *mehtzitz*, "peering through" a lattice as a deer appears amidst trees in the forest. So too are we meant to be reminded to live a mitzvah-centered life whenever our own or someone else's ritual fringes peek out at us.

We hear *tzitz* in one more important place in the reading of Torah: The high priest wore a gold forehead plate called a *tzitz* when he served in the Temple. Upon this headpiece *kodesh l'yud hey vav hey*, "Holy to G*d," was engraved in raised letters and affixed with a thread of *tehelet*, a color similar to cerulean blue that is described in the Midrash as the color of *shehinah*, of "Presence," and referred originally to the dominant color thread in each *tzitzit*. Wearing a *tallit* can be an experi-ence of being both held and holy, as the next story conveys.

When my sons, Adam and Mark, were toddlers, they would sometimes come to snuggle with me under my *tallit* during the *amidah*, the private, personal prayer portion of serv-ices. To hear them whispering the hopes, hurts, and happiness of their hearts as prayers filled me with awe. A common phrase in our liturgy is to be sheltered *tahat kanfei ha-shehinah*, "under the wings of *shehinah*." And ever-so-similarly would my boys describe themselves as baby birds under the *tallit* with me, where both *tallit* and Momma symbolized those sheltering wings, cosmically and intimately. To achieve this effect during parts of prayer when you want more privacy, it is common to lift your *tallit* into a kind of hooded shawl.

While the *tallit* can serve you powerfully during prayer, it also serves as a spiritual shelter at difficult times. A young stu-dent once called from a portable phone in a closet where she was hiding from an abusive uncle: "Rabbi, I called the police. They are coming," she whispered, "and I'm safely under my *tallit*, talking together with you and G*d." Another student once called from college to talk about a difficulty, saying that she'd wrapped herself in her *tallit* for the call and telling me that it had become a sacred space where she could cry and pray about her fears at this time in her life.

The Talmud records the opinion that those who engage in the mitzvah of *tzitzit* will have a *shehinah* experience, which was surely the case for these young people in distress. We have such traditions about our sages as well. The Maharshal, Rabbi Solomon Luria (1510–1574), for example, asked a close friend to be his ethical mirror, and during guidance sessions with this friend he would wrap himself in his *tallit*. It is easy to obtain a *tallit* online or through a local Jewish gift shop.

RECIPE #30:
Knot So Fast

Tying the knots for each corner of your *tallit* is a sacred activity you can do together with a special friend, family member, or mentor. Judaica shops sell precut sets of silk or cotton fringes for just this purpose. And is your present set quite frayed? It's fine to remove them and tie a new set on. As you may have heard, to prevent fraying, be sure to bind your fringes in foil for visits to the dry cleaner or else you could have Abe's experience: "The dry cleaner charged four times the usual price to clean my *tallit*!" Why was that, Abe—coffee stains? "No. He said it took him hours to get out all the knots!"

- Be sure to have a finished *tallit* nearby so you can see how a finished knotting looks.
- Remove three short strands and one long strand from the packet of fringes.
- Align them at one edge and slide them through the reinforced corner hole on one edge of the *tallit*. Continue until the three shorter strands are halfway through. (See a video at www.Reclaiming Judaism.org.)

- Now, with half the strands in one hand and half in the other, tie two tight knots just below the corner of the tallit.
- In order to fulfill the mitzvah of *tzitzit*, it is customary for you to say, *"l'shem mitzvat tzitzit,* for the sake of fulfilling the mitzvah of *tzitzit"* each time you tie a knot.
- Now, hold all the strands together and pull the longest one to the side. Wind the longest one seven times around all the strands, tightly under the first two knots.
- Now do two knots again, making sure to include the long strand each time when you are knotting; and wrap with the same longer strand eight times.
- Now do two knots again and wrap with the same longer strand eleven times.
- Now finally, do two knots and wrap with the same longer strand thirteen times.

Now close with two final tight knots and trim the *tzitzit* ends under the last two knots to a length that is appealing to you and won't drag on the floor when you're wearing your *tallit*. It is traditional to do this with your teeth rather than using a knife or scissors. As you've already learned, every Hebrew letter has a numerical value, and the value of the word *tzitzit* is 600; add to this 8 strands and 5 knots and each fringe is a visual reminder of the 613 mitzvot! For a powerful blessing ritual to use when preparing *tzitzit* for a bar/bat mitzvah student, visit the Bar/Bat Mitzvah section at www.Reclaiming Judaism.org. So, if *tzitzit* is such a significant mitzvah, surely we must talk about *kippah*!

KIPPAH AS OPPORTUNITY, KIPPAH AS CHALLENGE

I will not easily forget the day the lady at the Chinese takeout on New York City's Upper West Side would not give me a pint of Wonton soup. "You can't have it," she said.

"But I ordered and paid for it already." She goes to give me back my money. "No, I don't want the money, I want the soup."

She points at the *kippah* on my head, shakes her head no, and says, "Has pawlk, not for you." Then she points to the vegetarian side of the menu.

Of course, how could she know that I had just visited my ailing elderly Christian neighbor and offered to bring her the object of her craving, a carton of Wonton soup? So I had zipped across the street to bring her some, thus engaging the mitzvah of *ezrat holim*, "helping the ill," wearing, as I do every day if I'm not wearing a hat, one or another of my rainbow collection of *kippot* (pl).

All over the world, upon seeing my *kippah* every kind of Jewish person comes over to invite me to share Shabbat with them, or to ask a question about Jews or Judaism they've been carrying for some time, or to share a Jewish travel vignette or matter of the heart. And I also often stop someone wearing a *kippah* in a far-flung place to find out if there is a Jewish community, synagogue, or kosher restaurant nearby.

Kippah practice really makes the wearer aware of each action she is about to undertake, especially in public, because those who observe your actions and words will say to themselves, "So this is how a Jew acts."

Kippah is actually not a specific mitzvah; rather, it is a fairly recent custom for Jews, one unknown in biblical times. The Maharshal, a highly respected medieval sage, ruled wearing a *kippah* to be optional. Maimonides, one of the renowned innovators and codifiers of Jewish philosophy and law, who was also a full-time physician, didn't treat *kippah* as a law but simply offered the view that those who don't cover their heads don't take life seriously enough. Rashi, a vintner and scholar whose clear explanations of Torah and tradition are foundational to all Jewish study, recommended the wearing of a *kippah* as a sign of humility, a reminder that we did not create this amazing world teeming with abundance into which we were born. In Orthodox communities where gender differences are emphasized and affect permissible prayer and lifestyle practices, married women generally wear a hat, a scarf, or a wig called a *sheitl* rather than a *kippah* so as to convey an attitude of *tzniut,* "modesty," by more fully covering their hair. Single women signal singleness by leaving their hair uncovered until marriage.

While not a mitzvah per se, *kippah* is a simple and sometimes profound spiritual act. If it is not already your practice, consider locating a *kippah* of a size, shape, texture, and color that works for you and wear it for a few weeks. Or, if not all day, try adding a *kippah* when eating, while in services or private prayer, and during life-cycle events.

RECIPE #31:
What Color
Is Your
Kippah?

Notice if your life changes as people's perceptions and questions of you change, and as your sense of responsibility changes as a result of your walking in the world wearing this symbol.

It is fine to remove a *kippah* if you are in a situation where you feel that wearing it could be life-threatening. The Torah clearly says about Jewish practices, "You shall live by them" (Leviticus 18:5), and our sages understand this to also mean, "and not die by them." A famous example of this thinking is recounted by descendants of Rabbi Israel Lipkin of Salant (1810–1883) who, they say, made *kiddush*, drank wine, and ate a piece of cake on Yom Kippur during a typhus epidemic to emphasize to his congregants the priority of self-care under dire circumstances. And for the same reason it was considered proper to eat *treyf*, "nonkosher," if confined to a concentration camp during World War II.

Each practice guide herein is an opportunity.
Judaism is not meant to function as a cult.
No one can lock you into any particular denomination.
There's no one right way.
Jewish culture offers many variations on practices.
Different niches, even several niches, within Judaism
may serve your soul at different points in your life.
It's holy and healthy to experiment and explore.

THE TORAH OF MONEY

Heading to the subway, pass held tightly between my teeth, pulling luggage on both sides, a knapsack on my back, I realize this time I'll have to pass her by. "I'm sorry, my hands are so full. Will you be alright?" The woman to whom I always give change sits in the corner. She assesses my baggage and asks where I'm going. "To the Ukraine, a volunteer teaching assignment."

"Oh, my!" She exclaims, turning her cup of coins upside down and extending them toward me. "The people there are so very poor. Please give them my day's coins. They have so much less than me."

Jeffrey Dekro, coauthor of a work with the same title as this section, points out a remarkable passage in the Talmud:

> Rabbi Yishmael said: "One who wishes to acquire wisdom should study the way money works, for there is no greater area of Torah study than this. It is like an ever flowing stream."
>
> —*Bava Batra 175b*

Contributing to the flow of resources directed for the good of all, *tzedakah* seems like such a basic spiritual practice. Yet, to do this effectively, you must study the way money works; intelligent giving involves a learning process. Can the mitzvah of generosity be learned?

It is traditional to give children coinage, called H̲anukkah *gelt*, on H̲anukkah. The practice derives from the coins that were stamped by the Hasmoneans to commemorate their victory over the Greek Empire. As an alternative or complement to gift-giving, here's a way the guilt of *gelt* can be transformed through the mitzvah of learned giving.

RECIPE #32:
Reframing
Gelt

- Obtain a *pushkah*, a small donation container also known as a *tzedakah* box, for your home. You can make one from a coffee can by putting a hole in the lid or buy or fashion one of beauty; Judaica shops and catalogues carry many types.

- Encourage everyone in your family to regularly drop funds into the *pushkah*—money found in pockets in the wash, extra deposits when you feel especially blessed, or in honor of someone's memory or healing.

- On one of the nights of H̲anukkah, open all of the *tzedakah* boxes in the house and count the money. Announce the total and give the following assignment for another night of H̲anukkah: "Please bring a clipping about a cause you believe needs funding. Try to obtain a copy of the financial statement and program report of that organization; these are often online. Even better, visit the institutions associated with this cause if you can and report on what you see and learn. You will be the advocate for your cause. Also, bring three blank checks with you, just in case someone's presentation compels more than we have to allocate."

- On the day of your "*Gelt* Gathering" ask each person to present his or her cause, research, and analysis. For each cause, go around the table and invite questions, thoughts, ideas from all present. Ask each person to anonymously write down the percentage of the *tzedakah* money he or she recommends be allocated to each cause. Hand the results to one person, who will tally them for averages and place the *tzedakah* money in piles with a note indicating the amount and percentage going to each cause. One person will then write a check in those amounts for each cause and take the money for personal deposit.

- Now, set out envelopes labeled for each cause and ask those present to take out the three checks they've brought and decide to which causes they want to add funds. Once they've decided, place their checks in the appropriate envelopes. Some may want to enclose a note dedicating the donations in memory of a particular person. Seal and mail the envelopes. Now, remind those present to follow their cause—an advocate is a powerful and precious asset to a nonprofit.

> To fund a change in the world
> in the name of another
> is to fulfill two mitzvot:
> *zahor*, sacred memory, and *tzedakah*,
> the just sharing of your resources.

MITZVAH MYSTICISM

So how does holiness happen? Mitzvot are a remarkable part of the Jewish spiritual adventure. There is a mystical understanding of mitzvot articulated in the sacred work *Sefer Mivasair Tzedek*, which teaches that enlightenment is in part: "the moment when you realize that all your powers, virtues and qualities are nothing but aspects of G*d that have emanated into you, and a person is but a mere vessel. In the end, you will realize that you are only a piece of the Divine." In the words of Torah:

> A portion of G*d is G*d's people.
> —*Deuteronomy 32:9*

"Adam, we're almost done. Do you have any comment to make on the Torah reading?" We were at Dorshei Derech, a Reconstructionist community in Germantown, Pennsylvania, where everyone present gets a chance to make a comment on the weekly Torah reading. The difficult-to-interpret portion we were reading on the sacrificial system suggests that G*d loves *rey'ah hah'nee ho'ah*, "a savory smell." Adam was quite young, in second or third grade.

"Oh, yes. I think we have to see that for thousands of years people sacrificed 'aminals' because they believed G*d loved the smell of a barbecue and that if G*d smelled the Temple barbecue there would no more wars, storms, disease, volcanoes, or earthquakes.

"Then we figured out, well, G*d must not have a nose. So we worked on a new theory. G*d must have ears, and we prayed and prayed and prayed. But still there were wars, and storms, disease, volcanoes, and earthquakes.

"So I think my mommy's generation is working on a new theory—that G*d has hands." And young Adam reached out and took the hand of the people standing on either side of him, lifted their hands up high, and announced, "and these are the hands of G*d."

6

The Positive Power of Peoplehood

Originally indigenous to the Middle East,
Jews have lived, loved, partnered with,
and raised families within
every conceivable civilization.

Mighty empires dissipate in every age,
yet against overwhelming odds,
the Jewish people continue.

Is peoplehood
a spiritual practice?

A two-week vacation hiking around the perimeter of Iceland?
Perfect. No one in Iceland is likely to need rabbinic services.
A vacation out in nature—away from everyone and every-
thing in a busy life. Let's go!

At Icelandic Passport Control, the official looks me over
with unusual care. Finally, I inquire, "Is there is a problem?"

Agent: "I see that you are a rabbi."

"Yes." (Not anti-Semitism here!? How did she know? Oh dear, one of my business cards accidentally got sandwiched in the passport pages.)

Agent: "You're a rabbi. That means you're a Jew?"

"Quite so." (The agent looks like she's debating with herself about something. Oy, I wonder what?)

Agent: "Rabbi, I only know of one Jew who is a citizen of Iceland. I bet she'd love to meet you! Would you like me to put her in contact with you while you're here?"

Alas. She wasn't home.

Like baking soda in the cake of creation, the Jewish people live almost everywhere on the globe. For all that this book is full of Judaism, a person could disregard the previous chapters and still experience the benefits and challenges of Jewish peoplehood. A friend just back from an errand in Odessa put it this way: "When I speak to another Jew anywhere in the world, there's always something we can connect about, on some level, even if it's that we did observe Passover or we didn't, or finding someone we know in common, or asking if there's news about Israel, or if there's a synagogue nearby. Even those who don't go usually know."

You might say we have the matzah connection. Jews wonder about why a restaurant would serve it in August, because to us it is more than a food. Matzah has a definite season and conveys shared meaning—our core values: freedom, justice, family, community.

When Passover and spring break overlapped one year, we took our case of matzah along on the family ski trip to Copper Mountain, Colorado. Soon our table with its seder, seder plate, kiddush cup, wine, and matzah was surrounded by Jews from Mexico City proudly bearing their own boxes of matzah.

On another such occasion, we were hiking through the hill towns of northern Italy. We visited Pitigliano, a small, ancient walled city pristinely preserved and set like a gem into the side of a towering cliff where no car can enter. Wandering the cobbled streets, every footstep echoes back off the shuttered stone homes set into the walls, and I wondered, was Jericho once like this? Or Jerusalem? The smell of baking wafted our way. A family on horseback clattered by. What must the noise have been like when the streets were full of horses and heralds sounded their proclamations! It was just past dawn and the heat of the spring sunlight was beginning to shine uncomfortably on our faces. Around another bend. Ah. The bakery! We agreed to pause for espresso and pitzelle. But what's this? Hebrew on the door? A *hecksher*? Why would a bakery be certified kosher here? A mezuzah on the door? A robust, elderly Italian woman greets us. No pitzelle to be had, no canolli today. Passover cakes and matzah instead. "Is this a Jewish neighborhood?" I asked with excitement and incredulity.

"All gone." She shrugged. " My son and I, the only ones."

"So why have you koshered your bakery for Passover? Who will buy from you?"

A smile that could illuminate a dark castle enlivened her sad face, and her shoulders went back with pride: "Eh, we make-ah matzah for the Joint Distribution Committee. We supply-ah the whole region!"

Religious and secular, gastronomic Jews, social activist Jews, artistic Jews, Jewish intellectuals, and more, we rarely agree collectively about the meaning of a verse in Torah, guidelines for a service that we could all attend, or how best for Israel to survive and thrive as an ethical nation. Ah—well, we rarely agree on much that applies to us. But,

When it comes to working for
social welfare, human rights, the environment,
medical advances, education, libraries, and more,
Jews are involved in proportions far larger
than our percentage of the general population.

Why? Because we practice
collective memory and
collective consciousness.

We are not just random individuals.
We are all the souls
who were strangers in Egypt.

We are all the souls who stood at Sinai
and committed to a radical
new code for humane living.

Being religious or born into a Jewish family is not a prerequisite for being or becoming a member of the Jewish people. Perhaps one explanation for the wave of Europeans currently seeking to become Jewish is, as one woman described it to me: "There were not enough Jews left to give birth to all the returning Jewish souls after World War II. All of my life I have been drawn to Jewish people and Jewish practices. Your people are my people and I have begun studies to formally become a Jew."

The mystical aside, however, the Jewish people was originally forged out of an *eyrev rav*, a "mixed multitude" (Exodus

12:38). We arose from peoples indigenous to the Middle East who entered Egypt as guest workers when there was a widespread famine in the region and became enslaved over subsequent generations. Those who successfully fled and achieved freedom around 1280 BCE—the descendents of Abraham, Isaac, Jacob, and others—became a new, amalgamated people, *b'nei yisrael*—the "children of Israel." Jacob, the last of the founding patriarchs, received Israel as his sacred name. This new group, formed of his likely descendents and others, then became known as Israelites, the inheritors of his wisdom lineage, bound by radical, new, common accords that have come to us today in the form of the biblical commandments and the laws described in the Bible as having been given to Moses at Sinai. The descendents of the Israelites and all who have formally joined us since comprise the Jewish people.

As one of our peoplehood practices we hold ourselves responsible for caring for strangers. Thirty-six times the Torah mentions the mitzvah, the "sacred obligation," to care for others as a way of remembering our own people's experience. Let's look at just a few of those verses:

RECIPE #33:
We Were
Strangers

> You shall not abuse or oppress a stranger, for you were strangers in Egypt.
>
> —*Exodus 22:20*

> Do not oppress a stranger. You know the soul of the stranger for you were strangers in the land of Egypt.
>
> —*Exodus 23:9*

Love your neighbor as yourself.

—Leviticus 19:19

You shall love the stranger because you were strangers in the land of Egypt.

—Deuteronomy 10:19

"Love your neighbor as yourself"—this is the fundamental principle of Torah.

—Torah Kohanim, Rabbi Akiva

With a cluster of friends, compare and contrast these verses. The subtle addition of a word or a shift in phrasing are spiritual portals. The *hevruta* method described in chapter 3, "Taking Torah Personally," is recommended as a healthy and helpful way of studying the verses above. What do you notice as you compare the verses that might inform the way a Jew acts in the world as a representative of our people?

Notice in particular the verse "You know the *soul* of the stranger." Do you? Do we? How might this awareness translate into action?

In every generation Jews are moving through the world as strangers, hopefully seeking safe and productive havens. How would you say the awareness of being strangers has shaped the identity and spiritual path of our people?

When Rabbi Abraham Joshua Heschel joined the freedom march led by Reverend Martin Luther King, Rabbi Heschel later identified this as fulfilling the mitzvah of *zeyher yitziyat mitzrayim*, "remembering leaving Egypt." In your study circle, share stories about times when you have fulfilled this mitzvah and brainstorm ways to bring it to life in your life.

THE SOUL OF JUDAISM: CREATING MODELS FOR THE HUMAN FUTURE

As we have survived in a hostile world, the Jewish people has evolved, adapted, and grown into fresh approaches to living so powerful that they are often ahead of their time. In the words of Calvin Coolidge in a speech at a ceremony to lay the cornerstone to the Jewish Centre in Washington, D.C., on May 3, 1925: "Every inheritance of the Jewish people, every teaching of their secular history and religious experience, draws them powerfully to the side of charity, liberty, and progress." Here are some of the major conceptual contributions our people have made:

ONE G*D, NOT MANY. Instead of many gods, our people have carried, cultivated, and advocated the idea of one G*d, one Unified Field of Creation.

SHABBAT, AN INSTITUTION IN TIME NOT REQUIRING A TEMPLE. We have learned to build sacred space out of time, to let go of edifice as central to spiritual and religious life.

PRAYERS AND MITZVOT INSTEAD OF SACRIFICES. With the destruction of the Temple, we chose to no longer use burnt animal and food offerings. Prayer, charity, and deeds of consciousness have become the ways we offer our first fruits and best selves.

TIME AS BOTH CIRCULAR AND LINEAR; THINGS CAN CHANGE FOR THE BETTER. While respecting the cycle of seasons in nature and life, we also emphasize the cumulative importance of knowledge and working for positive change in all aspects of civilization.

ALL ETHICAL PEOPLES MERIT SALVATION; OURS IS NOT THE ONLY WAY. The Talmud derives from Genesis seven principles for living called the Noachide laws that are widely accepted by governments as the minimum pillars of civilization. These were acknowledged, for example, by the United States Congress in 1990. These principles declare as forbidden: stealing, abusive sexuality, eating meat from a living animal, murder, blasphemy, and idolatry. They make it obligatory to appoint judges and set up a court of law in order to pronounce just decisions. Maimonides taught that any human being who faithfully observes these laws earns a proper place in heaven. In other words, you need not be of a particular religion in order to be "saved," and, therefore, Jews have no reason to proselytize. Only souls who discover themselves to be drawn to a Jewish destiny and who determinedly seek out conversion are invited to study and see if our practices and legacy are truly their path.

MESSIAH AS A TIME AND PROCESS RATHER THAN A PERSON. The Jewish concept of a messiah is multifaceted. Originally it was that of a military leader who would take us from oppression and exile back to national sovereignty in Israel. We quite obviously have returned to Israel via other means. In chapter 2, "Reclaiming G*d with Integrity," we looked at how the word for messiah, *mashiah*, can be deconstructed and seen as having the root words *mae-siah*, "from dialogue." From this comes the idea held by many contemporary Jews that a dialogue within and between people can lead to a messianic age. Thus the expectation of an external agent is being transformed into a pragmatic, personal sense of responsibility to find our inner-messianic spark and join hands with a yearning humanity of all faiths to work toward sustainable world peace.

**HONORING TEACHERS AND LEARNING; EMPOWERING INDI-
VIDUAL FREEDOM OF THOUGHT.** Judaism is essentially nondogmatic and thoroughly encourages questioning. We honor
our teachers and raise our children to think of themselves as
teachers, scholars, innovators, architects of the human future
and the Judaism of the future.

PEOPLES, NOT BORDERS. The Jewish people learned how to
live as a dispersed civilization. Even today we live everywhere,
focused on being solid citizens, major contributors to the arts,
sciences, education, and economy wherever we dwell. It might
be said that we live an unarticulated new paradigm, that of a
universal people willing to be engaged citizens of every
country. Before the pogroms and World War II, we were proud,
active citizens of Germany, France, Latvia, the Netherlands,
and numerous other lands. It seems, however, that this practice
of being universal citizens was implemented too soon; it proved
to be too much of a stretch for a world accustomed to parochial
ways. Even as we came to look on the covenant of the
Promised Land largely as a utopian dreamscape, and Jerusalem
came to serve as a metaphor for harmony and the memory of
kingdom-times gone by, the dark side of human potential continued to reemerge—in the Russian pogroms of the late 1800s
and in the Nazi extermination camps—until, as World War II
ended and Jewish displaced citizens of nations that had offered
us up for incineration wandered homeless, it became clear that
we needed a safe space to call our own, to once more become
a landed nation. The idea of people being seen as citizens of
the world, safe and welcome to become citizens in all nations,
will have to wait, as a *go-hel-et bo-eh-ret*, a glowing coal of
hope, to be redeemed from the annals of possibility.

MODEL NATION-BUILDING. Jews have lived in Israel continuously for thousands of years and under every empire. The original biblical covenant, the Promised Land, beckoned as an ancient commitment to which our walking wounded responded after World War II with honor, passion, and hope. Had we almost forgotten that the mitzvah of *shivat tzion*, "returning to dwell in Zion," is a serious spiritual practice? Let us pause for a second and consider what that means from a modern, twenty-first-century point of view. Can we consider Zionism as the goal of building a model Middle Eastern society, dedicated as a labor of loving commitment to the One to whom we belong?

It has taken barely fifty years of statehood to realize just how much this is our people's and the eighty million Arab peoples' leading edge for growth. Nation-building is a practice in which we still need practice. And many of us do feel the pain of those who lived in the land while we were gone, many of whom have recently taken the name Palestinians. So we are challenged to again "remember that we were strangers" and to practice Zionism with integrity for *all* the land's indigenous peoples. That's a tall order for a spiritual practice that we're still trying to evolve. Whether together or side by side,

Respectful, successful coexistence —
cultivating, receiving, and giving it —
this is the current challenge.
We all have a lot to learn.

AND

As Herzl wrote in his novel *Altneuland*,
"If you will it, it is no dream!"

THE PEOPLEHOOD PRACTICE

In this volume so far, as in *Reclaiming Judaism as a Spiritual Practice*, your individual and family Jewish experience has been paid the greatest attention. But the hardest Jewish spiritual practice of all, the one thing that is the hardest to do but that can change everything—no, not belief in G*d; that's not required to be a Jew as long as we don't take on other gods— is for Jews to love one another.

The eighteenth-century sage known as the Baal Shem Tov noted that when all Jews can love each other—engage in the practice called *ahavat yisrael*, "loving the Jewish people"— then the fulfillment of the messianic vision of sustainable world peace becomes possible. The hardest thing for Jews to do is to suspend judgment of one another's different ways of manifesting "Jewishly" and instead to celebrate and savor each other. This has always been a spiritual challenge and a source of creative tension for us as individuals, denominations, sects, and as a people and a nation:

- The biblical prophets railed against our people's and the kings' lax practices.
- When Solomon died, ten of the tribes refused to have his son, Rehoboam, as their king, and so the Holy Land was split into Israel, with Jerusalem as the capital, and Judah, with Samaria as the capital. This situation then prevailed for some two hundred years.
- Maccabean and Hellenized Jews struggled furiously. Eventually the Maccabees saved the nation, but let's respect that the Talmud, the Haggadah, and many other major Jewish works are richly informed

by Greek thought and philosophy. The value to our
people of contacts with many cultures was first
noted by Rabbi Mordecai Kaplan, founder of
Reconstructionist Judaism, in the twentieth century. He pointed out that Judaism is an evolving
civilization, composed of innovations adopted from
our "host" countries and then adapted to our
system of ethics and practice.

• The major rift between the Sadducees and the
Pharisees in the Second Temple period was over
the maintenance of a sacrificial cult governed by a
priestly caste as opposed to an intellectually developed religion based on the interpretation of texts.
The latter triumphed, leading to rabbinic Judaism's
ability to adapt to statelessness and the destruction
of the Temple. And yet, the Talmud offers a model
for respectful inclusiveness. Citing differences that
arose—sometimes with a vengeance—among different sects over legal issues and day-to-day practices, the Talmud reports both the accepted and
the minority opinions. Interestingly, these minority
ideas are often drawn upon as essential resources
upon which to base new halahic developments by
later generations.

• In the twelfth century the Middle Eastern Jewish
community was sorely divided. There were
numerous Karaites, Jews keen on the sacrificial
system, who did not accept the elaborations of
Jewish law developed by contemporaneous
Rabbanites who would go on to formulate the
details of post–sacrificial-system Jewish life and law.

During that period Maimonides' innovations and interpretations provoked attacks on and even the burning of his works by his peers, but in our time, his works are read with great attention and respect by all who practice Judaism. Diverse expressions of Judaism have always existed. While the Karaites were quite sure their fundamentalism was essential to preserving a Jewish future—surprise!—it would turn out to be rabbinic Judaism that persisted with far greater success. None of us knows which of today's Judaisms will most strongly inform the Jewish future, though we all might wish to claim our own as the vanguard of future practice.

- As the Hasidic movement was developing in Europe some two hundred years ago, Hasidism had opponents in mainstream Orthodoxy called *mitnagdim*. While both attend closely to details of Jewish law, Hasidim add mystical and ecstatic experience to their practice. The original, generally more affluent *mitnagdim*, or "opposers," sought to have Hasidic leaders arrested and their practices disrupted. Today the descendants of these groups, under the rubric of Orthodoxy, often cooperate in Israel and abroad in lobbying on matters of religious concern and education.

- *Orthodoxy* as a term appears in Judaism in the nineteenth century in reaction to the emergence of Reform Judaism in Germany. The tension between the two might be seen as the opening for creation of what some now view as a middle ground, Conservative Judaism.

- From within Conservative Judaism emerged formerly Orthodox Rabbi Mordecai Kaplan, whose students founded Reconstructionism. And a growing coalition of Orthodox, Conservative, Reform, and Reconstructionist and unaffiliated Jews continue to collaborate with former H̲asidic rebbe Zalman Schachter-Shalomi to forge a new ethical/philosophical practice perspective called Jewish renewal.

So those who suggest that Jews were religiously homogeneous in exile are mistaken. The challenge of transcending differences within our people in order to attain the greatest mitzvah, *ahavat yisrael*, "loving the Jewish people," is a meta-practice of profound importance. Because that's so hard to do, one actually benefits from starting small.

Is your family Jewishly homogeneous?
Do you all fit on the same page of Judaism?
Ours doesn't.
Creation manifests neither one kind
of rose nor one kind of Jew.

RECIPE #34: The Bouquet of Respectful Pluralism

Make a list of your extended family by name and role and add a nonjudgmental description of their relationship to being Jewish. Here's an example from a family that gave permission to share theirs:

Eldest son: Organizes Friday night dinners with ḥallah and wine for the international students in his dorm; observes some of the traditions of Sukkot, Passover, and Ḥanukkah; has a cute and intelligent non-Jewish girlfriend; is active in Koach, college youth of the Conservative Movement. Says his Jewishness also inspires his passionate activism on environmental and social justice issues. Left wing on Middle East issues.

Youngest daughter: Eschewed religion in high school and now belongs to both the Chabad and Zen clubs on campus. She is actively searching for a Jewish boyfriend and has suddenly shown an interest in turning off all computers and media sources on Shabbat when together with the family to encourage more quality time. Right wing on Middle East issues.

Stepson: Became Christian to join his wife's path, and since having children they take them to church and also observe Friday night Shabbat rituals, Ḥanukkah, and Passover, saying the children can "choose" their religious identity when they get older.

Middle son: Age twenty, went to Israel for his junior year in college and became very excited about Judaism to the point of becoming an Orthodox *baal teshuvah*, "returnee." A medical student, he transferred to a school with kosher dining facilities, where he could also observe Shabbat. He brings his own prepared kosher food to family functions, does not travel on Shabbat, has his clothing checked for *shatnes*, "prohibited fiber combinations," that are derived from biblical verses, and gives generously to Jewish and secular charities.

Husband's ex-wife: Belongs to a Reform congregation, loves Jewish meal traditions, makes Shabbat dinners, and holds a family seder to which she invites his former wives and their families, who attend when available.

Ex-husband: Secular Zionist, contributes generously to social welfare programs for Jews and non-Jews.

Husband: Calls himself postdenominational, delights in Torah study and sweet Shabbat dinner gatherings, occasionally attends services, centrist on Middle East matters, left wing on American social justice issues.

Mother-in-law: Orthodox, makes wonderful Shabbat and holy day meals, attends Shabbat services regularly, and volunteers extensively for her synagogue. Dislikes when women lead public Jewish rituals other than candlelighting on Shabbat; very uncomfortable for her but she tolerates this development to support family cohesion.

Mother: Rebelled against the very strict Orthodox life she had as a child, but still keeps pork and shellfish out of her otherwise nonkosher home. Lights Shabbat candles, avoids religious services, and reads headlines closely with concern for the Jewish people. Loves to sing Yiddish show tunes.

Father: Allied soldier during World War II. Raised Orthodox but gave up attention to daily Jewish practices because of the Holocaust's effect on his faith. Does fast on Yom Kippur and celebrates major Jewish holidays with his children and grandchildren with a meal and some ritual. Left wing on American social welfare/justice issues; centrist on Middle East situation.

> A Jewish family is a bouquet,
> a snapshot of religious pluralism.
> Each member is a magnificent flower,
> one of the infinite faces of G*d.

- Write up the bouquet of pluralism that constitutes your family.
- If each person were a flower, what variety might you assign to each one?
- When you are done, step back to experience them as a whole bouquet.
- What do you feel? What do you need? What do you know?

A possible blessing for your family bouquet might incorporate one of the more mystical names of G*d:

n'vareh et ma'yan raz,	Let us bless the Well of Mystery,
borei minei yehudim.	Creator of the varieties of Jews.
ameyn!	Amen!

Note: At www.ReclaimingJudaism.org you will find successfully applied guidelines for ways Jews can join together respectfully in religious contexts. You might try them out in your community organizations.

WANDERING JEWS

Avadim hayeenu, "We were slaves": these words from the seder are part of our engraved memories of conscious peoplehood.

We are an ancient people with an amazing journey. After Egypt and some forty years of transformation in the wilderness, the Israelites eventually conquer a small section of the Fertile Crescent—the "Promised Land" described in the Torah. This area had been conquered in early 1300 BCE by the Canaanites. By the ninth century BCE the Israelites have kings; first David and then Solomon reign over Israel. By the eighth century BCE the biblical land is divided into two Israelite kingdoms because ten of the tribes refuse to be governed by Rehoboam, one of Solomon's sons, and in the sixth century BCE the Assyrians overrun what is known as the Northern Kingdom so that only the lower half of the "Promised Land," Judah, remains in Israelite hands. In the fifth century BCE the Babylonians overrun the brutal Assyrians, conquer the region, and destroy the Temple in Jerusalem. In the same century the Persians overtake the Babylonians and allow the Jewish people to return, but soon the Greek Empire swoops in, followed by the Roman Empire, which destroys the second Temple in 70 CE

From that time on, although small Jewish communities will re-form and remain in the land of Israel, continuing waves of Assyrian, Babylonian, and Roman oppression result in substantial death and forced exile for the Jewish people. This launches the historic traumatic traipse of our people throughout the earth. Ultimately the Romans fall, and in the third century CE the Byzantine Empire comes to take over the region, followed by the Islamic conquest. As with all empires, the Ottoman Empire also rises and falls, and eventually the British take the region, finally ceding it in 1948 when a vote of the United Nations gives governance of the Land of Israel to what remains of the Jewish people. We joyfully accept, only to have war declared on the reborn nation of Israel by the surrounding countries. The rest is rather recent history.

> We have survived landlessness,
> Crusades, Inquisition, and Holocaust.
> We have members from every race.
> People have joined our path
> from every religion.
> And we dwell in almost
> every nation on earth.

CITIZENS OF THE WORLD

The hill town Pitigliano, which was described earlier in this chapter, was once known as Little Jerusalem. Jews from Rome kept summer apartments there so that when the popes periodically decided to harvest Jewish businesses and homes for the church's treasury, the Jews could flee to the hills.

There are endless fascinating stories of how we made our way around the world and learned to adapt to new geographical, economic, religious, and cultural conditions. Many of us have heard from elders the conventional wisdom of the wandering Jew: "Your profession must be one that can fit in your head, be done with your own hands; your livelihood must be able to travel with you."

Awe, *yirah*, is a Jewish spiritual practice. And so, knowing the awesome path of the Jewish people that brought us to live among the nations of the world is, in itself, an important practice. Were we dispersed and do we continue to live throughout the world because it's a bad idea for us as a people to have all our "eggs in one basket" or because we are meant to lend our ideals and creative energy to every part of the planet? Perhaps both. Let's look in on how Jews came to live among the nations:

THE JEWS OF INDIA. The Jews of India include the Bene Israel, who arrived via inland trade routes during King Solomon's time. They became known as the *Shanwar Tellis*, Sabbath-observing (sesame) oil producers who kept their Hebrew first names and took Indian surnames. They started out on the prosperous western coast of India and moved to Bombay at the invitation of the East India Company in the late eighteenth century.

Benjamin of Tudela in 1167 described another group, the Cochin Jews on the Malabar coast, as, "black like their neighbors … observers of the law, and possessing the Torah of Moses." The Cochin claim to have survived the Inquisition, which was brought to India by the Portuguese, because of the protection of a local Raja who, in 1568, had them build their synagogue thirty yards from his own temple. It was not until the seventeenth century that the Bene Israel and the Cochin Jews of Southern India actually discovered each other!

To India also came the B'nai Menashe, who are possibly one of the original lost tribes. Having been enslaved by the Assyrians, the B'nai Menashe fled via the China-Burmese border to then arrive in East India. As a result of their isolation and exposure to missionary activity, most of them became Christians until, in 1951, their local chief revealed their ancient origins, and a return to Judaism became their passion. In 2005 Israel agreed to facilitate their return.

In Bombay and Calcutta you also find communities of Baghdadi Jews who fled oppression in Iraq, Syria, and Iran starting around 1796. Ashkenazi Jews are also found in small numbers in India. While some Jewish communities still remain, after 1948 most Indian Jews began emigrating to Israel, England, and the United States.

THE JEWS OF ENGLAND. Although today there are hundreds of thousands of British Jews, it was not until 1066 that William the Conqueror encouraged Jewish merchants and artisans from northern France to move to England. Others came from Germany, Italy, and Spain.

The Christian Crusades began in 1096 and under that aegis, in 1190, the Jews of York were massacred. Matters worsened until, in 1290, all Jews were expelled from England. It then took 350 years until Oliver Cromwell, influenced by a Dutch rabbi, Menasseh ben Israel, organized permission for Jews to worship openly in England. Resident Portuguese and Spanish Conversos, Jews forcibly converted to Christianity during the Inquisition who, under their Christian identities made their way to live in England, also became free to practice their Judaism openly. Still, it was not until the 1800s that foreign-born Jews could enter England and receive naturalization. From then on, the community thrived, growing naturally and through waves of Czechoslovakian and other Eastern European immigration.

THE JEWS OF FORMER SOVIET UNION. My own sons may well be descended from the Khazars, a Turkic tribe that migrated to the steppes of southern and eastern Ukraine by the fifth century. Their father, my "wasband," has a Simian/Mongolian fold on his palm (most people have a capital letter "M"), and both he and their grandmother have the high cheekbones and

Oriental eyes characteristic of that region. While scholars continue to debate the details, archaeological evidence mounts that in the ninth century the leaders of Khazaria requested conversion to Judaism, and by the eleventh century Khazars are reported by visiting merchants and dignitaries to be Jews, based on their having become entranced with it when one of them met a traveling Jewish trader. The Khazars brought Hebrew script into use in the region. Their communities also existed in Hungary, Transylvania, Lithuania, and central Ukraine. Most Jews of Ashkenazi Eastern European origin, however, likely descended from Yiddish-speaking immigrants who periodically flooded in from the west, from expulsions, and from persecution during the Crusades and thereafter.

THE JEWS OF SOUTH AFRICA. Though Dutch and British Jews accompanied some of the first white colonizers to South Africa in the mid-1800s, most Jewish immigrants after that time were from Latvia and Lithuania. In our family, Uncle Percy recalls arriving by ship with his father and another male relative when he was a young boy. The South African officials, it rapidly became apparent, required a per-person entry fee, and horrors, his father's assets proved to be sufficient for all but one of them. Who would have to go back to the terrors of Europe after the long, frightful journey? Young Percy was left on the ship, and days passed, but no one returned for him. What happened to them out there in Africa? Just hours before the ship was to set sail on its return voyage, Percy's father appeared with a group of leaders from the local Jewish council, the Board of Jewish Deputies, who had gathered funds to rescue the last member of the family.

The Jewish population of South Africa reached a high of

more than 100,000 citizens in the 1970s. Since that time, however, some 40,000 South African Jews have emigrated, many to Israel, North America, and Australia, while more than 10,000 Israelis have joined South Africa's Jewish communities.

Another of the lost communities of Jews appears to dwell in South Africa. The 300,000-member Venda tribe, which includes the 40,000-member Lemba tribe, observes rituals that include keeping kosher by pre-talmudic standards. This tribe also has priestly divisions as in Temple days of old, and their *Buba* clan, which has a role parallel to that of the *cohanim*, "priests," scored the highest of all groups ever tested for the priestly genetic type.

THE JEWS OF ARAB AND ISLAMIC LANDS. Jews first appeared in North Africa during Phoenician times and later, during the Greco-Roman period. Rabbi Akiba was among those who traveled to teach the Jews of Morocco and organize money and support to feed the Jewish rebellion against Rome. Little is known about the intervening years, but evidence has emerged that, led by a Jewish woman with a priestly name, Da<u>h</u>ya K'<u>h</u>ayna (Cohen), Jews and the indigenous Berbers lived and traveled together and, along with Christian forces, fought successfully for five years against the Muslims, who then swept across the region in the seventh century. In 1948 the Jewish population of Morocco was 265,000; today it is less than 5,000 as a result of the virulent and violent anti-Jewish efforts that spread as Islamic fundamentalism intensified. That said, Morrocco's King Hassan II protected the residual Jewish population and created the most tolerant country for Jews in the Arab world. He worked behind the scenes as a positive force in the Middle East peace process.

Jews in Islamic societies were not termed infidels; rather, both Christians and Jews were called "People of the Book" and considered somewhat spiritually evolved, although not sufficiently, since we didn't "yet" accept Mohammed as a prophet. Given this diminished status, we were called *dhimmi* (meaning "diminished"), allowed our own form of worship, but with varying degrees of enforcement were required to wear a yellow sash, pay special taxes, and observe other restrictions. Morocco became a French protectorate in 1912, and by 1955 independence was achieved by a Muslim government that joined the Arab League. After that, Jews attempting to leave the country were arrested and jailed until, in 1961, King Hassan II gave Jews the right to emigrate. Most were airlifted to Israel, some went to France, and today a substantial portion of French Jews are of Moroccan descent.

There are still Jews who continue to live in Arab lands, including the Tunisian island of Djerba, where elders chant aloud the Jewish mystical text, the Zohar, and survive by metalworking.

THE JEWS OF CHRISTIAN EUROPE. In 600 CE Reccard, a Visigoth king, forcibly converted some ninety thousand Jews in his kingdom to Christianity. Many of these Conversos continued to practice Judaism, at first quietly, and then openly under eight hundred years of Moorish rule. Then, Pope Innocent III (1198–1216) initiated the process of what would become known as the Inquisition, identifying Catholics as true believers, and defining all others as heretics. In 1479 Spanish King Ferdinand and Queen Isabella made a plan to unify their country under Catholicism and set up a system of inquisitors to purify their country of non-Catholics. In 1492 all Jews who had not converted were expelled. "New Christians," Protestants, and other non-Catholics were considered heretics to be identified by the general population. They were then given a chance to confess their heresy against the Catholic Church and were also "encouraged" to indict others. Those who admitted their "wrongs," often under extreme torture, and who survived their trials, were either released or remanded to secular courts for sentencing. If they would not admit their heresy or indict others, the accused were remanded to secular courts (so the "church" would not have blood on its hands), where they were sentenced to be publicly executed, often by being burned at the stake, or sentenced to life in prison. In the first twelve years, more than thirteen thousand Conversos were put on trial, and in the town of Seville alone some seven hundred were burned at the stake. All this resulted in a huge movement of peoples on the run in Catholic lands.

Many Spanish Jews fled to Portugal, but when the Portuguese conducted an Inquisition in 1497, survivors headed largely to Holland, and some to the more familiar Spanish culture of Mexico, where it was possible to practice Judaism openly until the arrival of the Inquisition forty years later.

THE JEWS OF NORTH AND SOUTH AMERICA. From Holland some Jews sailed to Brazil, started trade routes, and introduced sugar cane as a crop to the economy. When the Inquisition made its way to Brazil, sixteen ships were sent to remove the Jews. Some went back to Holland and others to islands throughout the Caribbean, where the English proved welcoming at the time. In about 1671, when Jews were given British citizenship in Surinam, it was our first full citizenship in any country during modern times.

From those Brazilian Jews who returned to Amsterdam would come many pioneers, among them the first rabbi and cantor to serve in the newest land of colonization, America. But North America's Jews were Converso Spanish colonists who were sent north from Mexico and homesteaded in what would become New Mexico. The Inquisition in Mexico City turned not only on Jews but also on those known to be converts who were sincerely practicing Christianity. Those who could, fled north and lived as Christians until their rediscovery of their Jewish roots in the twentieth century.

The Sephardim of Northern Europe arrived in America later, in colonial times, as traders. Among them were the Levi family of denim fame, as well as trappers, cowboys, financiers, educators, entertainers, and miners of turquoise. There were, essentially, no Jews in Canada, "New France," because Louis XIV had decreed that only Roman Catholics could settle the colony. The first Jewish settlers arrived with the British army that captured Montreal in 1760. Today more than 155,000 Jews live in Canada North America's story would be further enriched by numerous waves of Jewish immigrants, first from Germany, then from Eastern Europe, and, more recently, from the former Soviet Union, Israel, South Africa, Iran, and now Argentina.

Although many South American Jewish communities were originally composed of transplanted Conversos fleeing the Spanish Inquisition, by the 1800s French Jewish immigrants began to arrive in countries like Argentina, and in the late nineteenth century a third wave came fleeing poverty and the pogroms in Russia and other Eastern European countries. In 1889, 824 Russian Jews became *gauchos*, Argentinian cowboys, and founded a colony funded by the Baron Maurice de Hirsch Foundation called Moiseville. Immigration continued from Europe, Morocco, and the Ottoman Empire, and a rich Jewish culture developed and continues to this day. As World War II ended, however, Juan Perón halted Jewish immigration and allowed Argentina to become a haven for fleeing Nazis. In 1960 Adolf Eichmann was apprehended by Israeli agents in a Buenos Aires suburb. Between 1976 and 1983, the ruling juntas kidnapped and tortured Jews, who numbered 1,000 of the 9,000 known victims of state terrorism.

In 1998 Argentina elected as president Carlos Saul Menem, who was of Arab origin and who helped pass a law against racism and anti-Semitism that was adopted by the legislature. At present, poverty in Argentina is on the rise in all sectors of society, and new presidents are routinely installed. Some 200,000 Jews now live in Argentina; 10,000 emigrated in the early twentieth century, about 6,000 of them to Israel.

THE JEWS OF AUSTRALIA. Several Jews were among Australia's original population when it was settled as a penal colony in 1788. A thriving, hundred-thousand-strong Jewish community has since developed from successive waves of noncriminal European, Russian, South African, and Israeli immigration.

Population Estimates

World Population: 6,444,917,966
Jewish Population: 12,948,000

Jews are less than 0.2 percent of the world's population

44 percent of Jews live in North America
39 percent of Jews live in Israel
17 percent live in numerous other nations

There are many countries where transplanted Jews developed indigenous approaches to Jewishing. No doubt, we will some day attain citizenship in extraplanetary nations, serving kosher space burgers, *haroset* made from local produce, and matzah balls rendered edible for different degrees of gravity.

A CONSCIOUS COMMUNITY

Do most Jews know one another?
Of course not.
Do most of us care about one another?
Yes. Why?
We've learned that we have to.

While teaching much more in the way of Jewish history is beyond the purview of this volume, let's recall for one moment that in areas controlled by Nazi Germany 125 anti-Jewish laws were enacted between 1933 and 1937. Jews were banned from holding jobs in the civil service, courts, hospitals, and government, as well as from participating in sports, cultural activities, and education. Jewish books were publicly burned. Jewish shops and offices were marked with a "J" or "*Jude*." In September 1935 the Nuremberg Laws canceled Jewish citizenship and rendered illegal all marriages or sexual intercourse between Hitler's two invented racial groups: Jews and Aryans. Anti-Semitic handbooks were given to teachers. Jews were blamed for everything that had gone wrong in German society.

As early as 1922, in dialogue with Major Josef Hell, Hitler reported that if he came to power, the annihilation of Jews would be his first and foremost task. "Once the hatred and the battle against the Jews are really stirred up," he continued, "their resistance will inevitably break down in short order. They cannot protect themselves and no one will stand forth as their defenders." (Just in case you were wondering why Israel now has an army, navy, and air force.)

In 1938, thirty-two countries attended the Evian Conference, whose principal purpose was to find safe haven for the growing masses of refugees from Germany and Austria. However, Germany did not allow Jews to take their money and possessions when they were expelled, and sovereign countries tend not to welcome penniless immigrants. Only the Dominican Republic was willing to adjust its immigration quota and take in 100,000. Ultimately, 5,000 visas would be issued, but only 645 Jews would get there before it became virtually impossible to escape the Nazi roundups and death camps. By the war's end six million Jews would have been systematically murdered.

Golda Meir was at Evian, as a member of the uninvited delegation of Jews from Palestine. Her memoirs note: "Sitting there in that magnificent hall and listening to the delegates of thirty-two countries rise, each in turn, to explain how much they would have liked to take in substantial numbers of refugees and how unfortunate it was that they were not able to do so, was a terrible experience. I don't think that anyone who didn't live through it can understand what I felt at Evian—a mixture of sorrow, rage, frustration and horror."

NECESSARY NETWORKS

"Never again" became our people's slogan. Never again would we trust our destiny to others. Today, we do our best to maintain worldwide networks of Jewish social service, rescue, and relief agencies. These systems keep track of where our people are, and, when need be, we help one another move quickly to safe havens. Many of these agencies, such as the Jewish Agency for Israel, World ORT, Project Kesher, the Joint Distribution Committee, and the Hebrew Immigrant Aid Society, endeavor to help not only our people but also others who suffer in the regions where our agencies are based and we are in a position to be effective as a support system. This is part of our vision of fostering peace and cooperation on a universal scale.

The mitzvot of *pikuah nefesh*, saving a life, *pidyon shvu-im*, redeeming captives, and many others call out as spiritual practices asking us *al tifrosh min ha-tzibor*, "not to separate yourself from the community." In my lifetime I have been privileged to see this happen in the most amazing ways, showing the best side of what applied spirituality can bring out in people.

While I was on pregnancy leave from my position as executive director of the Jewish Federation of Cumberland County, New Jersey, a call came in. "You don't have to do this, but we knew you would want to know about a major event that's happening. One of the missing tribes has been discovered in Ethiopia, in the Gondar region. There have been political problems with getting them to Israel. Now it's clear that they are being persecuted, and there's a huge famine in their region right now. They are dying of starvation. A breakthrough has occurred! If those who can will walk the several hundred miles to Sudan, and risk the border-crossing, the Sudanese government will let us airlift them to freedom. It will cost $6,000 for each person we can get out. Do you want to be at the emergency fund raiser tonight?"

That afternoon an express package with videos of an African tribe calling themselves Beta Yisrael, House of Israel, arrives. Once a kingdom of more than 600,000 Jews, they date back to the time of the Temple and don't know about subsequent Jewish practices.

Infant seat, toddler seat, two children, and a mom barely past her C-section pop into the car for the forty-minute trek to the office. When I get there, the room is full of people, some I didn't even know were Jewish, and most of all, our community's Holocaust survivors and their children.

A man who lost his children in the Holocaust makes a call to mortgage his house to raise funds to rescue these people whom he has never met, doesn't resemble, and yet are his people, our people, in trouble. Teens get permission to withdraw money from their college funds. "Never again" is never said aloud, but we all hear it in our heart. In the Haggadah we read the parable of the four sons—one wise, one wicked, one simple, and one who does not yet know how to ask a question. "What does the wicked son say? 'What is this effort [remembering the Exodus] to you?' To *you* and not to him. Since he has taken himself out of the community's experience, he has denied the Essence." This means if you see the Jews over there as them and not you, then the practice of peoplehood, *ahavat yisrael*, is broken, the spirit leaks out, and something very precious may die.

HEALING FROM THE WOUNDS OF GROWING UP OR BECOMING JEWISH

Have you ever set yourself
outside the Jewish people or
thought to drop your Jewish identity?
I have.

Our Hebrew school met in a rented community room in the basement of the local bank. This one-room school was taught by Mr. Brody, a man who loved both Judaism and children. He taught us this simple song that had accompanying hand motions—do you know it? It went like this: *dah-veed mele*ḥ *yis-rael* ḥ*ai,* ḥ*ai, v'kah-yahm* ... "David, King of Israel, lives on [in our people]," not that I could have told you what it meant then. The day after learning that song, after school and with great enthusiasm, I taught the song and the hand motions to the children in the sprawl of interconnected backyards in our brand-new suburban tract development. Soon all the children on the swings were joyfully singing it together and running home to sing it for their parents.

That night a delegation of Irish and Italian Catholic mothers met mine at the front door. "We won't have your daughter trying to convert our children. She has been placed off-limits, and your yard and home are off-limits. Our children are not allowed to play with her anymore."

Raised in the intensely Jewish Lower East Side of New York and a section of Brooklyn called Canarsie, my mother was stunned into silence. Immediately our backyard seemed to have sprouted an invisible fence no neighborhood child would climb. Momma responded by learning how to drive so that she could take me to play at the homes of more tolerant families from diverse backgrounds, who also went to Friends School, as I did. I began to drain the bookmobile of reading material, inhaling stories, dwelling in fiction to salve the pain of loneliness and loss.

Then, a year later, came a special day. Drawn by the sound of young voices, I had climbed onto the ledge of the kitchen sink to peer into the backyard. The kids were back! The ban must be over! They were toting scraps of lumber and had set about building a house in our apple tree—one of the few mature fruit trees left standing when a farm and orchard were cleared for our development. It was August and it was hot, hot, hot.

In my bathing suit, I ran gleefully to meet them. "Hi kids! You're back?!" They turned, just six of them, ages maybe seven to twelve. The eldest boy called out: "It's the Jew! Father Martin says they killed Christ. Let's get her!" They ran at me brandishing their scrap lumber with protruding rusted nails. I sprinted for the sliding door at the back of our house, threw myself in and tugged the door shut, bleeding from a scrape I'd received when they tossed a piece of wood at me.

I never told my parents. That first visit from the neighbors had depressed my mother so much that it almost crushed her spirit. Were she to learn about this, it would have been too much. I write about it only now because I know that in her advanced stage of Alzheimer's she can no longer read.

When our first child was born, my first husband and I seriously debated whether it would be wise to give him a Jewish identity. But as we began to recall the beauty of Jewish tradition and the remarkable journey of the Jewish people across thousands of years, our protective parent filters were exchanged for wonder, and today both Adam and Mark have active Jewish lives, and one has even mentioned possibly becoming a rabbi one day. But we did talk about it. And that is important to do. It is best for a child to receive an identity not by default but rather one conferred with loving and focused intention.

Anti-Semitism is not the only way we receive wounds that impede our ability to connect meaningfully to Judaism. My hubbatzin, Barry, was raised in the dry, boring, formulaic post-Holocaust Orthodoxy of South Africa. His religious school teacher, who had no idea how to work with children, hit them on the hand with a two-by-four if they misbehaved. Only the warmth of his grandparents' Shabbat and holy day home stay with him, blossoming as important memories in our marriage.

When I teach my weeklong workshops, I sometimes incorporate a session called "Healing from the Wounds of Growing Up Jewish." Often, during our open-mike sharing, everyone wants to speak at some point. There are many real issues raised—by those who feel judged as too religious by their families and by those judged not religious enough; by those who suffered an overdose of precise Jewish observance growing up, and by those, most often women, given no meaningful Jewish education when they were young. Those who are children of survivors often speak of overprotective parents who feared losing a precious child in a crowd or at the beach. More recently, there are those who talk with great sadness about Israel's being abandoned by the political left and others who speak with equal sadness and pain about the Israeli government's approach to the Palestinian situation. When kept under the rug, these and other issues trip us up and form barriers to deep, joyful Jewishing.

RECIPE #35:
Recovering from the Wounds of Growing Up Jewish

Have you become or were you born Jewish? What are your wounds? Speaking this way is not treasonable. It is reasonable, and it offers an opening to a process of mourning and healing that will help you free up your heart to let the benefits of Jewish practices become ever more available to you.

- Uncover your inner dialogue about being Jewish. What has been challenging, what has been painful? Write your thoughts in a journal or shout them from a mountaintop, perhaps address them to G*d in the *hitbodedut* method described in chapter 2, "Reclaiming G*d with Integrity."
- Bring together a safe circle of those with whom you can share these kinds of awarenesses. If it is Passover time, you might start with a full *kiddush* cup and ask each person to pour out some wine after or as he begins to speak. When each person's inner *kiddush* cup is empty, allow for silence. As the *kiddush* says, *z'man heyruteynu mikra kodesh,* "times we are free holiness happens."
- Now, see if those present might be willing to read *Meaning and Mitzvah* or *Reclaiming Judaism as a Spiritual Practice* at home. If so, when they have begun to do so, meet weekly for discussions and each time pass the cup again. Let each person add something that comes up as an awareness to fill rather than deplete her cup of spirit.

Many post-Holocaust Jews have found spiritual support amid other world wisdom traditions—Hinduism, Buddhism, and Quakerism, to name but a few. Just as in the exercise above, it is powerful to speak about your Jewish journey with others. Have you been exploring other world wisdom traditions? Great! You are likely bringing back to the Jewish people

RECIPE #36:
Honoring
Your Journey

valuable skills and other nutrients for our people. What have you discovered on your spiritual journey that you would love to be able to connect back to being Jewish in a meaningful way?

The seeker's journey away from Judaism
is a pilgrimage that includes a return trip.
Those who were sheltered by the "ism" traditions—
Quakerism, Buddhism, Hinduism, Taoism, and others—
return bearing gifts of spirit.
Jewish meditation practitioners,
for example,
are putting the rest notes
back into the sound of being Jewish.
Jewish yoga teachers are
helping our people
back into their bodies.
A great holy healing is happening.

The discussion my husband and I had about raising the children as Jews? In the end we could not shake ourselves of the belief that our people exists for a reason, and that the individual survival of any one of us is not as important as the flow of our people and our practices through the river of earth's evolving civilizations. We agreed that raising our children in this covenant was important to the face of the future.

While I used to be allergic to the "G" word, today my sense is that G*d is working in part through the Jewish people and that our people is an important, enduring form of human organization. To understand the flow of history and hostility is not only to weep, it is to grow closer and stronger, to remember and to give because you feel yourself an ally or a member of our people, and you believe in what we stand for: We are the people of the *yud hey vav hey* revolution, carrying the living memory of the Power of Transformation. We can find a better way and we must model how to keep trying. Therefore, as the Haggadah says, *v'haggadtah l'vah-neh-hah*, "so tell it to your children."

"Mom."

"Adam, so nice of you to call."

"Mom, this is Mark, I'm on the other line too."

"Mom, our government is taking away essential freedoms and passing rules to limit constitutional rights. Noncitizens who have made their way here seeking a better life are being deported. Jewish history teaches that this is the opposite of spirituality and ethics. I just got a radio show to talk about this at my college. We all have to do something!"

"Mom, I'm organizing at my campus too. This is what you taught us, that activism is an important part of being spiritual and being a Jew. We called to talk about how you can get involved with our plans."

> Elijah would sigh over the honor of Israel every day,
> as if Israel were in danger
> of being annihilated from the world.
> In every generation that Elijah found righteous people,
> he would embrace and kiss them
> and bless the Holy One.
> —*Tanna d'Bei Eliyahu Rabbah 5:11*

APPENDIX: MITZVAH CARDS

Pikuah Nefesh **The Life Mitzvah** Acting to save a life. One who does is as one who saves the entire world.	*Bal Tash-hit* **The Environmental Mitzvah** Tolerating no wanton destruction of the planet.	*Ayd Shaheyr* **The Honest Witness Mitzvah** When you must say something, taking care to truthfully report what was said or done.
Lo Tikom **The Revenge Mitzvah** Dealing with anger and loss without multiplying wrongs or taking revenge.	*Lo Teteyn Mikshol* **The Stumbling Block Mitzvah** Being aware of how you can best set up environ-ments and situations so others won't be ethically or physically tripped up.	*Peah, leket, Shih'hah* **The Sharing Mitzvah** Viewing the fruits of your efforts as a field and finding ways to leave some gleanings for those in need.
Shalom Bayit **The Peace-Keeping Mitzvah** Performing conscious acts of self-restraint that may yield greater peace at home, work, and the world at large.	*Mezuzah* **The Sacred Space Mitzvah** Marking the rooms of your home as sacred space for loving and listening.	*Limmud Torah* **The Torah Mitzvah** Engaging in regular Torah study as a prism for awareness and growth.

G'nivat Da'at **The Marketing Mitzvah** Exercising truth in promotional advertising or speech.	*V'Hadarta P'nai Zaken* **The Elder Mitzvah** Receiving elders with respectful attention to their experience and needs.	*Dina d'Malḥuta Dina* **The Citizenship Mitzvah** Participating in society through your voice, taxes, service, and vote.
Ahavat Tzion **The Israel Mitzvah** Securing a defendable, just, beautiful State of Israel.	*Tzaar Baalei Hayim* **The Animal Mitzvah** Preventing unnecessary suffering of sentient beings.	*V'ahavta l'Rayeha* **The Love Mitzvah** Loving others as you could best love yourself.
Tzedakah **The Money Mitzvah** Achieving an equitable distribution of your personal resources so your life is good and many can thrive.	*Yizkor* **The Memory Mitzvah** Transforming the pain of loss into the gift of times together, remembered.	*Minyan* **The You Count Mitzvah** Having a network of caring friends and neighbors for whom you show up and who will show up for you.

Tanhui **The Community Pantry Mitzvah** Making sure everyone in your community has meals and a safe place to eat them.	*Hevra kaddisha* **The Burial Mitzvah** Ensuring respectful preparation of a soul's former body and seeing to its burial.	*Lih-yote b'Simha Tamid* **The Happiness Mitzvah** Living as though you are always at a *simha*, an especially happy occasion.
Shofar **The Wake-up Call Mitzvah** Relationships amiss any-where in your life? Let the shofar wake you up to make meaningful contact—now—don't wait another year!	*Sukkah* **The Nature Meditation Mitzvah** Tap together this fragile harvest home; gratefully hear the planet sing and sigh, build your inner life's circle—invite friends and neighbors to come by.	*Megillah* **The Masked Mitzvah** *Megillah* moments beckon us to remember that this life is just a mask. What's the hidden meaning? Esther's the one to ask.
Lo Tahmod **The Dangerous Desire Mitzvah** Noticing desire for others' possessions and practicing non-attachment to things.	*Nedarim* **The Promise Mitzvah** Taking care to honorably fulfill commitments you have made.	*Neehum Aveylim* **The Comforting Mitzvah** Supporting those in mourning through simply being present.

Teshuvah **The Returning Mitzvah** Facing difficult or desired changes—within you, with others, with the land, with the Source of Life—so that wholeness and holiness can return.	*Kashrut* **The Eating Mitzvah** Paying attention to what you choose to eat and how it is grown, packed, and prepared.	*Shabbat* **The Time Mitzvah** Consciously ceasing work, worldly news, investing and spending for one full day at each week's end.
Gemillut Hassadim **The Selfless Mitzvah** Performing deeds of loving-kindness for others.	*Aliyah l'Aretz* **The Pilgrimage Mitzvah** Letting your soul lift you up to live in, to experience, Jerusalem and Israel.	*Shmirat ha-Guf* **The Body Mitzvah** Caring for your body as the instrument that plays your life.
Mikvah **The Purification Mitzvah** Rebirthing yourself in living waters, the holy days, healing, and physical renewal.	*Hahnassat Orhim* **The Hospitality Mitzvah** Hosting in your home and out in the world as though all people are your honored guests.	*Tefillah* **The Prayer of Your Heart Mitzvah** Daily prayer practices to nourish your soul stream.

GLOSSARY

Aaron (ah-ha-rone): Served as the first high priest, brother of Moses and Miriam.

Abraham's mother: Unnamed in Torah. See midrash for the rabbinic imagination on her parenting abilities where she is called Emtelai or Emetlai.

Adam (ah-dahm): First human according to the biblical creation story, rooted in the word *adamah*, "earth," and *adom*, "red."

adon olam (ah-dohn oh-lahm): "Threshold of Eternity." Much-loved Jewish hymn found in almost every siddur and worship service because of its inspiring nature.

adonai (ah-doh-nai): Since it is a Jewish spiritual practice not to pronounce the tetragrammaton, the most sacred name of G*d, when it appears in prayers and scrolls this term, meaning "my Lord," which has as its root *ehden*, "threshold," is substituted. In some kabbalistic works *adonai* also has the attribute of *din*, "judgment," whereas the tetragrammaton would represent Presence and *shehinah*.

ahavah (ah-hah-vah): "Love." A core principle in Judaism is to infuse love into our actions and to draw inspiration from experiencing the greatest view of reality as having been created out of *ahavah u'v'ratzon*, love and desire, as the Shabbat *kiddush* prayer describes.

ahavat tzion, ahavas tzion (ah-hah-vaht tzee-yohn, ah-hah-vas tzee-yon): "Love of Zion." Caring for the Land of Israel as a sacred place and working for the full well-being of its land and peoples.

ahavat yisrael, ahavas yisroel (ah-hah-vaht yis-rah-ehl, ah-hah-vahs yis-roe-el): "Love of the Jewish people." The mitzvah of consciously caring for and making a point of getting along with other Jews; this mitzvah is said to be a prerequisite for bringing the messianic time.

akedah (ah-kay-dah): Term that denotes the "binding of Isaac" for apparent sacrifice by his father, Abraham, as instructed in the Bible by "G*d."

Akiva ben Yosef (a-kee-vuh ben yoseyf): Also known as Rabbi Akiba (born about 50 CE; martyred about 132 CE). Systematized Jewish law and formulated essential ways to work with it. Profoundly influential as a teacher of ethics. Tales of his great character and relationship with his wife, Rachel, abound.

Akkadian (uh-kay-dee-in): Semitic language of the group initially ruled by a Semitic king named Sargon in the area of the city of Akkad, Mesopotamia, around 2350 BCE. As in the Moses story, Sargon is sent downstream in a basket of rushes. His mother is known in lore as a priestess; his father is unknown. Sargon is described as raised by a gardener under the auspices of a goddess named Ishtar.

aleynu (ah-ley-nu): "It is upon us." Prayer toward the end of most Jewish services that includes a bowing to indicate we know we aren't responsible for nor in control of everything, while at the same time taking on the obligation to work for *tikkun olam*, "repair of the world," and recognizing that the fullness of this depends on awareness of the Unity of All Being becoming recognized by all beings.

aliyah, aliyot (pl) (ah-lee-yuh, ah-lee-yote): "Going up." Those who enter the covenant of being Jewish take turns fulfilling the mitzvah of standing at the Torah as it is read and reciting a blessing for the gift of Torah and the *hayyai olam*, eternal awareness that richly informs living, which springs from the gift of Torah.

aliyah l'aretz (ah-lee-yah la-ah-retz): "Going up to the Land." The mitzvah of making a pilgrimage to, or moving to, the Land of Israel.

Alkabetz, Rabbi Shlomo HaLevy (1505–1584): Kabbalist born in Salonica where he married. Taught in Adrianople, Turkey, and then moved to Safed, Israel, because he felt a person could only truly understand the secrets of Torah by living there. He wrote numerous works including the well-known Shabbat poem *l'hah dodi*.

al tifrosh min ha-tzibor (ahl tee-frosh mihn hah-tzee-boor): "Don't separate yourself from the community." The mitzvah of active engagement in community life, taking responsibility for guiding what Jewish communal decisions are to be in matters of religious life, social welfare, showing up for services and each other on both happy and sad occasions, advocating for needed change as well as ensuring that tradition is sustained with integrity and respect.

ameyn, **amen** (ah-meyn, au-mane): "Truly." Shares a root with *emunah,* "faith." Is also an acronym for *el meleh neh-ehman,* meaning "God is a faithful governing principle." "One who answers *amen* with all one's strength merits to have the gates of the Garden of Eden open before him" (Shabbat 119b). Also an Egyptian god of air and breath who was worshiped at Thebes.

ana el na r'fa na la (ah-na el nah r'fah nah lah): Moses' prayer for the healing of his sister Miriam when her skin flared up in a reaction to being put out of the leadership team with Moses and Aaron. This phrase is often used liturgically in Jewish healing services today.

Aramaic (ar-uh-may-ic): A Semitic language spoken by most Jews during the original developmental period of the Talmud. Also appears in many Jewish mystical writings such as the Zohar, and some traditional prayers, such as the *kaddish.*

aron kodesh (ah-rone koe-desh): "Holy ark." In the Temple during the sacrificial period the central point was the "holy of holies," which in a synagogue is represented by the cabinet-like enclosure for Torah scrolls.

arum(im) (ah-rum, ah-rue-mim): "Naked" and "cunning," as in the Eden story of the snake, Adam, and Eve.

asher (ah-sher): "That," "which."

ashrei yoshvei veiteha: "Happy are those who dwell in Your house" (Psalm 145:1). Those who recite it three times a day are said to find happiness. It is one of the earliest liturgical pieces added when the original service was expanded from being the *shema* and its surrounding blessings and the *amidah.*

assiyah (ah-see-yah): Dimension of physical being, of doing, one of the *arba olamot,* "Four Worlds" of spiritual awareness and practice elucidated within Jewish mysticism.

Assyria (us-seer-ee-ya): Mesopotamian kingdom formed after the Akkadians, with an economy based on trade.

atzilut (ah-tzee-lute): Transcendent level of the four dimensions of spiritual practice known as the *arba olamot*, "Four Worlds." This is where you connect beyond the known or conceivable and experience pure, unified Being.

Avraham (av-rah-hahm): Hebrew name for Abraham, founding patriarch of the Israelites and Judaism. His name was *avram* before his experience of G*d.

Avram (ahv-rum): Name of *avraham* (Abraham) in the Torah before he enters into awareness of G*d, whereupon the letter *hey* is added to his name, signifying his Israelite religion/culture.

ayd shaher (aid sha-her): "False witness." Phrase referring to the mitzvah of refraining from lying or misrepresenting the character, circumstances, or practices of another person.

Baal Shem Tov (bah-ahl shem tov): Rabbi Israel ben Eliezer (c. 1700–1760), also known by the acronym "Besht," considered the founder of modern Hasidism, taught based on the mystical methods of Rabbi Isaac Luria with accessibility for and love of the common person. Many beautiful stories of the Besht are told to this day.

Babylonian Empire: First arises in 2200 BCE. King Hammurabi was its most famous leader due to his code of justice, a small piece of which appears word for word in the Torah. Is conquered by the Assyrians but reemerges under King Nebuchadnezzar in 626 BCE.

Baer, Rabbi Dov (dove bear) (1773–1827): Son of the founder of Chabad Hasidism; prolific writer and mystical teacher who moved his father's followers from Liady to Lubavitch, Russia.

bal tash-hit (bahl tash-heet): "No destruction." Mitzvah of respect for the planet and its resources.

Bar Kochba (bar koh-bah): Aramaic for "son of a star," also known as Simeon ben Kosiba. He led a promising Jewish rebellion against the Roman domination of Israel in 132–135 CE. He was thought by Rabbi Akiva to be the awaited messiah who would restore the Jews to sovereignty in the Land of Israel.

bar mitzvah (bar mitz-vah): Rite of passage of a Jewish male upon reaching thirteen years of age to the status of adult empowerment to take responsibility for fulfillment of the mitzvot. Originally the parents would undertake this ritual themselves by reciting a blessing of release from responsibility for monitoring the youth's relationship to the mitzvot. Today bar mitzvah involves an extensive period of study, preparation, and mentoring for the youth, who enhances the transition with an *aliyah* to the Torah, a blessing, in most cases a teaching about the Torah portion directed to his community, and a chanting of the text of the Torah and *Haftarah*.

baruh (bah-ruh, often transliterated "baruch"): "Bless." Shares a root with the Hebrew words for knee, pond, bow, and blessing.

bat mitzvah (bat mitz-vah): Parallel rite to the ritual of bar mitzvah, introduced in the twentieth century for females. Some communities consider this appropriate for age twelve and up; others stay with age thirteen, as became the custom for males. Many communities have identical ritual practices for girls, except among the Orthodox where norms are still evolving for this practice and, at the time of this writing, if girls ascend to and read from the Torah, it is done in a women-only gathering.

beit midrash (beit mid-rahsh): "House of inquiry." Technical term for a room or building dedicated for Jewish sacred text studies.

Bene Yisrael (beh-ney yis-ra-el): Largest community of Jews of India who today reside primarily in Bombay and Israel.

Benjamin of Tudela: Jewish scholarly author of a medieval travelogue prized by scholars for its rich information on local customs of Spain, Italy, Greece, Israel, Turkey, China, India, and Egypt.

bensch (ben-ch): Yiddish for gathering for a blessing, generally applies to *ha-motzi*, the blessing for a meal that includes bread, and to *birkat ha-mazon*, "blessing the meal," a sequence of blessings of gratitude and awareness chanted after such a meal. One can also *bensch gomel*, say a prayer of gratitude for those who have narrowly escaped death—from an accident, crime, or major surgery.

beriyah (bree-yah): One of the four dimensions of spirituality known as the *arba olamot* of the kabbalists; this one concerns ideas, thoughts, abstraction, and innovations.

Beta Yisrael (bey-tah yis-rah-el): Name preferred by Ethiopian Jews discovered living in the Gondar province, many of whom were airlifted to Israel during the late twentieth century. The North American Conference on Ethiopian Jewry (NACOEJ) continues to advocate for, feed, and educate those who remain on a waiting list for emigration.

B'nai Menashe (b'nei men-ah-sheh): Region of northern India, bordering Burma and Bangladesh, that is home to about five thousand people who consider themselves Jews and descendents of one of the lost tribes, that of Menashe.

British Mandate: Period in World War I during which the Turks were defeated by the British and, from July 24, 1922, to

May 15, 1948, the British ruled the Land of Israel, which they called Palestine.

b'tzelem elohim (b'tzeh-lem eh-loe-him): Passage in Genesis that describes humans as created "in the image of G*d."

Buba (bu-bah): Priestly group of the African Venda tribe with the highest incidence of genetic evidence of any group for descent from the *cohanim*, "priestly class," of Temple times.

Byzantine Empire: Term invented in 1557 by a German historian to describe a period of the superpower Roman Empire spanning from the third century CE to the fifteenth century, when it was conquered by the Ottoman Empire.

Cabbalah: See Kabbalah.

caliph (kay-liff): From the Arabic term *khalifa*, a vice-regent in the spiritual leadership hierarchy.

Canaan: Term for a region roughly corresponding to present-day Israel (including the West Bank), western Jordan, southern Syria, and southern Lebanon. The Canaanite town Ugarit was rediscovered in 1928 and most modern knowledge about the Canaanites stems from excavation in this area.

Cochin: Region of India where a few members of the once-substantial Cochin Jewish community still live.

Code of Hammurabi: A code of law written by Babylonian King Hammurabi, who reigned from 1792 to 1750 BCE. His name means "the Amoiritic god Hammu is great." He turned Babylon into the center of an empire with hegemony over all of Mesopotamia. A section of this code appears in the Torah.

cohen, cohanim (pl) (coe-heyn, coe-hah-nim): "Priest." Became a common Jewish surname.

Conversos: One of the terms for those who had to convert to Christianity during the Spanish Inquisition in order to survive. Also known as Marranos and called *anusim* in Hebrew.

Crusades: The first crusade, in 1096 CE, was launched by Pope Urban II with the intention of taking back Jerusalem, which first came under Muslim rule in 637 CE. Waves of religiously, politically, and economically motivated Crusades, campaigns to bring lands and peoples under Christian rule and religion, voluntarily or by force, would continue for nearly a thousand years. Lands conquered along the way were taken to create new kingdoms, and the face of Europe was forever changed. The eighth crusade started in 1270.

Cushite: Cush was the gold capital of ancient Africa. Moses had a relationship not appreciated by Miriam and Aaron, possibly a marriage, with a Cushite woman. As head of a nation moving through other people's territories, marital alliances with daughters of heads of other nations could be something Moses would have undertaken.

Dahya K'hayna (dah-yuh k'hay-nah): "Dahya Cohen." Jewish woman warrior who led the Berber invasion of North Africa in the seventh century.

daven (dah-vehn): Yiddish for heartfelt praying.

davenology: Term introduced by Rabbi Zalman Schachter-Shalomi for cultivating an in-depth understanding of the spiritual infrastructure and flow of Jewish prayer.

devarim (d'vah-rim): "Words" or "things." Also the Hebrew name for the biblical book of Deuteronomy.

devekut (d'vey-kute): "Cleaving" or "intimacy." Principle and practices developed within Hasidism and adopted by many Jews that create an experience of reaching for at-one-ment. Shares the root letters of *debek*, "glue."

dhimmi (dih-mee): "Diminished." Category of local resi-dent status developed by Muslims for non-Muslims who are not pagans, since Jews and Christians also believe in one G*d.

dina d'mal<u>h</u>uta dina (deena d'mahl-hoo-tah deena): "The law of the regency is the law." Principle that unless it contravenes Torah, we must obey the laws of the land in which we reside.

divrei torah (dihv-ray toe-rah): An explanation or inter-pretation you write, read, or hear given by a contemporary that sheds insight on the weekly Torah portion.

d'oraita (d'or-aye-tuh): Aramaic term meaning "from the Torah." Some scholars say possibly from the Hebrew word *or*, "light."

eeshah (ee-shah): "Woman."

ehden (eh-den): "Threshold" or "window sill." Root of *adonai*. Also appears as root of term for "connecting socket" in Exodus 27:16, regarding construction of the Tabernacle.

ehyeh asher ehyeh (eh-yeh ah-sheyr eh-yeh): Moses asks at the burning bush for a name of the "G*d" he has encoun-tered and the answer can be translated in the durative—"I am what I am"—which is the same verb form as the future tense, so an equally valid translation would be "I am becoming what I am becoming" or "I will be what I will be."

Eichmann, Adolf (1906–1962): Headed the Gestapo Department of Jewish Affairs and moved up from a clerk spe-cializing in information about Jews to a corporal at the Dachau death camp to helping organize the Wannsee Conference in Berlin and other aspects of the "final solution." Following the surrender of Nazi Germany in May of 1945, Eichmann was arrested but managed to escape. In 1950, with the help of the

SS underground, he fled to Argentina and lived under the assumed name Ricardo Klement for ten years until Israeli Mossad agents abducted him on May 11, 1960. Eichmann went on trial in Jerusalem for crimes against the Jewish people, crimes against humanity, and war crimes, and was hanged.

eish *(ey-sh)*: "Fire."

eish-ah (eysh-ah): "Her fire."

eitz hayyim, atzei hayyim (pl) (eytz hah-yim, atzei hah-yim): "Tree of Life." One of two significant trees in the Garden of Eden narrative that continues to appear as a major Jewish symbol and metaphor. The Torah is called a "tree of life" and this is also the name of the reality map with many associated texts and meditation practices developed by the kabbalists.

el, elim (pl) (ehl, ey-lim): "G*d," "gods." Hebrew and other early languages use this as a generic term for the concept of a god and sometimes as a name of G*d, as in Beth El, "House of G*d."

Elat Chayyim (ey-laht hah-yeem): Retreat center in Accord, New York, about two hours north of New York City in the Catskill Mountains that draws seekers and teachers of Jewish spiritual practice from every denomination of Judaism. Visit www.elatchayyim.org.

Elijah, Eliyahu (Ee-lie-jah, el-ee-yah-hu): Ninth-century BCE prophet during the rule of King Ahab; considered precursor of the messiah in a variety of liturgical pieces.

elohim (eh-loe-him): Of the many names for G*d in Judaism, this is the earliest, the third word in the Torah, and is considered to be about the power of nature.

emet (eh-meht): "Truth." Composed of the first, middle, and last letters of the Hebrew alphabet; Jewish mystics see this word as signifying that truth is constantly changing and is composed of your past, present, and future.

Evian Conference: In 1938 representatives of thirty-two countries met at the French resort of Evian for an International Conference initiated by U.S. President Franklin D. Roosevelt with the goal of moving Jews into safe countries and away from the Nazi regime. Declaring themselves under economic duress and unable to absorb more immigrants, most of the world's nations abstained from taking Jews. Only the Dominican Republic was willing to adjust its quotas to take in Jews, and a few hundred went there before Germany made emigration impossible.

eyrev rav (ey-rev rahv): "Mixed multitude." Expression given in Exodus 12:38 to describe the diverse group of Israelite and non-Israelite slaves who escape from Egypt. They become one group known as Israelites during their collective experience and vocal commitment at Sinai.

ezrat ḥolim (ez-raht ho-lim): "Helping the ill" is a mitzvah.

Federation: A system that involves affiliating Jewish social welfare and education agencies in a given region so that fund raising and services can be coordinated more effectively. Various names of Jewish federations are the national umbrella, United Jewish Communities (UJC), the Israel fund component, United Jewish Appeal (UJA), and many local federations.

forshpeis (for-shpice): Yiddish for appetizer or snack before a meal; can be used to refer to a physical or intellectual mini-experience as well.

gematria (g'mah-tree-uh): "Numerology" practice whereby, since every Hebrew letter has a numerical value and creative force, the sum of a word or phrase can be found and compared with other terms of similar value as a way of seeking deeper insight into the meaning of a verse of Torah. There are a number of anagram-like ways of assigning numerical values that extend the challenges and opportunities of this practice.

Gendlin, Dr. Gene: Psychologist and philosopher who developed the best-selling work and technique for connecting with your body's intuitive ways of knowing called Focusing. Visit www.focusing.org.

Gikatilla, Rabbi Joseph (1248–1323): Spanish kabbalist who carried on the work of Abraham Abulafia, he also knew secular science and philosophy. Author of many works including *Ginot Egoz* and *Shaarei Orah*.

gamal (gah-mahl): "Camel."

gashmiut (gahsh-mee-ute): "Materiality." The physical world as we know it.

gemilut hasadim (g'mee-lute hah-sah-dim): "Deeds of loving-kindness." Mitzvah of thoughtful actions to be distinguished from the mitzvah of *tzedakah*, giving of money.

g'nivat da'at (g'nee-vaht dah-aht): "Theft of knowledge." It is a mitzvah to not engage in deceptive advertising practices.

Gold, Rabbi Shefa: Spiritual teacher of chanting, devotional healing, spiritual community-building, and meditation, and composer of sacred music and chant, she reintroduced chanting meditation as a Jewish practice and directs the C-Deep Center for Devotional Energy and Ecstatic Practice. Visit www.rabbishefagold.com.

goy (goy): "Nation." The Israelites are enjoined to lead mitzvah-centered lives in order to be a *goy kadosh*, "a holy nation." Non-Jews are often termed *goyim*, "nations."

Hagar (hah-gahr): Servant of Sarah who becomes a surrogate mother and bears Abraham's first son, Ishmael.

Haggadah (hah-gah-dah): From *haggid*, "telling," the booklet containing the liturgy for the Passover seder ritual.

ha̲hnassat or̲him (ha̲h-nah-saht ohr-̲him): Mitzvah of treating those around you as guests.

halleluyah (hah-leh-lu-yah): "Praise G*d." *Hallal* means "praise." *Yah*, "G*d," is composed of the first two letters of the tetragrammaton with the addition of a vowel sound and often appears in words as a way of placing G*d into a name or term, as is the case here. Among modern mystics of the Jewish Renewal movement *yah* is a popular term for G*d because of its relative gender neutrality and breath-like sound.

ha-makom (ha mah-comb): "The Place." One of the many metaphoric names for G*d.

ha-na-ah (hah-nah-ah): "Benefit" or "pleasure."

Hananiah ben Teradyon: Convicted of teaching Torah during the Hadrianic persecutions, he was condemned to be wrapped in a Torah scroll and burned at the stake.

Hannah: Name meaning "grace." She appears in 1 Samuel 1:1 as an infertile woman crying and expressing the prayer of her heart in the Temple. She is held as the model for personal prayer, as the sacrificial system was still active at that time. Hannah spoke her heart aloud to G*d and did conceive a son, Samuel. She dedicated Samuel to serve in the Temple, and he went on to become a judge and prophet.

Hansen's disease: A chronic disease characterized by skin and muscle nodules and deteriorioration, which epidemiologists find did not exist on earth during the biblical period and does not at all match the biblical account of the symptoms of *tzara'at*, which used to be viewed as meaning *leprosy*.

Hanukkah (hah-new-kah): Winter equinox holiday commemorating the Maccabean revolt and restoration of the Temple. Based on *hinuh*, "dedication," or "education."

hanukkat ha-bayit (hah-new-kaht hah-bah-yit): Ritual for dedicating a home with the placing of a mezuzah on a doorpost.

hareini: "Behold me." Expression for being present and ready to undertake a mitzvah.

har ha-elohim: "Mountain of the G*d." Place where Moses goes on his vision quest and encounters the burning bush.

hashem (hah-shehm): "The Name." Term used by Moses in Deuteronomy to refer to his burning bush experience of G*d and used today in place of saying any form of G*d's names out loud during study or discussion so as to reserve them for use only as "callings" to or honoring of Presence during prayer.

Hasidism (hah-sih-dizm): Orthodox religious movement founded some two hundred years ago in Eastern Europe that expanded on the meditation and mysticism in Judaism in addition to retaining the laws and customs. Clusters of different approaches generally took on the name of the town of their main teacher; many were wiped out during the Holocaust, and rerooted throughout the world.

King Hassan II: King of Morocco [1929–1999], who made significant efforts to promote the safety and practice of the remaining Jews in his country and who worked behind the scenes to facilitate the Middle East peace process.

havdalah (hav-dah-lah): Beautiful ritual for ending the Sabbath, based on a root word meaning "difference." Involves blessings over wine, sweet-smelling spices, and a braided candle.

havurah (hah-vu-rah): Group that gathers regularly for friendship in the context of Jewish prayer or study. Visit www.havurah.org.

hayah (hai-yuh): "Lively." The fourth of the five levels of the soul, this refers to the soul's capacity for intuition and endurance. Also used as a female first name.

Herzl, Theodore (1860–1904): Studied in Vienna, lived in Paris, witnessed the Kishinev pogrom in 1903. Philosopher and political theorist and politician, architect of modern Zionism, author of *Der Judenstaat* and also *Altneuland*, he also proposed bringing Jews to live in Uganda as a temporary measure of rescue from the pogroms. He died in Vienna in 1905 and his remains are buried on Mt. Herzl in Israel.

Heschel, Rabbi Abraham Joshua (1907–1972): Author, civil rights activist in the United States, and advocate for freedom for Soviet Jewry; professor of philosophy, Kabbalah, and Hasidism. Escaped Nazi Germany and served briefly at the Reform movement's seminary, Hebrew Union College, then transferred for a lengthy term to the Conservative movement's Jewish Theological Seminary. Major works include: *Man Is Not Alone*, *G*d in Search of Man*, *The Sabbath*, and *The Prophets*.

hevra kaddisha (heh-vruh kah-dee-shah): "Holy friends." An organization of those in the community who are dedicated to preparing the body of a Jewish person for burial.

hevruta (hehv-rue-tah): One-to-one text study with a peer where you help one another understand and discover layers of meaning. Based in the root word *haver*, "friend," and indeed, this practice most often leads to enduring friendship.

HIAS (high-ahs): Acronym for the nonprofit Hebrew Immigrant Aid Society established to assist in immigrant absorption and relocation. To date HIAS has helped more than 4.5 million people, including Jews fleeing the Holocaust, Morocco, and Russia, as well as non-Jews from Afghanistan, Bosnia, Bulgaria, Czechoslovakia, Ethiopia, Haiti, Hungary, Iran, Morocco, Poland, Romania, Tunisia, Vietnam, and the successor states to the former Soviet Union. Visit www.hias.org.

hiddur mitzvah (hee-door meetz-vah): "To embroider" a mitzvah. The practice of making an act or sacred object more beautiful than if you just did it in a simple, straightforward way. Judaism is an aesthetic tradition, not an ascetic one.

hineini (hee-nay-nee): "Here I am." The response given when G*d twice calls the names of specific persons in Torah, such as Adam, Moses, and Samuel. This same response is used to open a meditation, to strengthen doing a mitzvah, or by the cantor to indicate humility at serving as the congregation's conduit of spirit.

hinuh (hee-nuh): "Education." The root word of Hanukkah.

hitbodedut (hit-boe-d'doot): Practice of solitary praying from the heart in a great outpouring, often done in nature.

hitgashmiut (hit-gahsh-mee-ute): Practice of losing your sense of materiality through ecstatic practice, often dance.

hityashvut (hit-yahsh-vute): Hasidic concept of finding equanimity, a "settling" of the soul that mentors can guide during the maturation process.

hoda'ah (hoe-dah-ah): "Gratitude."

Honi (Hoe-ni): In Greek, *Onias*. In Hebrew *honi ha-me'aggel*, "Honi the Circle Drawer." The Talmud and midrashim offer stories of this teacher who was known to Josephus as being unafraid to speak truth to power and who, lore has it, had extraordinary powers.

humash (hoo-mahsh): Often spelled Chumash. The Five Books of Moses in book form, based on the root letters for the word *five*.

hutzpah (hutz-pah, hutz-puh): Yiddish for creative audacity. Often spelled chutzpah.

Ibn Ezra (c. 1089–1164): Abraham Meir Ibn Ezra. Grammarian, commentator, poet, philosopher, and astronomer; born in Tudela, Spain. He traveled widely and wrote a number of ethical treatises, poems, and other works. One of the most important authors of biblical commentary, his interpretations were Neoplatonic and often rationalistic. He was the inspiration for Robert Browning's "Rabbi Ben Ezra."

Ibn Gabirol (1021–1058): Rabbi Solomon ben Judah Ibn Gabirol. Philosopher and poet, he was the first to teach Neoplatonism in Europe. Considered a heretic by religious Jews of his time, ironically his theological liturgical work *adon olam* became one of the most enduring and popular liturgical works in Judaism and is found in almost every Jewish prayer service and prayer book.

idit (ee-deet): "Witness." Also known as Irit, these are names given in rabbinic literature for Lot's wife, who isn't named in the Bible.

Inquisition (1391–1869): Term for the process of purifying Spain and eventually other lands of non-Catholics via horrific methods of torture as a form of "inquiry" and conversion, with those found guilty of heresy often burned at the stake.

Isaac: *Yitzhak* in Hebrew. Son of Abraham; father of Jacob and Esau.

Ishmael (ish-mah-el): "Man from G*d." Son of Abraham through Sarah's surrogate, Hagar.

Jacob: *Yaakov* in Hebrew. Son of Isaac, father of the twelve tribes and daughters, only one of whom, Dina, is named.

Jewish Agency for Israel: Rescues Jews in distress, funds and organizes for the absorption of Jewish immigrants to Israel, and promotes a healthy understanding of Zionism worldwide. Visit www.Jafi.org.

Joint Distribution Committee: Founded in 1914 to assist Palestinian Jews caught in the throes of World War I, the JDC has aided millions of Jews in more than eighty-five countries, providing education and social welfare support. www.JDC.org.

Kabbalah (kah-bah-lah): Jewish mystical practice, texts, and stories that have been evolving since biblical times. From the verb *l'kabeyl*, "to receive."

kaddish (kah-deesh, kah-dish): Prayer about the holiness and evolving nature of All Being and the possibility of peace and wholeness that appears in a variety of forms as a bridge throughout Jewish services. Forms include the abbreviated version, *hatzi kaddish*; the full version, *kaddish Shalem*; the *kaddish* remembering scholars and teachers, *kaddish d'rabbanan*; a special funeral *kaddish d'ithadata*; and the *kaddish* said by mourners, *kaddish yatom*. Based on the root term *kadosh*, "holy."

Kaplan, Rabbi Mordecai (1881–1983): Born in Lithuania, he helped to found the Young Israel Orthodox movement in America and went on to be ordained at the Conservative movement's Jewish Theological Seminary. His original philosophy and ideas about how to harmonize Judaism with the emerging values of changing times led his students to successfully urge him to join them in founding a new seminary, the Reconstructionist Rabbinical College. He was the first to institute bat mitzvah in North America and also made liturgical changes in the prayer book to remove the idea of "chosenness." Best known among his many fascinating works is *Judaism as a Civilization*.

Karaites (kahr-ites): In about 800 CE a movement that started out to emphasize Torah fundamentalism arose; its leader was named Anan. Evolved into large numbers by Maimonides' time, eventually taking on some of the philosophical necessities of rabbinic Judaism because the Torah requires interpretation to remain a living religious code. Some Karaite groups exist to this day as a sect distinct from Judaism.

kashrut (kash-root, kash-rus): "Kosher." Practices of food purchase and preparation that delineate which foods can be eaten and in what combinations, and how to organize cookware to support this practice of conscious eating that emphasizes compassion for life.

kavannah (kah-vah-nah, kav-vuh-nuh): "Intention." Shares the root *kav*, "line," and indicates a practice whereby you focus your intention before prayer or action.

kiddush (kee-dush, kih-dush): Blessing over the wine done on Shabbat, on holy days, and during some life-cycle events. Wine is the symbol for blood in its representation of life and vitality.

kippah (kee-pah, kee-paw): Skullcap; yarmulke (Yiddish). Round headcovering that signifies the wearer is engaged in prayer or a meal, or wears it throughout the day as a reminder and symbol of living a mitzvah-centered life.

kishkas (kish-kus): Yiddish for gut emotions, as when something gets to you before you even think about what it means. *Kishka* also literally means the guts of an animal, and an Eastern European Jewish delicacy is to serve it cooked with a savory stuffing.

klal yisrael (klal yis-rah-el): "All of Israel." Term for the mitzvah of engaging in caring, committed peoplehood.

klippot (klee-pote): "Shards," "husks." Hardenings that block your full self-expression. Also, in the kabbalists' model, broken bits of creation that we are here to find and repair so that creation attains its highest possible realization.

koa<u>h</u> (koe-ah): "Strength." Also the name of the Conservative movement's college youth organization.

Kook, Rabbi Avraham (1865–1935): Trained at the Volozhin Yeshiva but descended from a <u>H</u>asidic family. While living in England during World War I, he participated in the efforts that led to the Balfour Declaration. After the war, Rav Kook became Israel's first Ashkenazi chief rabbi. A mystic and poet with many writings to his credit, including a complete commentary on the prayer book called *Olat R'AYaH*.

k'sheleg (k'sheh-leg): "Like snow." Description of how pale Miriam turned when she was thrust out of the leadership triumvirate consisting of herself, Moses, and Aaron. Considered to be a symptom of a disorder caused by such experiences called *tza-ra'at*.

kvetch (k'vetch): Yiddish for "complain."

lasua<u>h</u> (la-sua<u>h</u>): "Dialogue" or "meditate."

leekboa (leek-boe-ah): "Affix." As in a mezuzah.

leket (leh-keht): "Gleanings." That which is collected from the sides of the field by the poor, a practice of biblical times that we can fulfill by being sure to leave something from our own production for others.

Lemba Tribe: South African tribe that claims to be descended from one of the Lost Tribes, the Lemba seek out Jewish learning and practice, and some have asked for permission to move to Israel.

levi, leviim (pl) (ley-vi, l'vee-im): Levites. The workers who kept the Temple and sacrificial system functioning. Some Jews have kept track through the years of whether their paternal relatives were Levites, and they come up to the Torah when called for the second *aliyah*, reserved by tradition for a representative of this group. Named for one of the twelve tribes.

Levi Yitzhak of Berditchev (1740–1810): Author of *Kedushat Levi* and disciple of the Maggid of Mezrich. Served as rabbi in the cities of Britchval, Zelichov, and Pinsk, and for the last twenty-five years of his life was the rabbi of Berditchev, which, under his inspired leadership, grew into a flourishing center of Hasidism. Known for his love of G*d and the Jewish people, he would argue with G*d and plead for an end to exile.

leyn (layn): "Chant." Yiddish term for chanting the Torah and other sacred scroll texts aloud at services.

l'hah dodi (l'ha doe-dee): "To you my Beloved." Shabbat prayer written by kabbalist Shlomo ben Moses Alkabetz (circa 1505 CE) that emphasizes enlightenment as part of the process of bringing Shabbat into your spirit so that you create the ambience of a bride being reunited with Awareness.

Lipkin, Rabbi Israel (1810–1883): Major developer of the *mussar* movement, which emphasized teaching and practice of Jewish ethics and the cultivation of self for this purpose. Also known as Rabbi Israel Salanter.

Litman, Rabbi Jane: Early leader of Jewish feminism; graduate of the Reconstructionist Rabbinical College and coauthor of *Lifecycles* (see Suggestions for Further Reading).

Lot: Abraham's nephew.

Lot's wife: Unnamed in Torah, she is known in Midrash as Idit or Irit.

l'shem (l'shehm): "For the sake of." A phrase used to introduce certain acts as being done for the sake of their inherent holiness, such as writing a Torah and making love.

Luria, Rabbi Isaac (1534–1572): Lived in Sefad and known as the Ari, a magnificent kabbalist who taught his system to Rabbi Hayyim Vital (1542–1620).

ma'ariv (mah-ah-riv, mah-ah-reev): "Evening." Term for the evening service.

madrega (mahd-rey-gah): "Step" or "level." Can be physical or spiritual.

mae-siah (mae see-ah): "From dialogue." Possible way to separate letters of the Hebrew word for *messiah* so as to find the way to peace within and between each of us.

maggid (mah-geed): "Teller." Term for a professional storyteller.

Maggid of Mezrich (1710–1772): The Baal Shem Tov's disciple and the first of the Hasidic rebbes who held court and gave personal advice. His disciples are among the most famous of the early Hasidic masters, including Levi Yitzhak of Berditchev, Zusya of Hanipoli, Solomon ben Meir Ha-Levi of Kariln, Elimelekh of Lyzhansk, and Moshe Leib of Sassov.

Maharal (1525–1609): Rabbi Judah Loew, known for the stories of the Golem that are associated with him. His educational philosophy was that the student should be educated according to his intellectual faculties and so not learn the Talmud and its commentaries at too early an age. His writings include a commentary on Rashi's commentary to the Torah, writings on Passover, exile, and redemption; on *Pirkei Avot*; and on development of character.

Maharshal (1510–1574): Rabbi Solomon Luria, one of the great Ashkenazi devisors of Jewish law and teachers of his time. Known for his work on *halahah*, *Yam Shel Shlomo*, and his talmudic commentary *Chochmat Shlomo*.

Maimonides (1135–1204): Rabbi Moshe ben Maimon, also called the Rambam. Born in Córdoba, Spain, under Muslim rule, his family fled to Morocco after the fall of Córdoba to the Almohads. In Morocco he studied at the University of Fez, where he composed his acclaimed commentary on the *Mishnah*. Next he briefly lived in Israel and finally settled in Fostat, Egypt, where he was doctor to the Grand Vizier Alfadhil and/or the Sultan Saladin of Egypt. There he composed most of his life's work, including the *Mishneh Torah*. He died in Fostat, and was buried in Tiberias, Israel.

mashiah,   moshiah (mah-shee-a<u>h</u>,   moe-shee-a<u>h</u>): "Messiah."

Masoretes (maz-or-eetes): Research teams who, between the seventh and tenth century CE, compiled a system of critical notes, symbols, and notations to represent vowel sounds and music, to ensure that the Torah would be maintained in the most authentic and original wording and chanting possible.

matzah (mah-tzah, mah-tzuh): Flat bread that is part of the Passover ritual. Symbolizes the bread of the poor and oppressed. Its ingredients can touch water no longer than eighteen minutes lest the matzah rise and become leavened. The luxury of leavened foods is not allowed on Passover so as to heighten the experience of reenacting leaving slavery for freedom, which is the basis of the Passover seder.

mayyim (mah-yim): "Water."

mayyim hayyim (mah-yim hah-yim): "Living Waters." Needed for purification rituals so that your soul, body, and even your dishes can transition to a reclaimed sense of sacred service. Also see *mikvah*.

mazel tov (mah-zahl tov): "Good star." Blessing derived originally from astrology and given on special occasions to ensure that the event would be happening under an auspicious star or constellation.

Meir, Golda (1898–1978): Born in Kiev, Russia, lived in America, and served in many leadership capacities for the State of Israel, including ambassador to Russia and prime minister. The Yom Kippur War occurred during her tenure.

mem (mehm): Middle letter of the Hebrew alphabet with the value of forty; symbolic of transformation.

meshuganosis (muh-shuh-guh-no-sis): Term coined by Rabbi Goldie Milgram to refer to the condition of irrational thinking that exceeds a midline of normalcy.

mezuzah (m'zoo'zah): Box with a scroll inside that instructs us to "listen" so that we can "love"; is a mitzvah to place one on every doorpost of your dwelling except for the bathroom.

mikvah (mihk-vuh, mik-veh): Ritual purification of the soul through immersion in the Cosmic Womb as symbolized by a lake, river, ocean, or indoor facility with rainwater added. Undertaken after menstruation, miscarriage, a wet dream, and in anticipation of a holiday or wedding; also for washing a corpse during *taharah,* the ritual preparation for burial.

minei (mee-nay): "Types" or varieties of something.

min<u>h</u>ah (mihn-<u>h</u>uh): Afternoon service, named after the afternoon offerings of Temple times.

minyan (mihn-yahn): Ten people who are required to gather in order to hold a full formal service; women are not counted for this in Orthodox settings, although some synagogues in Israel have made a creative adjustment and now require ten men and ten women to be present to start a formal service.

Miriam (meer-yahm): Moses' sister, who places him, as a baby, into a basket in a river to be found downstream. She alerts the pharaoh's daughter to a possible midwife, his mother; and she finds water sources in the wilderness and leads the people in song.

mi shebeirah (mee-sheh-bey-rah): "One who blessed." Opening of a blessing for healing, naming, or memorial that invokes the presence of the Source of all blessing.

Mishnah (mish-nuh): Completed in approximately 200 CE under the editorship of Rabbi Yehudah Hanasi ("Judah the Prince"), this was the first normative, postbiblical compilation of Jewish law.

mitnagdim, misnagdim (meet-nahg-dim, mis-nahg-dim): "Opposers." Term for those who find G*d in the details more than via the balance of the Hasidic model of deep halahic and ecstatic practice.

mitzvah, mitzvot (meetz-vah, meetz-vote): The 613 sacred acts identified within the Torah that, when observed, texture life with consciousness, compassion, justice, and joy.

m'kuballim (m'koo-bah-lim): "Receivers." When you get an understanding of a mystical work so that a portal of significant new understanding and connection opens, you become one of these sacred transducers of G*d awareness.

m'leetvah (m'leet-vah): Russian word for prayer.

mohin d'gadlut (moe-hin d'gahd-lute): "Large mind." Expanded consciousness.

mohin d'katnut (moe-hin d'kaht-nute): "Small mind." Contracted or personal consciousness of the immediate pains and pleasures of life.

Mosheh (moe-sheh): Hebrew for the English name Moses, who led the Israelites out of Egypt and up to the Promised Land.

Na<u>h</u>man of Breslov (1772–1810): Great-grandson of the Baal Shem Tov and founder of the Breslov <u>H</u>asidim. He died of tuberculosis at age thirty-eight. His stories and writings on spiritual approaches to prayer and relief of depression are popular today and his *Thirteen Tales* series is said to have influenced Franz Kafka. His scribe Natan (Nossan) of Nemirov helped develop his major publication, *Likutey Moharan,* a collection of powerful teachings.

Na<u>h</u>um of Chernobyl (1730–1797): Pioneer of the <u>H</u>asidic movement who was a disciple of the Baal Shem Tov and author of a mystical Torah commentary called *Me'or Einayim.*

nee<u>h</u>um avelim (nee-<u>h</u>um ah-vey-lim): "Comforting mourners." It is a mitzvah to attend to the needs of mourners, not by being in their face with words but rather by hanging around quietly to listen and support their needs.

neshamah (n'sha-mah, n'shuh-meh): One of five words in Hebrew for the soul.

netilat yadayim (n'tee-laht yah-dah-yim): "Lifting up hands." Last words of the prayer for washing the hands before meals as a way of purifying your intentions before eating alone or in community.

Noachide laws: Seven principles of civilized behavior derived from the Torah in relation to the descendants of Noah that define righteous gentiles: No murder, theft, false gods, cursing or abuse of the name of G*d, sexual misconduct, removing and eating a limb from a live animal, and the requirement to establish a justice system and courts of law and enforcement. This code was acknowledged by the United States government as well.

Noah's wife: While not named in the Bible, she is given the name *Naamah* in Midrash Genesis Rabbah 23:4.

Nuremberg laws: Formalized measures taken against Jews in Germany up to 1935; so named because they were announced at a Nazi party rally in Nuremberg. Had two parts: The Law for the Protection of German Blood and German Honor prohibited sex and marriage between Jews and Germans and the employment of German women under age forty-five in Jewish households; the Reich Citizenship Law stripped Jews of German citizenship.

or ayn sof (ohr ayn sofe): "Light without End"; how kabbalists refer to the original light of creation as an emanation of *ayn sof*, G*d "without limits."

orhim (ohr-him): "Guests."

ORT: Acronym of the Russian words *Obshestvo Remeslenofo zemledelcheskofo Truda*, meaning the Society for Trades and Agricultural Labor, an organization founded in Russia that today is an educational and training nonprofit of international scope. Learn more at www.ort.org.

Otiyot Hayyot (oh-tee-ote hai-oat): Embodying the Hebrew letters to express their mystical significance. "Each soul has its letters, and their life energy comes through them," says founder Yehudit Goldfarb, who has trained teachers worldwide. Visit www.otiyot.com.

Ottoman Empire: Covered southwest Asia, northeast Africa, and southeast Europe; created by the Ottoman Turks in the thirteenth century and lasted until the end of World War I. Although initially small, it expanded until it superseded the Byzantine Empire.

parparot l'hohmah (par-par-ote l'hoh-ma): "Butterflies to wisdom." Affectionate description of the function of *gematria*.

parsha, parshiot (par-shah, par-shee-ote): "Portion." As in each individual Torah portion read in sequence throughout the year.

peah, peyoht (pey-ah, pey-oht): "Sides or edges," as in a field, or the sidelocks of hair worn by Hasidim, as a reminder to leave gleanings from your earnings and production for those less fortunate.

penimi, penimiut (puh-nee-mee, p'nee-mee-ute): "Inside meaning" of a verse, word, prayer, or practice where what is apparent often turns out to be only one of many possible interpretations.

pikuah nefesh (pee-koo-ah neh-fesh): "Noticing a soul." The mitzvah of saving a life takes precedence over the regular mitzvot of daily living.

pikuah shvu-im (pee-koo-ah sh'voo-im): "Noticing captives." The mitzvah of redeeming those unjustly held captive, as in the work of Amnesty International.

pluralism: Used in this work in the sense of respectful inclusion of all, even if their views or practices do not agree with yours, as long as they/we do not proselytize.

pokeah ivrim (poe-kay-ah iv'rim): "Opens the eyes of the blind." One of the morning blessings that asks us to consider how we are blind in the way we go about our lives.

posek, poskim (pl) (poe-sayk, poce-kim): One who is trained in Jewish law to such an advanced point that others, including rabbis, turn to this individual for guidance in difficult matters.

Prager, Rabbi Marcia: Second woman in Jewish history to head a program of rabbinic ordination. A rabbinical graduate of the Reconstructionist Rabbinical College, she went on to head the Aleph Ordination Program, originally established by Rabbi Zalman Schachter-Shalomi. Author of *The Path of Blessings* (see Suggestions for Further Reading).

Project Kesher: Grassroots organization that partners Western women with Jewish women in the independent states of the former Soviet Union (FSU). Project Kesher provides a process, an infrastructure, and resources to help the FSU women define and address their own needs in their own communities. Its priorities have proved to be renewing Jewish life, empowering women financially, and securing women's health and safety. Visit www.projectkesher.org.

p'shat (p'shaht): "Simple." The surface meaning of a text or prayer, what it "apparently" means.

pushkah (puhsh-kuh): *Tzedakah* (charity) box. Yiddish for a container used for the solicitation or placing of charitable funds on a regular, individual basis.

Qaballah: See Kabbalah.

Pharisees (phar-uh-sees): The name, in Hebrew, means "separatists." They developed a process of interpretation of the Torah, and their teachings evolved into the Mishnah and Talmud, and thus constitute the basis of rabbinic Judaism. Stressed the religious importance of study and denied that knowledge was the prerogative of the priesthood.

Rabbeynu Gershom (approximately 960–1028 CE): Leading halahic authority and head of the academy in Mainz, Germany, Gershom ben Yehuda was also known as *Me'or ha-Golah*, "Light of the Diaspora." Recent research has shown that the ban on polygamy attributed to him was, in fact, instituted a century or two later. He did issue several ordinances that were accepted as binding by the Jews of Europe—bans against polygamy, against divorcing a woman without her consent, against reading letters addressed to others, and against scoffing at converts who returned to Judaism.

Rashbam (rash-bahm) (1083–1174): Samuel ben Meir, grandson of Rashi and important Torah commentator. A liturgical poet, as a scholar he objected to his grandfather's use of midrash and exegesis.

Rashi (rah-shee) (1040–1105): Acronym for Rabbi Shlomo Yitzhaki who lived mostly in Troyes, France. A vintner and prolific Jewish scholar who wrote commentaries on the entire Hebrew Bible and the Talmud that are considered essential to understanding those texts. His Torah commentary was the first Hebrew text ever printed on a printing press.

ratso v'shov (ratzo-v'showv): "Running and returning." Characteristic of the soul's yearning for oneness with all and need to remain linked to the body in this life.

ravveen (rah-veen): Russian for "rabbi."

Rebecca: *Rivkah* in Hebrew. Biblical matriarch due to her marriage to Isaac and lineage to Abraham.

ruah (rue-ah): "Breath," "wind," or "spirit."

Sadducees (sad-u-sees): First century CE major Temple faction, largely made up of priests and aristocrats, insistent on the exclusive centrality of the Temple. They rejected the Pharisaic supernatural beliefs, the doctrine of the resurrection of the body, and the immortality of the soul, and rejected the belief in the existence of angels and ministering spirits. The principle of "an eye for an eye" was interpreted literally and not as referring to monetary compensation, which was the view adopted by the Pharisees.

Sarai (sah-rai): Sarah's name before she experienced G*d and had a *hey* added to indicate her Israelite religious connection.

seah (say-ah): Talmudic unit of measurement of fluid. There are forty *seah* required for a ritual bath, a *mikvah*.

seder (sey-dr): "Order." Passover evening ritual of reenacting through liturgy the experience of leaving Egypt.

Sephardim (she-far-dim): Jews of Spain, Morocco, and the Mediterranean region with unique culture and religious practices.

seyhel (sey-hl): Yiddish for having smarts.

Shabbat (shah-baht, shah-bos): Sabbath. The practice of reserving one day each week to refrain from use of money, work, media, and creation of new physical things, except for procreation.

Shabbatai Tzvi (shah-bah-tie tzvee): Self-declared sixteenth-century messiah who convinced much of the Jewish population to sell their businesses, pack up, and prepare to move to Israel. When confronted by the Caliph of the Ottoman Empire about this disturbance to the workings of his region, Shabbatai Tzvi converted to Islam.

shaharit, shaharis (shah-reet, shah-rihs): Often spelled *Shacharit*. Morning service, from *shahar*, "dawn."

shalom bayit (shah-lome bah-yeet, bah-yihs): The mitzvah of engaging in or refraining from particular words or action for the sake of a more peaceful home.

Shanwar Tellis: "Sabbath observing oil pressers." Jews of Bombay, India, today known as the Bene Israel.

shehinah (shuh-hee-nah): Often spelled *shechinah* or *shekhinah*. G*d as presence and flow.

sheitl (shy-tl): Marriage wig.

shema (sh'mah): "Listen." Prayer from Deuteronomy declaring the Oneness of All Being found throughout Jewish services, in *tefillin*, the mezuzah, and said at sleep time and upon approaching sure death.

shidduh (shih-duh): A person "makes a *shidduh*," as in helping someone to find a marriage partner.

shivat tzion (shee-vaht tzee-yohn): "Return to Zion." The mitzvah of pilgrimage to Israel.

shviti (shee-vee-tee): "I set before me." Practice of being aware of G*d's presence by placing a physical reminder, such as a work of art containing the tetragrammaton in rooms you frequent, and pausing to contemplate it.

shmirat ha-guf (shmeer-aht ha-goof): Mitzvah of caring for your body.

shmutz (sh'muhtz): Yiddish for filth or dirt that you can get on your clothes or your soul.

Shoah (show-ah): Holocaust. Hebrew for "complete destruction."

shofar (show-far): Ram's horn blown to announce the New Year, the sound of which fills the soul even more deeply with connections to themes of hoped-for personal change and awareness of awe of G*d.

shomer Shabbat (shomer Shabbat): Mitzvah of keeping the Sabbath.

shuckle (shuh-kl): Swaying movement characteristic of Jews who are praying.

siddur(im) (see-dur, see-dur-im): "Prayer book." Shares the root of *seder*, "order."

siman tov (see-man tohv): A "good sign." A blessing for a special occasion, incorporating the hope that the stars be aligned auspiciously for good things.

sofer (so-fehr): Scribe who does the calligraphy for Torah scrolls, *megillot, tefillin,* mezuzot, and ritual documents such as a divorce paper known as a *get.*

sotah (sew-tah): Biblical ritual for women accused of infidelity by their husbands; thought by some scholars to have been designed to deal with inappropriately jealous husbands.

sukkah (sue-kah, suh-kuh): Harvest hut built in Torah times for shelter in the fields. It has become a mitzvah to set up a *sukkah* at your own home to host guests out in nature during the festival called Sukkot.

Sumeria(n): Present-day southern Iraq was home to this Mesopotamian people from the fifth millennium BCE. By 3000 BCE a flourishing civilization existed there, which gradually exerted power over the surrounding area and culminated in the Akkadian dynasty. The Sumerians are believed to have invented the cuneiform system of writing.

takannah (tah-kah-nah): "Repair." An edict issued by a high-ranking rabbi that would shift Jewish practice in its time and that was intended for all time; for example, the edict that outlawed polygamy.

tallit, tallis; tallitot (pl) (tah-leet, tah-lis; tah-lee-tote): "Prayer shawl." With rare exceptions, worn at morning services and during morning practices at home.

Talmud (tahl-mood): Record of discussions on Jewish law, ethics, customs, legends, and stories that forms the basis for all later codes of Jewish law. Talmud cititations are often incorporated into Jewish literature. There are two forms of Talmud, respectively developed by Jewish academies in Babylonia and Israel over a period of three hundred years, concluding around 500 CE. Known as the Talmud Bavli and Talmud Yerushalmi, both share a core text, the *Mishnah*, a record of early oral law, redacted by the rabbinic scholar Judah ha-Nasi. Surrounding the *Mishnah* is the Gemara, which analyzes and comments upon the meaning and application of the *Mishnah* for living. Surrounding both the *Mishnah* and the Gemara are commentaries by subsequent generations, including the most recent added in our times by Rabbi Adin Steinsaltz.

Tanakh (tah-na<u>h</u>): Acronym for the entirety of Jewish Scripture—Torah (the Five Books of Moses), *Neviim* (Prophets), and *Ketuvim* (Writings).

tanhui (tan-hoo-ee): "Soup Kitchen." It is a mitzvah to maintain soup kitchens and food pantries for the poor wherever you live.

Tanya (tahn-yuh): Classic <u>H</u>asidic work written by Rabbi Shne'ur Zalman of Liadi, the first Lubavitcher rebbe. Through this work, we enter into a world that integrates kabbalistic notions of the cosmos with the most basic issues of human existence in relation to the Divine: the nature of the soul, Torah, and mitzvot, and the battle between good and evil within ourselves.

targum(im) (tar-goom, tar-goo-mim): "Translation." Translations of the Torah in Aramaic with rich interpretive slant that were read aloud starting from the Second Temple period so that common people could understand these interpretations in their native languages.

tefillin (t'fee-leen, t'fill-in): Meditation aid for morning contemplation that is made up of two sets of leather straps, each with a small box on it that contains excerpts from the

Torah. One is wrapped onto the nondominant arm and one around the forehead.

teshuvah (t'shoo-vah): Process of healing damaged relationships with self, others, and G*d that is emphasized as the High Holy Days approach and is practiced steadily throughout the year.

tihel (tih-<u>h</u>el): Headscarf worn by Orthodox woman for reasons of modesty because women's hair is considered to be alluring.

tikkun olam (tee-kune oh-lahm): "Repair of the world." A core Jewish value to engage in social welfare and environmental activism.

Tosafot (toe-sah-fote): Commentaries by students of Rashi.

treyf (trayf): Non-kosher.

tzaar baalei <u>h</u>ayyim (tzah-ar bah-ahlei <u>h</u>ah-yim): Mitzvah of inflicting no unnecessary pain on anything sentient.

tza-ra'at (tzah-rah-aht): A skin eruption, referred to in the Bible, that afflicts biblical characters when they experience shame or great distress, especially in regard to their relationship with G*d. Was wrongly labeled leprosy due to a mistranslation when the Bible was translated from Greek to English.

tzedakah (tzeh-dah-kah): Giving money to help the poor, the arts, education, and the like; charitable giving is a mitzvah.

Tzion (tzee-yone): Zion, the Land of Israel.

Tzipora (tzih-poe-rah): Wife of Moses, daughter of Yitro, a Midianite priest.

tzitzit (tzee-tzeet): Fringes that are specially knotted onto the four corners of a *tallit*, "prayer shawl."

ufruf (uf-roof): Yiddish for coming up to the Torah for a blessing in preparation for your wedding.

v'ahavta l'reya<u>h</u>ah kamo<u>h</u>ah (v'ah-hav-tah l'ray-ah-ha kah-moe-<u>h</u>a): Mitzvah of caring for friends and neighbors with the quality of attention you would ideally give yourself.

Venda (Vehn-da): Also known as Lemba. Malawi, Zimbabwean, and South African Bantu-speaking people whom scholars find to be the descendents of Semitic traders who entered Africa around 696 CE. They consider themselves to be Jews, seek out Jewish teachers to come to their region, and are famous for metalwork and pottery. They have a priestly class called the *Buba* that tests very high for a gene trait associated with the *cohanim*, high priests of Temple times. Under apartheid a region was created for them of 6,500 square kilometers.

v'hadarta p'nai zaken (v'<u>h</u>ah-dahr-tah puh-ney zah-ken): Honoring elders is the mitzvah of honoring their accomplishments and seeing to their needs; some rise when an elder enters the room as a tradition connected to this commandment.

Visigoths (vih-zi-goths): A people who invaded the Roman Empire in 268 CE, overrunning the Balkan peninsula and even threatening Italy itself. At its height, before a major defeat in 507, the Visigothic kingdom included almost all of the Iberian peninsula. The Visigoths had their own form of Christianity called Arianism but later became Catholics.

wasband (wuz-band): Ex-husband, term innovated by Rabbi Goldie Milgram in 1979.

ye<u>h</u>idah (yuh-hee-dah): The fifth level of the soul in which your individual soul cannot be distinguished from the energy of all of life any more than the candle's heat or light can be said to formally end and the rest of the space around it begin.

yehidut, yehidus (yuh-hee-doot, yuh-hee-duhs): "Spiritual intimacy." The experience of a couple's first private time together after their wedding ceremony. Also refers to private time with your rebbe during which your soul is recharged through the profoundness of the contact. Also refers to a peak experience of at-one-ment with G*d.

yehudi, yehudim (pl) (yeh-hoo-di, yeh-hoo-dim): "Jew(s)." From the son of Jacob, *yehuda*, Judah, after whom one of the ten tribes was named. When the biblical kingdom split into two after the death of King Solomon, those who lived in the kingdom of Judah became known as *yehudim*. In the sixth century BCE, Assyria conquered the Northern Kingdom, Israel, so the term *yehudi* continued to define the citizens of Judah and the term became generally used as the Hebrew term for a member of the Jewish people.

yeshiva, yeshivot (pl) (y'shee-vah, y'sheevote): Institute of Jewish learning. Can refer to an advanced setting or a day school. From the root word *yashav*, "sat."

yitzhak (yitz-hak): Isaac; son of Abraham.

Yiddish (yih-dish): Fusion language derived mostly from medieval German dialects, Hebrew, Aramaic, several Slavic languages, Old French, and Old Italian. Originally extensively spoken as a vernacular by Ashkenazi Jews of Central and Eastern Europe, Yiddish is currently experiencing a revival in very Orthodox communities and among those interested in preserving this aspect of Jewish culture. Has an extensive literature and is written in Hebrew script.

yiddisheh kup (yih-dish-eh cup): Yiddish for a compliment indicating that your thinking was quite clever.

yizkor (yihz-ker): Memorial service for deceased loved ones said on Yom Kippur, Passover, Shavuot, and Sukkot.

Those who do so are said to bring merit and honor to the soul(s) that have passed on to the next world.

Yom Kippur (yom kee-poor): Day of Atonement, major Jewish holy day that is the culmination of processes of ethical self-reflection and efforts to restore relationships with yourself, your family, your coworkers, and with G*d.

y'rei hashem (y'rei ha-shem): Those who are in fear/awe of G*d. A core principle and mitzvah in Judaism is to live with great respect for the remarkable gift of life and the beauty and power within and perhaps beyond the world as we know it.

yud hey vav hey: It is a strong practice to say *adonai* rather than to adopt any pronunciation for the tetragrammaton, the four-letter name of G*d that is considered most sacred in the Jewish religion This practice serves to prevent the human imagination from fully defining what G*d might be, which is a way of honoring the mystery of the Source of Life and Creation.

zahor (zah-hohr): "Remember."

zeyher yitziyat mitzrayim (zey-hair y'tzee-yaht meetz-rah-yim): "Remember leaving Egypt." A mitzvah that helps us keep faith that things do change no matter how hard they get.

Zion (zae-yahn): King David captured this southeastern hill of what became known as Jerusalem from the Jebusites (Joshua 15:63; 2 Samuel 5:7), built a citadel and palace and Temple upon it, and this comes to be known as the City of David (1 Kings 8:1; 2 Kings 19:21, 31; 1 Chronicles 11:15). Eventually the term refers to all of Jerusalem and sometimes the Israelites (Psalms 51:28; 87:5), and today to all of the State of Israel.

Zionism (zae-yahn-izm): Movement to reestablish the Jewish homeland that arose in the late nineteenth century in response to anti-Semitism and today is practiced by those con-cerned with the support and development of the State of Israel.

Zohar (zo-hahr): Jewish mystical texts written in Hebrew and Aramaic that came to light in Spain in the thirteenth century and are foundational to Kabbalah.

Zornberg, Aviva Gottlieb: Born in London in 1944 and grew up in Glasgow, Scotland. Her father was head of the Rabbinical Court of Glasgow. She taught English literature at the Hebrew University from 1969 to 1976. Since 1980, she has taught Torah to classes in Jerusalem, at Matan, Lindenbaum, Pardes, and the Jerusalem College for Adults. Author of *Genesis: The Beginning of Desire* and *The Particulars of Rapture: Reflections on Exodus.*

SUGGESTIONS FOR FURTHER READING

Abrams, Judith Z. *The Talmud for Beginners: Prayer*, vol. 1. Northvale, NJ: Jason Aronson, 1992. Also visit her website, www.maqom.com, to get turned on to the amazing learning, spirit, ethics, and passion in the Talmud.

Alter, Judah Aryeh Leib, Arthur Green (translator), and Shai Gluskin. *The Language of Truth: The Torah Commentary of Sefat Emet*. Philadelphia: Jewish Publication Society, 1998. Makes accessible to all the inspiring words of a remarkable Hasidic commentator; open to Jews from every part of Judaism.

Aron, Isa. *Becoming a Congregation of Learners: Learning As a Key to Revitalizing Congregational Life*. Woodstock, VT: Jewish Lights, 2000. Excellent template for helping congregations to develop the depth of infrastructure and understanding to deeply enjoy and cultivate Jewish learning.

Artson, Bradley Shavit. *It's a Mitzvah: Step-by-Step to Jewish Living*. Springfield, NJ: Behrman House, 1995. Clear, accessible, meaningful, useful, and spiritual guide to the wide range of mitzvot.

Berenson-Perkins, Janet. *Kabbalah Decoder: Revealing the Messages of the Ancient Mystics*. Hauppauge, NY: Barron's Educational Series, 2000. Graphically beautiful and user-friendly presentation on how the Tree of Life fits together and works as a system of spiritual practice.

Bonder, Nilton. *The Kabbalah of Envy: Transforming Hatred, Anger and Other Negative Emotions*. Boston: Shambhala, 1997. Lots of sources and supportive, creative ways into this topic through the Jewish perspective of a South American rabbi with a spiritual orientation. Also recommended:

———. *The Kabbalah of Food: Conscious Eating for Physical, Emotional and Spiritual Health*. Boston: Shambhala, 1998.

———. *The Kabbalah of Money: Jewish Insights on Giving, Owning and Receiving*. Boston: Shambhala, 2001.

Boorstein, Sylvia, and Stephen Mitchell. *That's Funny, You Don't Look Buddhist: On Being a Faithful Jew and a Passionate Buddhist*. San Francisco: HarperSanFrancisco, 1998. Boorstein's many books make nice gifts for Jews who meditate and haven't yet connected with Jewish meditation.

Brener, Anne. *Mourning and Mitzvah: A Guided Journal for Walking the Mourner's Path through Grief to Healing*. Woodstock, VT: Jewish Lights, 2001. The most powerful book I've seen on loss and mourning. *Meaning & Mitzvah* and its companion volume, *Reclaiming Judaism as a Spiritual Practice*, were inspired by her approach, although the title of *Meaning and Mitzvah* arose via a friend in Holland and was not related to Anne's work.

Bush, Lawrence, and Jeffrey Dekro. *Jews, Money, and Social Responsibility: Developing a "Torah of Money" for*

Contemporary Life. Washington, DC: B'nai B'rith Book Service, 1993. The best work on spirituality and money around—solid and helpful.

Buxbaum, Yitzhak. *Jewish Spiritual Practices*. Northvale, NJ: Jason Aronson, 1994. Excellent source reader on H̲asidic spirituality; a large compendium, for folks who enjoy scanning text for fascinating stories and inspiring passages.

Cooper, David A. *God Is a Verb: Kabbalah and the Practice of Mystical Judaism*. New York: Riverhead, 1998. A classic. Accessible, powerful combination of contemporary philosophy, H̲asidic spirituality, and a Jewish Renewal rabbi's understanding of meditation as a way to connect with G*d and meaning via his time spent in Buddhist practice and studies.

———. *The Handbook of Jewish Meditation Practices: A Guide for Enriching the Sabbath and Other Days of Your Life*. Woodstock, VT: Jewish Lights, 2000. A master teacher who will take you along step by step, both higher and deeper. He has many works; all are valuable for the meditatively inclined.

Davis, Avram, ed. *Meditation from the Heart of Judaism: Today's Teachers Share Their Practices, Techniques and Faith*. Woodstock, VT: Jewish Lights, 1999. Excellent collection of essays by some of the early North American teachers of Jewish meditation.

Diamant, Anita. *The Red Tent*. New York: Picador, 1998. Magnificent novel full of new midrashic interpretations of the Torah of women's lives and the midrash of the rabbis.

Dosick, Wayne. *Soul Judaism: Dancing with God into a New Era*. Woodstock, VT: Jewish Lights, 1999. Introduction to aspects of Jewish spirituality. Easy to read; recommends specific Hasidic melodies for most topics.

Elon, Ari, Naomi Mara Hyman, and Arthur Waskow. *Trees, Earth and Torah: A Tu B'Shvat Anthology*. Philadelphia: Jewish Publication Society, 2000. Copious, carefully translated, and discussed sources for engaged Jewish environmental studies.

Frankel, Ellen, and Betsy Platkin Teutsch. *The Encyclopedia of Jewish Symbols*. Northvale, NJ: Jason Aronson, 1992. Two hundred and fifty images and explanations of Jewish symbols, useful for creating *shviti* and other Jewish sacred art.

Frankiel, Tamar. *The Gift of Kabbalah: Discovering the Secrets of Heaven, Renewing Your Life on Earth*. Woodstock, VT: Jewish Lights, 2003. Introduction to Kabbalah, easy to read and implement.

Frankiel, Tamar, and Judy Greenfeld. *Entering the Temple of Dreams: Jewish Prayers, Movements, and Meditations for the End of the Day*. Woodstock, VT: Jewish Lights, 2000. Combines yoga-type movement traditions with Jewish prayer; nicely done.

————. *Minding the Temple of the Soul: Balancing Body, Mind, and Spirit through Traditional Jewish Prayer, Movement, and Meditation*. Woodstock, VT: Jewish Lights, 1997. Combines yoga-type movement traditions with Jewish prayer in an easy-to-follow and easy-to-integrate-into-your-own-life format.

Fuchs-Kreimer, Nancy. *Parenting as a Spiritual Journey: Deepening Ordinary and Extraordinary Events into Sacred Occasions*. Woodstock, VT: Jewish Lights, 1998. Excellent. Great ideas.

Gefen, Nan Fink. *Discovering Jewish Meditation: Instruction and Guidance for Learning an Ancient Spiritual Practice*. Woodstock, VT: Jewish Lights, 1999. User-friendly introduction.

Goldstein, Elyse. *ReVisions: Seeing Torah through a Feminist Lens*. Woodstock, VT: Jewish Lights, 2001. Clear explanations of new ways women find of studying Jewish sacred text.

———, ed. *The Women's Haftarah Commentary: New Insights from Women Rabbis on the 54 Weekly Haftarah Portions, the 5 Megillot and Special Shabbatot*. Woodstock, VT: Jewish Lights, 2004. Brings the voices of a gender and generation to light and into Jewish life.

———, ed. *The Women's Torah Commentary: New Insights from Women Rabbis on the 54 Weekly Torah Portions*. Woodstock, VT: Jewish Lights, 2001. Great collection; groundbreaking effort.

Green, Arthur. *Ehyeh: A Kabbalah for Tomorrow*. Woodstock, VT: Jewish Lights, 2004. Courageous offering of a Kabbalah-based theology for today.

———. *Seek My Face: A Jewish Mystical Theology*. Woodstock, VT: Jewish Lights, 2003. Solid Jewish philosophy through a deep soul for the times in which we live.

———. *Tormented Master: The Life and Spiritual Quest of Rabbi Nahman of Breslov*. Woodstock, VT: Jewish Lights, 1992. Biography of Nahman of Breslov. You may be surprised by this well-written scholarly biography.

Hoffman, Joel. *In the Beginning: A Short History of the Hebrew Language*. New York: New York University Press, 2004. Intensely fascinating presentation on the importance of the *yud hey vav* letters in human literacy development and also teachings on the role of the Masoretes in conforming the Torah text to a norm.

Hoffman, Lawrence A. My *People's Prayer Books—Traditional Prayers, Modern Commentaries*, vols. 1–9. Woodstock, VT: Jewish Lights, 1997–. Unique format brings many views together to help the prayer book come alive.

Idel, Moshe. *Kabbalah: New Perspectives*. New Haven, CT: Yale University Press, 1990. Scholarly classic.

Jacobson, Simon. *Toward a Meaningful Life: The Wisdom of the Rebbe Menachem Mendel Schneerson*. New York: Perennial Currents, 2004. Beautiful adaptations of the teachings of the Lubavitcher rebbe for soulful Jews, regardless of denomination.

Kamenetz, Rodger. *The Jew in the Lotus: A Poet's Re-Discovery of Jewish Identity in Buddhist India*. San Francisco: HarperSanFrancisco, 1995. This book has left a lasting impact on the souls of many who hope to find spirituality in their Jewish roots.

Kaplan, Aryeh. *Inner Space: Introduction to Kabbalah, Meditation and Prophecy*. Brooklyn, NY: Moznaim Publishing, 1990. Delicious way to explore for those inclined to meditation, cosmology, and Kabbalah.

———. *Jewish Meditation: A Practical Guide*. New York: Schocken, 1995. Classic, accessible, deep. Try each meditation that he recommends.

———. *Meditation and the Bible*. Northvale, NJ: Jason Aronson, 1995. More from this, alas, deceased master of Jewish meditation. He has several other works; each are excellent and most worthy of your attention.

———. *Sefer Yetzirah: The Book of Creation*. Boston: Weiser Publishing, 1997. Fascinating, foundational text in Kabbalah.

Kaplan, Mordecai. *Judaism as a Civilization: Toward a Reconstruction of American Jewish Life*. Philadelphia: Jewish Publication Society, 1994. Deeply empowering explanation of how Judaism has always evolved and continues to do so.

Kushner, Lawrence. *Eyes Remade for Wonder: A Lawrence Kushner Reader*. Woodstock, VT: Jewish Lights, 1998. Moving stories of Jewish spirituality. There are numerous works by this author. Every one is helpful for those entering the study of Kabbalah, mysticism, and Jewish spiritual connection.

Lamm, Norman. *The Shema: Spirituality and Law in Judaism*. Philadelphia: Jewish Publication Society, 2000. A wonderful collection of teachings and stories about the *shema*.

Lerner, Michael. *Jewish Renewal: A Path to Healing and Transformation*. San Francisco: Perennial, 1995. Foundational work that has helped enoble and empower the Jewish spiritual renaissance.

———. *The Politics of Meaning: Restoring Hope and Possibility in an Age of Cynicism*. Reading, MA: Addison-Wesley, 1997. Creative ideas for restoring social justice.

Locks, Gutman G. *The Spice of Torah-Gematria*. New York: Judaica Press, 1985. Pick a number and look up which word in the Torah has that numerical value. The opening essay is also a great introduction to *gematria*. Perfect resource for those who like this form of Torah study.

Lowin, Joseph. *Hebrew Talk: 101 Hebrew Roots and the Stories They Tell*. Berkeley, CA: EKS Publishing, 2004. The author of *Hadassah* magazine's Hebrew column, which takes one Hebrew root for each column and creatively shows the many words that grow from it, has compiled many of those columns into this work that is superb for developing your vocabulary.

Matlins, Stuart M., ed. *The Jewish Lights Spirituality Handbook: A Guide to Understanding, Exploring and Living a Spiritual Life*. Woodstock, VT: Jewish Lights, 2001. A potpourri of ways into Jewish spiritual practice that will introduce you to a variety of teachers.

Matt, Daniel. *The Essential Kabbalah: The Heart of Jewish Mysticism*. San Francisco: Harper San Francisco, 1996. User-friendly translations of segments of the Zohar.

———. *God and the Big Bang: Discovering Harmony between Science and Spirituality*. Woodstock, VT: Jewish Lights, 1998. Easy to read; insightful.

———. *Zohar: Annotated and Explained*. Woodstock, VT: SkyLight Paths, 2002. Lovely collection of translations and interpretations by one who is able to help entry-level folks experience meaning in difficult places.

———. *The Zohar: Pritzker Edition*, vol. 1. Stanford, CA: Stanford University Press, 2003. The best translation available; amazing scholarship.

Milgrom, Jo. *Handmade Midrash: Workshops in Visual Theology*. Philadelphia: Jewish Publication Society, 1992. Great for artists, parents, and teachers.

Orenstein, Debra, with Jane Rachel Litman. *Lifecycles, Vol. 1: Jewish Women on Biblical Themes in Contemporary Life*. Woodstock, VT: Jewish Lights, 2000. First major work to put a plethora of women's voices and unique vantage points into the Torah commentary of our people.

Ouaknin, Marc-Alain. *Mysteries of the Kabbalah*. New York: Abbeville Press, 2000. Clear description of history, major aspects of Kabbalah, and beautiful expression of the heart of the matter.

Ouaknin, Marc-Alain, and Josephine Bacon. *Mysteries of the Alphabet: The Origins of Writing*. New York: Abbeville Press, 1999. Fascinating and beautifully presented.

Ouaknin, Marc-Alain, and Llewellyn Brown. *The Burnt Book*. Princeton, NJ: Princeton University Press, 1998. Tells the story of why Talmud is moving, powerful, and at the center of major issues and developments in Jewish life.

Pearl, Judea, and Ruth Pearl, eds. *I Am Jewish: Personal Reflections Inspired by the Last Words of Daniel Pearl*. Woodstock, VT: Jewish Lights, 2005. How do some of the most interesting and inspiring Jews find meaning through being Jewish? This is a powerful collection for all of us to read and discuss.

Prager, Marcia. *Amidah Cards*. Beautifully illustrated with descriptions of each blessing that help to impart its spiritual possibilities. Order through www.aleph.org.

———. *The Path of Blessing: Experiencing the Energy and Abundance of the Divine*. Woodstock, VT: Jewish Lights, 2003. Great reading, inspiring, spiritual, and educational.

Rapp, Steven A. *Aleph-Bet Yoga: Embodying the Hebrew Letters for Physical and Spiritual Well-Being*. Woodstock, VT: Jewish Lights, 2002. Delightful, effective guide to integrating yoga, movement, and the Hebrew letters.

Ribner, Melinda. *Everyday Kabbalah: A Practical Guide to Jewish Meditation, Healing, and Personal Growth*. New York: Citadel Press, 1998. User-friendly, visualization-based introduction.

Ribner, Mindy. *Kabbalah Month by Month: A Year of Spiritual Practice and Personal Transformation*. San Francisco: Jossey-Bass, 2002. Astrology plays an active role throughout the Talmud and medieval Judaism. This work shows how to renew those practices in contemporary terms as a way of enriching your personal life.

Schachter-Shalomi, Zalman. *Paradigm Shift*. Northvale, NJ: Jason Aronson, 2000. Creative options for Jewish prayer and ritual. A groundbreaking work for those seriously engaged in renewing Jewish spiritual life.

————. *Wrapped in a Holy Flame: Teachings and Tales of the Hasidic Masters*. San Francisco: Jossey-Bass, 2003. User-friendly insight into the lives of Hasidic teachers and the contemporary applications of their teachings.

Schachter-Shalomi, Zalman, and Donald Gropman. *First Steps to a New Jewish Spirit: Reb Zalman's Guide to Recapturing the Intimacy and Ecstasy in Your Relationship with God*. Woodstock, VT: Jewish Lights, 2003. Reprint of the first work to inspire Jewish spiritual connection—beautiful.

Schachter-Shalomi, Zalman, and Joel Segel. *Jewish with Feeling: A Guide to Meaningful Practice*. New York: Riverhead, 2005. Heart-opening guide to joyful Jewishing.

Shapira, Kalonymus Kalman. *Conscious Community: A Guide to Inner Work*. Northvale, NJ: Jason Aronson, 1996. Very interesting to read and reflect on your own community in regard to the view of the Piacetzna rebbe. Cotranslated by Rabbi Andrea Cohen-Kiener and Yosef Grodsky.

Shapiro, Rami. *Minyan: Ten Principles for Living a Life of Integrity*. New York: Bell Tower, 1997. Very spiritual, clear, simple, and a loving guide to Jewish spirituality from a rabbi also heavily influenced by Buddhism. Author of several excellent books. Also visit his website for online works: www.rabbirami.com.

Shire, Michael. *To Life! L'Chaim!: Prayers and Blessings for the Jewish Home*. San Francisco: Chronicle Books, 2000. A beautiful gift and spiritually elegant work.

Siegel, Daniel, ed. *Siddur Kol Koreh*. Spiritually uplifting translations of every prayer in the Shabbat service and many very moving contemporary liturgical additions and explanations. Available through www.aleph.org.

Silberman, Neil Asher. *Heavenly Powers: Unraveling the Secret History of the Kabbalah*. New York: Penguin/Putnam, 1998. Very interesting historical presentation.

Steinsaltz, Adin. *A Guide to Jewish Prayer*. New York: Schocken Books, 2002. Important guide, gives background and flow of service.

————. *Opening the Tanya: Discovering the Moral and Mystical Teachings of a Classic Work of Kabbalah*. San Francisco: Jossey-Bass, 2003. Takes you deeply into Jewish mysticism with ease. Every one of this author's many works is worthwhile reading for contemporary Jewish spiritual seekers.

Strassfeld, Michael. *The Jewish Holidays: A Guide and Commentary*. New York: HarperResource, 1993. Very helpful resource for basic Jewish holiday practices through a spiritual lens. Seek out other works of this early pioneer of Jewish spirituality in this millennium.

Telushkin, Joseph. *Words That Hurt, Words That Heal: How to Choose Words Wisely and Well*. New York: Perennial Currents, 1998. Eloquent and easy-to-grasp principles of the highest spirituality—how we speak to and treat others. Author of many valuable works.

Waskow, Arthur. *Down-to-Earth Judaism: Food, Money, Sex and the Rest of Life—A Spiritual Guide*. New York: Perennial Currents, 1997. Lots of sources in here interpreted from a very liberal perspective. See his website, www.shalomctr.org, for many free online teachings and program ideas.

———. *Godwresting—Round 2: Ancient Wisdom, Future Paths.* Woodstock, VT: Jewish Lights, 1998. Deep theological questions illuminated in accessible format.

Weinberg, Matis. *Frameworks.* Stanford, CA: Foundation for Jewish Publication, 1998. Series of teachings on each book of the Torah—very accessible and highly spiritual commentary; sometimes sexist, but very much worth including in your library.

Wiener, Shohama, ed. *The Fifty-Eighth Century: A Jewish Renewal Sourcebook.* Northvale, NJ: Jason Aronson, 1996. Even more creative essays on Jewish spirituality.

Wiener, Shohama, and Jonathan Omer-Man. *Worlds of Jewish Prayer: A Festschrift in Honor of Rabbi Zalman M. Schachter-Shalomi.* Northvale, NJ: Jason Aronson, 1993. Lots of creative essays on joyful, deep, spiritual Jewishing.

Winkler, Gershon. *Sacred Secrets: The Sanctity of Sex in Jewish Law and Lore.* Northvale, NJ: Jason Aronson, 1998. Don't let the title fool you: This little book is a hidden secret of neat things to know about Judaism and sexuality.

———. *The Way of the Boundary Crosser: An Introduction to Jewish Flexidoxy.* Northvale, NJ: Jason Aronson, 1998. Very helpful understanding of how to deal with the apparent inflexibility of *halahah* when your spirituality and personal values seem in conflict with Judaism. A fascinating, accessible read for serious Jewishing.

Yerushalmi, Yosef Hayim. *Zakhor: Jewish History and Jewish Memory.* Seattle: University of Washington Press, 1996. A gem. Essays that touch the heart of memory.

Zaslow, David. *Ivdu Et HaShem B'Simcha: A Siddur for Spiritual*

Renewal. 1997. (Orders via the author, 692 Elkader St., Ashland, OR 97520; e-mail ShalomRav@aol.com.) Excellent softcover siddur to have at home and in religious schools; very rich resource for songs, translations, and spiritual orientation of translations.

Zemer, Moshe. *Evolving Halakhah: A Progressive Approach to Traditional Jewish Law*. Woodstock, VT: Jewish Lights, 2003. Opens up new ways of thinking about and living through *halahah*.

Zornberg, Aviva Gottlieb. *The Beginning of Desire: Reflections on Genesis*. New York: Image Books, 1996. Scholarship and spirit combine to yield a fascinating and highly informative tour into the biblical book of Genesis.

———. *The Particulars of Rapture: Reflections on Exodus*. New York: Image Books, 2002. More of the above, applied to Exodus.

INDEX

Children's Books

What You Will See Inside a Synagogue

By Rabbi Lawrence A. Hoffman and Dr. Ron Wolfson; Full-color photos by Bill Aron

A colorful, fun-to-read introduction that explains the ways and whys of Jewish worship and religious life. Full-page photos; concise but informative descriptions of the objects used, the clergy and laypeople who have specific roles, and much more. For ages 6 & up.

8½ x 10½, 32 pp, Full-color photos, Hardcover, ISBN 1-59473-012-1 **$17.99** *(A SkyLight Paths book)*

Because Nothing Looks Like God

By Lawrence and Karen Kushner

What is God like? Introduces children to the possibilities of spiritual life. Real-life examples of happiness and sadness invite us to explore, together with our children, the questions we all have about God.

11 x 8½, 32 pp, Full-color illus., Hardcover, ISBN 1-58023-092-X **$16.95** *For ages 4 & up*

Also Available: **Because Nothing Looks Like God Teacher's Guide**

8½ x 11, 22 pp, PB, ISBN 1-58023-140-3 **$6.95** *For ages 5–8*

Board Book Companions to *Because Nothing Looks Like God*

5 x 5, 24 pp, Full-color illus., SkyLight Paths Board Books *For ages 0–4*

What Does God Look Like? ISBN 1-893361-23-3 **$7.95**

How Does God Make Things Happen? ISBN 1-893361-24-1 **$7.95**

Where Is God? ISBN 1-893361-17-9 **$7.99**

The 11th Commandment: Wisdom from Our Children

by The Children of America

"If there were an Eleventh Commandment, what would it be?" Children of many religious denominations across America answer in their own drawings and words.

8 x 10, 48 pp, Full-color illus., Hardcover, ISBN 1-879045-46-X **$16.95** *For all ages*

Jerusalem of Gold: Jewish Stories of the Enchanted City

Retold by Howard Schwartz. Full-color illus. by Neil Waldman.

A beautiful and engaging collection of historical and legendary stories for children. Based on Talmud, midrash, Jewish folklore, and mystical and Hasidic sources.

8 x 10, 64 pp, Full-color illus., Hardcover, ISBN 1-58023-149-7 **$18.95** *For ages 7 & up*

The Book of Miracles: A Young Person's Guide to Jewish Spiritual Awareness

By Lawrence Kushner. All-new illustrations by the author.

6 x 9, 96 pp, 2-color illus., Hardcover, ISBN 1-879045-78-8 **$16.95** *For ages 9–13*

In Our Image: God's First Creatures

By Nancy Sohn Swartz

9 x 12, 32 pp, Full-color illus., Hardcover, ISBN 1-879045-99-0 **$16.95** *For ages 4 & up*

Also Available as a Board Book: **How Did the Animals Help God?**

5 x 5, 24 pp, Board, Full-color illus., ISBN 1-59473-044-X **$7.99** *For ages 0–4 (A SkyLight Paths book)*

From SKYLIGHT PATHS PUBLISHING

Becoming Me: A Story of Creation

By Martin Boroson. Full-color illus. by Christopher Gilvan-Cartwright.

Told in the personal "voice" of the Creator, a story about creation and relationship that is about each one of us.

8 x 10, 32 pp, Full-color illus., Hardcover, ISBN 1-893361-11-X **$16.95** *For ages 4 & up*

Ten Amazing People: And How They Changed the World

By Maura D. Shaw. Foreword by Dr. Robert Coles. Full-color illus. by Stephen Marchesi.

Black Elk • Dorothy Day • Malcolm X • Mahatma Gandhi • Martin Luther King, Jr. • Mother Teresa • Janusz Korczak • Desmond Tutu • Thich Nhat Hanh • Albert Schweitzer.

8½ x 11, 48 pp, Full-color illus., Hardcover, ISBN 1-893361-47-0 **$17.95** *For ages 7 & up*

Where Does God Live? *By August Gold and Matthew J. Perlman*

Helps young readers develop a personal understanding of God.

10 x 8½, 32 pp, Full-color photo illus., Quality PB, ISBN 1-893361-39-X **$8.99** *For ages 3–6*

Children's Books
by Sandy Eisenberg Sasso

Adam & Eve's First Sunset: God's New Day
Engaging new story explores fear and hope, faith and gratitude in ways that will delight kids and adults—inspiring us to bless each of God's days and nights.
9 x 12, 32 pp, Full-color illus., Hardcover, ISBN 1-58023-177-2 **$17.95** *For ages 4 & up*

But God Remembered
Stories of Women from Creation to the Promised Land
Four different stories of women—Lillith, Serach, Bityah, and the Daughters of Z—teach us important values through their faith and actions.
9 x 12, 32 pp, Full-color illus., Hardcover, ISBN 1-879045-43-5 **$16.95** *For ages 8 & up*

Cain & Abel: Finding the Fruits of Peace
Shows children that we have the power to deal with anger in positive ways. Provides questions for kids and adults to explore together.
9 x 12, 32 pp, Full-color illus., Hardcover, ISBN 1-58023-123-3 **$16.95** *For ages 5 & up*

God in Between
If you wanted to find God, where would you look? This magical, mythical tale teaches that God can be found where we are: within all of us and the relationships between us.
9 x 12, 32 pp, Full-color illus., Hardcover, ISBN 1-879045-86-9 **$16.95** *For ages 4 & up*

God's Paintbrush: Special 10th Anniversary Edition
Wonderfully interactive, invites children of all faiths and backgrounds to encounter God through moments in their own lives. Provides questions adult and child can explore together.
11 x 8½, 32 pp, Full-color illus., Hardcover, ISBN 1-58023-195-0 **$17.95** *For ages 4 & up*

Also Available: **God's Paintbrush Teacher's Guide**
8½ x 11, 32 pp, PB, ISBN 1-879045-57-5 **$8.95**

God's Paintbrush Celebration Kit
A Spiritual Activity Kit for Teachers and Students of All Faiths, All Backgrounds
Additional activity sheets available:
8-Student Activity Sheet Pack (40 sheets/5 sessions), ISBN 1-58023-058-X **$19.95**
Single-Student Activity Sheet Pack (5 sessions), ISBN 1-58023-059-8 **$3.95**

In God's Name
Like an ancient myth in its poetic text and vibrant illustrations, this award-winning modern fable about the search for God's name celebrates the diversity and, at the same time, the unity of all people.
9 x 12, 32 pp, Full-color illus., Hardcover, ISBN 1-879045-26-5 **$16.99** *For ages 4 & up*

Also Available as a Board Book: **What Is God's Name?**
5 x 5, 24 pp, Board, Full-color illus., ISBN 1-893361-10-1 **$7.99** *For ages 0–4* *(A SkyLight Paths book)*

Also Available: **In God's Name video and study guide**
Computer animation, original music, and children's voices. 18 min. **$29.99**

Also Available in Spanish: **El nombre de Dios**
9 x 12, 32 pp, Full-color illus., Hardcover, ISBN 1-893361-63-2 **$16.95** *(A SkyLight Paths book)*

Noah's Wife: The Story of Naamah
When God tells Noah to bring the animals of the world onto the ark, God also calls on Naamah, Noah's wife, to save each plant on Earth. Based on an ancient text.
9 x 12, 32 pp, Full-color illus., Hardcover, ISBN 1-58023-134-9 **$16.95** *For ages 4 & up*

Also Available as a Board Book: **Naamah, Noah's Wife**
5 x 5, 24 pp, Full-color illus., Board, ISBN 1-893361-56-X **$7.95** *For ages 0–4* *(A SkyLight Paths book)*

For Heaven's Sake: Finding God in Unexpected Places
9 x 12, 32 pp, Full-color illus., Hardcover, ISBN 1-58023-054-7 **$16.95** *For ages 4 & up*

God Said Amen: Finding the Answers to Our Prayers
9 x 12, 32 pp, Full-color illus., Hardcover, ISBN 1-58023-080-6 **$16.95** *For ages 4 & up*

Current Events/History

The Story of the Jews: A 4,000-Year Adventure—A Graphic History Book
Written & illustrated by Stan Mack
Witty, illustrated narrative of all the major happenings from biblical times to the twenty-first century. 6 x 9, 288 pp, illus., Quality PB, ISBN 1-58023-155-1 **$16.95**

Hannah Senesh: Her Life and Diary, the First Complete Edition
By Hannah Senesh; Foreword by Marge Piercy; Preface by Eitan Senesh
6 x 9, 352 pp, Hardcover, ISBN 1-58023-212-4 **$24.99**

The Jewish Prophet: Visionary Words from Moses and Miriam to Henrietta Szold and A. J. Heschel *By Rabbi Michael J. Shire*
6½ x 8½, 128 pp, 123 full-color illus., Hardcover, ISBN 1-58023-168-3 **Special gift price $14.95**

Shared Dreams: Martin Luther King, Jr. & the Jewish Community
By Rabbi Marc Schneier. Preface by Martin Luther King III.
6 x 9, 240 pp, Hardcover, ISBN 1-58023-062-8 **$24.95**

"Who Is a Jew?": Conversations, Not Conclusions *By Meryl Hyman*
6 x 9, 272 pp, Quality PB, ISBN 1-58023-052-0 **$16.95**

Ecology

Ecology & the Jewish Spirit: Where Nature & the Sacred Meet
Edited by Ellen Bernstein 6 x 9, 288 pp, Quality PB, ISBN 1-58023-082-2 **$16.95**

Torah of the Earth: Exploring 4,000 Years of Ecology in Jewish Thought
Vol. 1: Biblical Israel: One Land, One People; Rabbinic Judaism: One People, Many Lands
Vol. 2: Zionism: One Land, Two Peoples; Eco-Judaism: One Earth, Many Peoples
Edited by Rabbi Arthur Waskow
Vol. 1: 6 x 9, 272 pp, Quality PB, ISBN 1-58023-086-5 **$19.95**
Vol. 2: 6 x 9, 336 pp, Quality PB, ISBN 1-58023-087-3 **$19.95**

Grief/Healing

Against the Dying of the Light: A Parent's Story of Love, Loss and Hope
By Leonard Fein
Unusual exploration of heartbreak and healing. Chronicles the sudden death of author's 30-year-old daughter and shares the wisdom that emerges in the face of loss and grief.
5½ x 8½, 176 pp, Quality PB, ISBN 1-58023-197-7 **$15.99;** Hardcover, ISBN 1-58023-110-1 **$19.95**

Grief in Our Seasons: A Mourner's Kaddish Companion *By Rabbi Kerry M. Olitzky*
4½ x 6½, 448 pp, Quality PB, ISBN 1-879045-55-9 **$15.95**

Healing of Soul, Healing of Body: Spiritual Leaders Unfold the Strength & Solace in Psalms *Edited by Rabbi Simkha Y. Weintraub, C.S.W.*
6 x 9, 128 pp, 2-color illus. text, Quality PB, ISBN 1-879045-31-1 **$14.99**

Jewish Paths toward Healing and Wholeness: A Personal Guide to Dealing with Suffering *By Rabbi Kerry M. Olitzky. Foreword by Debbie Friedman.*
6 x 9, 192 pp, Quality PB, ISBN 1-58023-068-7 **$15.95**

Mourning & Mitzvah, 2nd Edition: A Guided Journal for Walking the Mourner's Path through Grief to Healing *By Anne Brener, L.C.S.W.*
7½ x 9, 304 pp, Quality PB, ISBN 1-58023-113-6 **$19.95**

The Perfect Stranger's Guide to Funerals and Grieving Practices
A Guide to Etiquette in Other People's Religious Ceremonies *Edited by Stuart M. Matlins*
6 x 9, 240 pp, Quality PB, ISBN 1-893361-20-9 **$16.95** *(A SkyLight Paths book)*

Tears of Sorrow, Seeds of Hope: A Jewish Spiritual Companion for Infertility and Pregnancy Loss *By Rabbi Nina Beth Cardin*
6 x 9, 192 pp, Hardcover, ISBN 1-58023-017-2 **$19.95**

A Time to Mourn, A Time to Comfort, 2nd Edition: A Guide to Jewish Bereavement and Comfort *By Dr. Ron Wolfson*
7 x 9, 336 pp, Quality PB, ISBN 1-58023-253-1 **$19.99**

When a Grandparent Dies: A Kid's Own Remembering Workbook for Dealing with Shiva and the Year Beyond *By Nechama Liss-Levinson, Ph.D.*
8 x 10, 48 pp, 2-color text, Hardcover, ISBN 1-879045-44-3 **$15.95** *For ages 7–13*

Abraham Joshua Heschel

The Earth Is the Lord's: The Inner World of the Jew in Eastern Europe
5½ x 8, 128 pp, Quality PB, ISBN 1-879045-42-7 **$14.95**

Israel: An Echo of Eternity *New Introduction by Susannah Heschel*
5½ x 8, 272 pp, Quality PB, ISBN 1-879045-70-2 **$19.95**

A Passion for Truth: Despair and Hope in Hasidism
5½ x 8, 352 pp, Quality PB, ISBN 1-879045-41-9 **$18.99**

Holidays/Holy Days

Leading the Passover Journey
The Seder's Meaning Revealed, the Haggadah's Story Retold
By Rabbi Nathan Laufer
Uncovers the hidden meaning of the Seder's rituals and customs
6 x 9, 208 pp, Hardcover, ISBN 1-58023-211-6 **$24.99**

Reclaiming Judaism as a Spiritual Practice: Holy Days and Shabbat
By Rabbi Goldie Milgram
Provides a framework for understanding the powerful and often unexplained intellectual, emotional, and spiritual tools that are essential for a lively, relevant, and fulfilling Jewish spiritual practice. 7 x 9, 272 pp, Quality PB, ISBN 1-58023-205-1 **$19.99**

7th Heaven: Celebrating Shabbat with Rebbe Nachman of Breslov
By Moshe Mykoff with the Breslov Research Institute
Explores the art of consciously observing Shabbat and understanding in-depth many of the day's spiritual practices. 5⅛ x 8¼, 224 pp, Deluxe PB w/flaps, ISBN 1-58023-175-6 **$18.95**

The Women's Passover Companion
Women's Reflections on the Festival of Freedom
Edited by Rabbi Sharon Cohen Anisfeld, Tara Mohr, and Catherine Spector
Groundbreaking. A provocative conversation about women's relationships to Passover as well as the roots and meanings of women's seders.
6 x 9, 352 pp, Hardcover, ISBN 1-58023-128-4 **$24.95**

The Women's Seder Sourcebook
Rituals & Readings for Use at the Passover Seder
Edited by Rabbi Sharon Cohen Anisfeld, Tara Mohr, and Catherine Spector
Gathers the voices of more than one hundred women in readings, personal and creative reflections, commentaries, blessings, and ritual suggestions that can be incorporated into your Passover celebration.
6 x 9, 384 pp, Hardcover, ISBN 1-58023-136-5 **$24.95**

Creating Lively Passover Seders: A Sourcebook of Engaging Tales, Texts & Activities
By David Arnow, Ph.D. 7 x 9, 416 pp, Quality PB, ISBN 1-58023-184-5 **$24.99**

Hanukkah, 2nd Edition: The Family Guide to Spiritual Celebration
By Dr. Ron Wolfson. Edited by Joel Lurie Grishaver.
7 x 9, 240 pp, illus., Quality PB, ISBN 1-58023-122-5 **$18.95**

The Jewish Family Fun Book: Holiday Projects, Everyday Activities, and Travel Ideas
with Jewish Themes *By Danielle Dardashti and Roni Sarig. Illus. by Avi Katz.*
6 x 9, 288 pp, 70+ b/w illus. & diagrams, Quality PB, ISBN 1-58023-171-3 **$18.95**

The Jewish Gardening Cookbook: Growing Plants & Cooking for
Holidays & Festivals *By Michael Brown* 6 x 9, 224 pp, 30+ illus., Quality PB, ISBN 1-58023-116-0 **$16.95**

The Jewish Lights Book of Fun Classroom Activities: Simple and Seasonal
Projects for Teachers and Students *By Danielle Dardashti and Roni Sarig*
6 x 9, 240 pp, Quality PB, ISBN 1–58023–206–X **$19.99**

Passover, 2nd Edition: The Family Guide to Spiritual Celebration
By Dr. Ron Wolfson with Joel Lurie Grishaver 7 x 9, 352 pp, Quality PB, ISBN 1-58023-174-8 **$19.95**

Shabbat, 2nd Edition: The Family Guide to Preparing for and Celebrating the Sabbath
By Dr. Ron Wolfson 7 x 9, 320 pp, illus., Quality PB, ISBN 1-58023-164-0 **$19.95**

Sharing Blessings: Children's Stories for Exploring the Spirit of the Jewish Holidays
By Rahel Musleah and Michael Klayman
8½ x 11, 64 pp, Full-color illus., Hardcover, ISBN 1-879045-71-0 **$18.95** *For ages 6 & up*

Inspiration

God in All Moments
Mystical & Practical Spiritual Wisdom from Hasidic Masters
Edited and translated by Or N. Rose with Ebn D. Leader
Hasidic teachings on how to be mindful in religious practice and cultivating every-day ethical behavior—*hanhagot.* 5½ x 8¼, 192 pp, Quality PB, ISBN 1-58023-186-1 **$16.95**

Our Dance with God: Finding Prayer, Perspective and Meaning in the
Stories of Our Lives *By Karyn D. Kedar*
Inspiring spiritual insight to guide you on your life journeys and teach you to live and thrive in two conflicting worlds: the rational/material and the spiritual.
6 x 9, 176 pp, Quality PB, ISBN 1-58023-202-7 **$16.99**

Also Available: **The Dance of the Dolphin** (Hardcover edition of *Our Dance with God*)
6 x 9, 176 pp, Hardcover, ISBN 1-58023-154-3 **$19.95**

The Empty Chair: Finding Hope and Joy—Timeless Wisdom from a Hasidic Master,
Rebbe Nachman of Breslov *Adapted by Moshe Mykoff and the Breslov Research Institute*
4 x 6, 128 pp, 2-color text, Deluxe PB w/flaps, ISBN 1-879045-67-2 **$9.95**

The Gentle Weapon: Prayers for Everyday and Not-So-Everyday Moments—
Timeless Wisdom from the Teachings of the Hasidic Master, Rebbe Nachman of Breslov
Adapted by Moshe Mykoff and S. C. Mizrahi, together with the Breslov Research Institute
4 x 6, 144 pp, 2-color text, Deluxe PB w/flaps, ISBN 1-58023-022-9 **$9.95**

God Whispers: Stories of the Soul, Lessons of the Heart *By Karyn D. Kedar*
6 x 9, 176 pp, Quality PB, ISBN 1-58023-088-1 **$15.95**

An Orphan in History: One Man's Triumphant Search for His Jewish Roots
By Paul Cowan. Afterword by Rachel Cowan. 6 x 9, 288 pp, Quality PB, ISBN 1-58023-135-7 **$16.95**

Restful Reflections: Nighttime Inspiration to Calm the Soul, Based on Jewish Wisdom
By Rabbi Kerry M. Olitzky & Rabbi Lori Forman 4½ x 6½, 448 pp, Quality PB, ISBN 1-58023-091-1 **$15.95**

Sacred Intentions: Daily Inspiration to Strengthen the Spirit, Based on Jewish Wisdom
By Rabbi Kerry M. Olitzky and Rabbi Lori Forman 4½ x 6½, 448 pp, Quality PB, ISBN 1-58023-061-X **$15.95**

Kabbalah/Mysticism/Enneagram

Seek My Face: A Jewish Mystical Theology
By Dr. Arthur Green
This classic work of contemporary Jewish theology, revised and updated, is a profound, deeply personal statement of the lasting truths of Jewish mysticism and the basic faith claims of Judaism. A tool for anyone seeking the elusive presence of God in the world. 6 x 9, 304 pp, Quality PB, ISBN 1-58023-130-6 **$19.95**

Zohar: Annotated & Explained
Translation and annotation by Dr. Daniel C. Matt. Foreword by Andrew Harvey
Offers insightful yet unobtrusive commentary to the masterpiece of Jewish mysticism. Explains references and mystical symbols, shares wisdom of spiritual masters, and clarifies the *Zohar*'s bold claim: We have always been taught that we need God, but in order to manifest in the world, God needs us.
5½ x 8½, 160 pp, Quality PB, ISBN 1-893361-51-9 **$15.99** *(A SkyLight Paths book)*

Cast in God's Image: Discover Your Personality Type Using the Enneagram and Kabbalah
By Rabbi Howard A. Addison
7 x 9, 176 pp, Quality PB, Layflat binding, 20+ journaling exercises, ISBN 1-58023-124-1 **$16.95**

Ehyeh: A Kabbalah for Tomorrow *By Dr. Arthur Green*
6 x 9, 224 pp, Quality PB, ISBN 1-58023-213-2 **$16.99**; Hardcover, ISBN 1-58023-125-X **$21.95**

The Enneagram and Kabbalah: Reading Your Soul *By Rabbi Howard A. Addison*
6 x 9, 176 pp, Quality PB, ISBN 1-58023-001-6 **$15.95**

Finding Joy: A Practical Spiritual Guide to Happiness *By Dannel I. Schwartz with Mark Hass*
6 x 9, 192 pp, Quality PB, ISBN 1-58023-009-1 **$14.95**

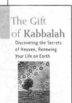

The Gift of Kabbalah: Discovering the Secrets of Heaven, Renewing Your Life on Earth
By Tamar Frankiel, Ph.D.
6 x 9, 256 pp, Quality PB, ISBN 1-58023-141-1 **$16.95**; Hardcover, ISBN 1-58023-108-X **$21.95**

The Way Into Jewish Mystical Tradition *By Lawrence Kushner*
6 x 9, 224 pp, Quality PB, ISBN 1-58023-200-0 **$18.99**; Hardcover, ISBN 1-58023-029-6 **$21.95**

Life Cycle
Marriage / Parenting / Family / Aging

Jewish Fathers: A Legacy of Love
Photographs by Lloyd Wolf. Essays by Paula Wolfson. Foreword by Harold S. Kushner.
Honors the role of contemporary Jewish fathers in America. Each father tells in his own words what it means to be a parent and Jewish, and what he learned from his own father. Insightful photos. 9½ x 9⅞, 144 pp with 100+ duotone photos, Hardcover, ISBN 1-58023-204-3 **$30.00**

The New Jewish Baby Album: Creating and Celebrating the Beginning of a Spiritual Life—A Jewish Lights Companion
By the Editors at Jewish Lights. Foreword by Anita Diamant. Preface by Sandy Eisenberg Sasso.
A spiritual keepsake that will be treasured for generations. More than just a memory book, *shows you how—and why it's important*—to create a Jewish home and a Jewish life. 8 x 10, 64 pp, Deluxe Padded Hardcover, Full-color illus., ISBN 1-58023-138-1 **$19.95**

The Jewish Pregnancy Book: A Resource for the Soul, Body & Mind during Pregnancy, Birth & the First Three Months
By Sandy Falk, M.D., and Rabbi Daniel Judson, with Steven A. Rapp
Includes medical information, prayers and rituals for each stage of pregnancy, from a liberal Jewish perspective. 7 x 10, 208 pp, Quality PB, b/w illus., ISBN 1-58023-178-0 **$16.95**

Celebrating Your New Jewish Daughter: Creating Jewish Ways to Welcome Baby Girls into the Covenant—New and Traditional Ceremonies
By Debra Nussbaum Cohen 6 x 9, 272 pp, Quality PB, ISBN 1-58023-090-3 **$18.95**

The New Jewish Baby Book, 2nd Edition: Names, Ceremonies & Customs—A Guide for Today's Families *By Anita Diamant* 6 x 9, 336 pp, Quality PB, ISBN 1-58023-251-5 **$19.99**

Parenting As a Spiritual Journey: Deepening Ordinary and Extraordinary Events into Sacred Occasions *By Rabbi Nancy Fuchs-Kreimer* 6 x 9, 224 pp, Quality PB, ISBN 1-58023-016-4 **$16.95**

Judaism for Two: A Spiritual Guide for Strengthening and Celebrating Your Loving Relationship *By Rabbi Nancy Fuchs-Kreimer and Rabbi Nancy H. Wiener*
Addresses the ways Jewish teachings can enhance and strengthen committed relationships. 6 x 9, 208 pp, Quality PB, ISBN 1-58023-254-X **$16.99**

Embracing the Covenant: Converts to Judaism Talk About Why & How
By Rabbi Allan Berkowitz and Patti Moskovitz 6 x 9, 192 pp, Quality PB, ISBN 1-879045-50-8 **$16.95**

The Guide to Jewish Interfaith Family Life: An InterfaithFamily.com Handbook
Edited by Ronnie Friedland and Edmund Case 6 x 9, 384 pp, Quality PB, ISBN 1-58023-153-5 **$18.95**

Introducing My Faith and My Community
The Jewish Outreach Institute Guide for the Christian in a Jewish Interfaith Relationship
By Rabbi Kerry M. Olitzky 6 x 9, 176 pp, Quality PB, ISBN 1-58023-192-6 **$16.99**

Making a Successful Jewish Interfaith Marriage: The Jewish Outreach Institute Guide to Opportunities, Challenges and Resources
By Rabbi Kerry M. Olitzky with Joan Peterson Littman 6 x 9, 176 pp, Quality PB, ISBN 1-58023-170-5 **$16.95**

The Creative Jewish Wedding Book: A Hands-On Guide to New & Old Traditions, Ceremonies & Celebrations *By Gabrielle Kaplan-Mayer*
Provides the tools to create the most meaningful Jewish traditional or alternative wedding by using ritual elements to express your unique style and spirituality. 9 x 9, 288 pp, b/w photos, Quality PB, ISBN 1-58023-194-2 **$19.99**

Divorce Is a Mitzvah: A Practical Guide to Finding Wholeness and Holiness When Your Marriage Dies *By Rabbi Perry Netter. Afterword by Rabbi Laura Geller.*
6 x 9, 224 pp, Quality PB, ISBN 1-58023-172-1 **$16.95**

A Heart of Wisdom: Making the Jewish Journey from Midlife through the Elder Years
Edited by Susan Berrin. Foreword by Harold Kushner. 6 x 9, 384 pp, Quality PB, ISBN 1-58023-051-2 **$18.95**

So That Your Values Live On: Ethical Wills and How to Prepare Them
Edited by Jack Riemer and Nathaniel Stampfer 6 x 9, 272 pp, Quality PB, ISBN 1-879045-34-6 **$18.95**

Theology/Philosophy

Aspects of Rabbinic Theology
By Solomon Schechter. New Introduction by Dr. Neil Gillman.
6 x 9, 448 pp, Quality PB, ISBN 1-879045-24-9 **$19.95**

Broken Tablets: Restoring the Ten Commandments and Ourselves
Edited by Rachel S. Mikva. Introduction by Lawrence Kushner. Afterword by Arnold Jacob Wolf.
6 x 9, 192 pp, Quality PB, ISBN 1-58023-158-6 **$16.95**; Hardcover, ISBN 1-58023-066-0 **$21.95**

Creating an Ethical Jewish Life
A Practical Introduction to Classic Teachings on How to Be a Jew
By Dr. Byron L. Sherwin and Seymour J. Cohen
6 x 9, 336 pp, Quality PB, ISBN 1-58023-114-4 **$19.95**

The Death of Death: Resurrection and Immortality in Jewish Thought
By Dr. Neil Gillman 6 x 9, 336 pp, Quality PB, ISBN 1-58023-081-4 **$18.95**

Evolving Halakhah: A Progressive Approach to Traditional Jewish Law
By Rabbi Dr. Moshe Zemer
6 x 9, 480 pp, Quality PB, ISBN 1-58023-127-6 **$29.95**; Hardcover, ISBN 1-58023-002-4 **$40.00**

Hasidic Tales: Annotated & Explained
By Rabbi Rami Shapiro. Foreword by Andrew Harvey, SkyLight Illuminations series editor.
5½ x 8½, 240 pp, Quality PB, ISBN 1-893361-86-1 **$16.95** *(A SkyLight Paths Book)*

A Heart of Many Rooms: Celebrating the Many Voices within Judaism
By Dr. David Hartman 6 x 9, 352 pp, Quality PB, ISBN 1-58023-156-X **$19.95**

The Hebrew Prophets: Selections Annotated & Explained
Translation & Annotation by Rabbi Rami Shapiro. Foreword by Zalman M. Schachter-Shalomi
5½ x 8½, 224 pp, Quality PB, ISBN 1-59473-037-7 **$16.99** *(A SkyLight Paths book)*

Keeping Faith with the Psalms: Deepen Your Relationship with God Using the
Book of Psalms *By Daniel F. Polish* 6 x 9, 272 pp, Hardcover, ISBN 1-58023-179-9 **$24.95**

The Last Trial
On the Legends and Lore of the Command to Abraham to Offer Isaac as a Sacrifice
By Shalom Spiegel. New Introduction by Judah Goldin.
6 x 9, 208 pp, Quality PB, ISBN 1-879045-29-X **$18.95**

A Living Covenant: The Innovative Spirit in Traditional Judaism
By Dr. David Hartman 6 x 9, 368 pp, Quality PB, ISBN 1-58023-011-3 **$18.95**

Love and Terror in the God Encounter
The Theological Legacy of Rabbi Joseph B. Soloveitchik
By Dr. David Hartman
6 x 9, 240 pp, Quality PB, ISBN 1-58023-176-4 **$19.95**; Hardcover, ISBN 1-58023-112-8 **$25.00**

Seeking the Path to Life
Theological Meditations on God and the Nature of People, Love, Life and Death
By Rabbi Ira F. Stone 6 x 9, 160 pp, Quality PB, ISBN 1-879045-47-8 **$14.95**

The Spirit of Renewal: Finding Faith after the Holocaust
By Rabbi Edward Feld 6 x 9, 224 pp, Quality PB, ISBN 1-879045-40-0 **$16.95**

Tormented Master: The Life and Spiritual Quest of Rabbi Nahman of Bratslav
By Dr. Arthur Green 6 x 9, 416 pp, Quality PB, ISBN 1-879045-11-7 **$19.99**

Your Word Is Fire: The Hasidic Masters on Contemplative Prayer
Edited and translated by Dr. Arthur Green and Barry W. Holtz
6 x 9, 160 pp, Quality PB, ISBN 1-879045-25-7 **$15.95**

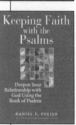

I Am Jewish
Personal Reflections Inspired by the Last Words of Daniel Pearl
Almost 150 Jews—both famous and not—from all walks of life, from all around the world, write about Identity, Heritage, Covenant / Chosenness and Faith, Humanity and Ethnicity, and *Tikkun Olam* and Justice.
Edited by Judea and Ruth Pearl
6 x 9, 304 pp, Deluxe PB w/flaps, ISBN 1-58023-259-0 **$18.99**; Hardcover, ISBN 1-58023-183-7 **$24.99**
Download a free copy of the *I Am Jewish Teacher's Guide* **at our website:**
www.jewishlights.com

Spirituality/The Way Into... Series

The Way Into... Series offers an accessible and highly usable "guided tour" of the Jewish faith, people, history and beliefs—in total, an introduction to Judaism that will enable you to understand and interact with the sacred texts of the Jewish tradition. Each volume is written by a leading contemporary scholar and teacher, and explores one key aspect of Judaism. *The Way Into...* enables all readers to achieve a real sense of Jewish cultural literacy through guided study.

The Way Into Encountering God in Judaism   *By Neil Gillman*
6 x 9, 240 pp, Quality PB, ISBN 1-58023-199-3 **$18.99**; Hardcover, ISBN 1-58023-025-3 **$21.95**

Also Available: **The Jewish Approach to God: A Brief Introduction for Christians**
By Neil Gillman 5½ x 8½, 192 pp, Quality PB, ISBN 1-58023-190-X **$16.95**

The Way Into Jewish Mystical Tradition   *By Lawrence Kushner*
6 x 9, 224 pp, Quality PB, ISBN 1-58023-200-0 **$18.99**; Hardcover, ISBN 1-58023-029-6 **$21.95**

The Way Into Jewish Prayer   *By Lawrence A. Hoffman*
6 x 9, 224 pp, Quality PB, ISBN 1-58023-201-9 **$18.99**; Hardcover, ISBN 1-58023-027-X **$21.95**

The Way Into Torah   *By Norman J. Cohen*
6 x 9, 176 pp, Quality PB, ISBN 1-58023-198-5 **$16.99**; Hardcover, ISBN 1-58023-028-8 **$21.95**

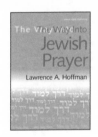

Spirituality in the Workplace

Being God's Partner
How to Find the Hidden Link Between Spirituality and Your Work
By Rabbi Jeffrey K. Salkin. Introduction by Norman Lear.
6 x 9, 192 pp, Quality PB, ISBN 1-879045-65-6 **$17.95**

The Business Bible: 10 New Commandments for Bringing Spirituality & Ethical Values into the Workplace   *By Rabbi Wayne Dosick*
5½ x 8½, 208 pp, Quality PB, ISBN 1-58023-101-2 **$14.95**

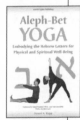

Spirituality and Wellness

Aleph-Bet Yoga
Embodying the Hebrew Letters for Physical and Spiritual Well-Being
By Steven A. Rapp. Foreword by Tamar Frankiel, Ph.D., and Judy Greenfeld. Preface by Hart Lazer
7 x 10, 128 pp, b/w photos, Quality PB, Layflat binding, ISBN 1-58023-162-4 **$16.95**

Entering the Temple of Dreams
Jewish Prayers, Movements, and Meditations for the End of the Day
By Tamar Frankiel, Ph.D., and Judy Greenfeld
7 x 10, 192 pp, illus., Quality PB, ISBN 1-58023-079-2 **$16.95**

Jewish Paths toward Healing and Wholeness: A Personal Guide to Dealing with Suffering   *By Rabbi Kerry M. Olitzky. Foreword by Debbie Friedman.*
6 x 9, 192 pp, Quality PB, ISBN 1-58023-068-7 **$15.95**

Minding the Temple of the Soul
Balancing Body, Mind, and Spirit through Traditional Jewish Prayer, Movement, and Meditation   *By Tamar Frankiel, Ph.D., and Judy Greenfeld*
7 x 10, 184 pp, illus., Quality PB, ISBN 1-879045-64-8 **$16.95**
Audiotape of the Blessings and Meditations: 60 min. **$9.95**
Videotape of the Movements and Meditations: 46 min. **$20.00**

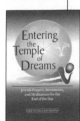

Spirituality

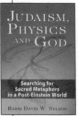

Does the Soul Survive?: A Jewish Journey to Belief in Afterlife, Past Lives & Living with Purpose   *By Rabbi Elie Kaplan Spitz. Foreword by Brian L. Weiss, M.D.*
Spitz relates his own experiences and those shared with him by people he has worked with as a rabbi, and shows us that belief in afterlife and past lives, so often approached with reluctance, is in fact true to Jewish tradition.
6 x 9, 288 pp, Quality PB, ISBN 1-58023-165-9 **$16.95**; Hardcover, ISBN 1-58023-094-6 **$21.95**

First Steps to a New Jewish Spirit: Reb Zalman's Guide to Recapturing the Intimacy & Ecstasy in Your Relationship with God
By Rabbi Zalman M. Schachter-Shalomi with Donald Gropman
An extraordinary spiritual handbook that restores psychic and physical vigor by introducing us to new models and alternative ways of practicing Judaism. Offers meditation and contemplation exercises for enriching the most important aspects of everyday life.   6 x 9, 144 pp, Quality PB, ISBN 1-58023-182-9 **$16.95**

God in Our Relationships: Spirituality between People from the Teachings of Martin Buber   *By Rabbi Dennis S. Ross*
On the eightieth anniversary of Buber's classic work, we can discover new answers to critical issues in our lives. Inspiring examples from Ross's own life—as congregational rabbi, father, hospital chaplain, social worker, and husband—illustrate Buber's difficult-to-understand ideas about how we encounter God and each other. 5½ x 8½, 160 pp, Quality PB, ISBN 1-58023-147-0 **$16.95**

Judaism, Physics and God: Searching for Sacred Metaphors in a Post-Einstein World   *By Rabbi David W. Nelson*
In clear, non-technical terms, this provocative fusion of religion and science examines the great theories of modern physics to find new ways for contemporary people to express their spiritual beliefs and thoughts.
6 x 9, 352 pp, Hardcover, ISBN 1-58023-252-3 **$24.99**

The Jewish Lights Spirituality Handbook: A Guide to Understanding, Exploring & Living a Spiritual Life   *Edited by Stuart M. Matlins*
What exactly is "Jewish" about spirituality? How do I make it a part of my life? Fifty of today's foremost spiritual leaders share their ideas and experience with us.
6 x 9, 456 pp, Quality PB, ISBN 1-58023-093-8 **$19.95**; Hardcover, ISBN 1-58023-100-4 **$24.95**

Bringing the Psalms to Life: How to Understand and Use the Book of Psalms
By Dr. Daniel F. Polish
6 x 9, 208 pp, Quality PB, ISBN 1-58023-157-8 **$16.95**; Hardcover, ISBN 1-58023-077-6 **$21.95**

God & the Big Bang: Discovering Harmony between Science & Spirituality
By Dr. Daniel C. Matt   6 x 9, 216 pp, Quality PB, ISBN 1-879045-89-3 **$16.95**

Godwrestling—Round 2: Ancient Wisdom, Future Paths
By Rabbi Arthur Waskow   6 x 9, 352 pp, Quality PB, ISBN 1-879045-72-9 **$18.95**

One God Clapping: The Spiritual Path of a Zen Rabbi   *By Rabbi Alan Lew with Sherril Jaffe*
5½ x 8½, 336 pp, Quality PB, ISBN 1-58023-115-2 **$16.95**

The Path of Blessing: Experiencing the Energy and Abundance of the Divine
By Rabbi Marcia Prager   5½ x 8½, 240 pp., Quality PB, ISBN 1-58023-148-9 **$16.95**

Six Jewish Spiritual Paths: A Rationalist Looks at Spirituality   *By Rabbi Rifat Sonsino*
6 x 9, 208 pp, Quality PB, ISBN 1-58023-167-5 **$16.95**; Hardcover, ISBN 1-58023-095-4 **$21.95**

Soul Judaism: Dancing with God into a New Era
By Rabbi Wayne Dosick   5½ x 8½, 304 pp, Quality PB, ISBN 1-58023-053-9 **$16.95**

Stepping Stones to Jewish Spiritual Living: Walking the Path Morning, Noon, and Night   *By Rabbi James L. Mirel and Karen Bonnell Werth*
6 x 9, 240 pp, Quality PB, ISBN 1-58023-074-1 **$16.95**; Hardcover, ISBN 1-58023-003-2 **$21.95**

There Is No Messiah... and You're It: The Stunning Transformation of Judaism's Most Provocative Idea   *By Rabbi Robert N. Levine, D.D.*
6 x 9, 192 pp, Quality PB, ISBN 1-58023-255-8 **$16.99**; Hardcover, ISBN 1-58023-173-X **$21.95**

These Are the Words: A Vocabulary of Jewish Spiritual Life   *By Dr. Arthur Green*
6 x 9, 304 pp, Quality PB, ISBN 1-58023-107-1 **$18.95**

Spirituality/Lawrence Kushner

Filling Words with Light: Hasidic and Mystical Reflections on Jewish Prayer
By Lawrence Kushner and Nehemia Polen
Reflects on the joy, gratitude, mystery, and awe embedded in traditional prayers and blessings, and shows how you can imbue these familiar sacred words with your own sense of holiness. 5½ x 8½, 176 pp, Hardcover, ISBN 1-58023-216-7 **$21.99**

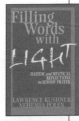

The Book of Letters: A Mystical Hebrew Alphabet
Popular Hardcover Edition, 6 x 9, 80 pp, 2-color text, ISBN 1-879045-00-1 **$24.95**
Collector's Limited Edition, 9 x 12, 80 pp, gold foil embossed pages, w/limited edition silkscreened print, ISBN 1-879045-04-4 **$349.00**

The Book of Miracles: A Young Person's Guide to Jewish Spiritual Awareness
6 x 9, 96 pp, 2-color illus., Hardcover, ISBN 1-879045-78-8 **$16.95** *For ages 9–13*

The Book of Words: Talking Spiritual Life, Living Spiritual Talk
6 x 9, 160 pp, Quality PB, ISBN 1-58023-020-2 **$16.95**

Eyes Remade for Wonder: A Lawrence Kushner Reader *Introduction by Thomas Moore*
6 x 9, 240 pp, Quality PB, ISBN 1-58023-042-3 **$18.95**; Hardcover, ISBN 1-58023-014-8 **$23.95**

God Was in This Place & I, i Did Not Know
Finding Self, Spirituality and Ultimate Meaning 6 x 9, 192 pp, Quality PB, ISBN 1-879045-33-8 **$16.95**

Honey from the Rock: An Introduction to Jewish Mysticism
6 x 9, 176 pp, Quality PB, ISBN 1-58023-073-3 **$16.95**

Invisible Lines of Connection: Sacred Stories of the Ordinary
5½ x 8½, 160 pp, Quality PB, ISBN 1-879045-98-2 **$15.95**

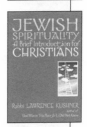

Jewish Spirituality—A Brief Introduction for Christians
5½ x 8½, 112 pp, Quality PB Original, ISBN 1-58023-150-0 **$12.95**

The River of Light: Jewish Mystical Awareness 6 x 9, 192 pp, Quality PB, ISBN 1-58023-096-2 **$16.95**

The Way Into Jewish Mystical Tradition
6 x 9, 224 pp, Quality PB, ISBN 1-58023-200-0 **$18.99**; Hardcover, ISBN 1-58023-029-6 **$21.95**

Spirituality/Prayer

Pray Tell: A Hadassah Guide to Jewish Prayer
By Rabbi Jules Harlow, with contributions from Tamara Cohen, Rochelle Furstenberg, Rabbi Daniel Gordis, Leora Tanenbaum, and many others
A guide to traditional Jewish prayer enriched with insight and wisdom from a broad variety of viewpoints—from Orthodox, Conservative, Reform, and Reconstructionist Judaism to New Age and feminist.
8½ x 11, 400 pp, Quality PB, ISBN 1-58023-163-2 **$29.95**

My People's Prayer Book Series
Traditional Prayers, Modern Commentaries *Edited by Rabbi Lawrence A. Hoffman*
Provides diverse and exciting commentary to the traditional liturgy, helping modern men and women find new wisdom in Jewish prayer, and bring liturgy into their lives. Each book includes Hebrew text, modern translation, and commentaries from all perspectives of the Jewish world.
Vol. 1—The Sh'ma and Its Blessings
  7 x 10, 168 pp, Hardcover, ISBN 1-879045-79-6 **$24.99**
Vol. 2—The Amidah
  7 x 10, 240 pp, Hardcover, ISBN 1-879045-80-X **$24.95**
Vol. 3—P'sukei D'zimrah (Morning Psalms)
  7 x 10, 240 pp, Hardcover, ISBN 1-879045-81-8 **$24.95**
Vol. 4—Seder K'riat Hatorah (The Torah Service)
  7 x 10, 264 pp, Hardcover, ISBN 1-879045-82-6 **$23.95**
Vol. 5—Birkhot Hashachar (Morning Blessings)
  7 x 10, 240 pp, Hardcover, ISBN 1-879045-83-4 **$24.95**
Vol. 6—Tachanun and Concluding Prayers
  7 x 10, 240 pp, Hardcover, ISBN 1-879045-84-2 **$24.95**
Vol. 7—Shabbat at Home
  7 x 10, 240 pp, Hardcover, ISBN 1-879045-85-0 **$24.95**
Vol. 8—Kabbalat Shabbat (Welcoming Shabbat in the Synagogue)
  7 x 10, 240 pp, Hardcover, ISBN 1-58023-121-7 **$24.99**

Meditation

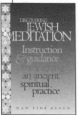

The Handbook of Jewish Meditation Practices
A Guide for Enriching the Sabbath and Other Days of Your Life
By Rabbi David A. Cooper
Easy-to-learn meditation techniques. 6 x 9, 208 pp, Quality PB, ISBN 1-58023-102-0 **$16.95**

Discovering Jewish Meditation: Instruction & Guidance for Learning an Ancient Spiritual Practice *By Nan Fink Gefen, Ph.D.* 6 x 9, 208 pp, Quality PB, ISBN 1-58023-067-9 **$16.95**

A Heart of Stillness: A Complete Guide to Learning the Art of Meditation
By Rabbi David A. Cooper 5½ x 8½, 272 pp, Quality PB, ISBN 1-893361-03-9 **$16.95**
(A SkyLight Paths book)

Meditation from the Heart of Judaism: Today's Teachers Share Their Practices, Techniques, and Faith *Edited by Avram Davis*
6 x 9, 256 pp, Quality PB, ISBN 1-58023-049-0 **$16.95**

Silence, Simplicity & Solitude: A Complete Guide to Spiritual Retreat at Home
By Rabbi David A. Cooper 5½ x 8½, 336 pp, Quality PB, ISBN 1-893361-04-7 **$16.95**
(A SkyLight Paths book)

The Way of Flame: A Guide to the Forgotten Mystical Tradition of Jewish Meditation *By Avram Davis* 4½ x 8, 176 pp, Quality PB, ISBN 1-58023-060-1 **$15.95**

Ritual/Sacred Practice/Journaling

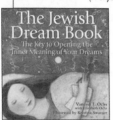

The Jewish Dream Book: The Key to Opening the Inner Meaning of Your Dreams *By Vanessa L. Ochs with Elizabeth Ochs; Full-color illus. by Kristina Swarner*
Instructions for how modern people can perform ancient Jewish dream practices and dream interpretations drawn from the Jewish wisdom tradition. For anyone who wants to understand their dreams—and themselves.
8 x 8, 120 pp, Full-color illus., Deluxe PB w/flaps, ISBN 1-58023-132-2 **$16.95**

The Jewish Journaling Book: How to Use Jewish Tradition to Write Your Life & Explore Your Soul *By Janet Ruth Falon*
Details the history of Jewish journaling throughout biblical and modern times, and teaches specific journaling techniques to help you create and maintain a vital journal, from a Jewish perspective. 8 x 8, 304 pp, Deluxe PB w/flaps, ISBN 1-58023-203-5 **$18.99**

The Book of Jewish Sacred Practices: CLAL's Guide to Everyday & Holiday Rituals & Blessings *Edited by Rabbi Irwin Kula and Vanessa L. Ochs, Ph.D.*
6 x 9, 368 pp, Quality PB, ISBN 1-58023-152-7 **$18.95**

Jewish Ritual: A Brief Introduction for Christians
By Rabbi Kerry M. Olitzky and Rabbi Daniel Judson
5½ x 8½, 144 pp, Quality PB, ISBN 1-58023-210-8 **$14.99**

The Rituals & Practices of a Jewish Life: A Handbook for Personal Spiritual Renewal *Edited by Rabbi Kerry M. Olitzky and Rabbi Daniel Judson*
6 x 9, 272 pp, illus., Quality PB, ISBN 1-58023-169-1 **$18.95**

Science Fiction/ Mystery & Detective Fiction

Mystery Midrash: An Anthology of Jewish Mystery & Detective Fiction
Edited by Lawrence W. Raphael. Preface by Joel Siegel.
6 x 9, 304 pp, Quality PB, ISBN 1-58023-055-5 **$16.95**

Criminal Kabbalah: An Intriguing Anthology of Jewish Mystery & Detective Fiction
Edited by Lawrence W. Raphael. Foreword by Laurie R. King.
6 x 9, 256 pp, Quality PB, ISBN 1-58023-109-8 **$16.95**

More Wandering Stars: An Anthology of Outstanding Stories of Jewish Fantasy and Science Fiction *Edited by Jack Dann. Introduction by Isaac Asimov.*
6 x 9, 192 pp, Quality PB, ISBN 1-58023-063-6 **$16.95**

Wandering Stars: An Anthology of Jewish Fantasy & Science Fiction
Edited by Jack Dann. Introduction by Isaac Asimov.
6 x 9, 272 pp, Quality PB, ISBN 1-58023-005-9 **$16.95**

Spirituality/Women's Interest

The Quotable Jewish Woman: Wisdom, Inspiration & Humor from the Mind & Heart *Edited and compiled by Elaine Bernstein Partnow*
The definitive collection of ideas, reflections, humor, and wit of over 300 Jewish women.
6 x 9, 496 pp, Hardcover, ISBN 1-58023-193-4 **$29.99**

Lifecycles, Vol. 1: Jewish Women on Life Passages & Personal Milestones
Edited and with introductions by Rabbi Debra Orenstein 6 x 9, 480 pp, Quality PB, ISBN 1-58023-018-0 **$19.95**

Lifecycles, Vol. 2: Jewish Women on Biblical Themes in Contemporary Life
Edited and with introductions by Rabbi Debra Orenstein and Rabbi Jane Rachel Litman
6 x 9, 464 pp, Quality PB, ISBN 1-58023-019-9 **$19.95**

Moonbeams: A Hadassah Rosh Hodesh Guide *Edited by Carol Diament, Ph.D.*
8½ x 11, 240 pp, Quality PB, ISBN 1-58023-099-7 **$20.00**

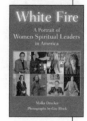

ReVisions: Seeing Torah through a Feminist Lens *By Rabbi Elyse Goldstein*
5½ x 8½, 224 pp, Quality PB, ISBN 1-58023-117-9 **$16.95**

White Fire: A Portrait of Women Spiritual Leaders in America
By Rabbi Malka Drucker. Photographs by Gay Block.
7 x 10, 320 pp, 30+ b/w photos, Hardcover, ISBN 1-893361-64-0 **$24.95** *(A SkyLight Paths book)*

Women of the Wall: Claiming Sacred Ground at Judaism's Holy Site
Edited by Phyllis Chesler and Rivka Haut 6 x 9, 496 pp, b/w photos, Hardcover, ISBN 1-58023-161-6 **$34.95**

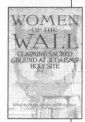

The Women's Haftarah Commentary: New Insights from Women Rabbis on the 54 Weekly Haftarah Portions, the 5 Megillot & Special Shabbatot
Edited by Rabbi Elyse Goldstein 6 x 9, 560 pp, Hardcover, ISBN 1-58023-133-0 **$39.99**

The Women's Torah Commentary: New Insights from Women Rabbis on the 54 Weekly Torah Portions *Edited by Rabbi Elyse Goldstein*
6 x 9, 496 pp, Hardcover, ISBN 1-58023-076-8 **$34.95**

The Year Mom Got Religion: One Woman's Midlife Journey into Judaism
By Lee Meyerhoff Hendler 6 x 9, 208 pp, Quality PB, ISBN 1-58023-070-9 **$15.95**

See Holidays for *The Women's Passover Companion: Women's Reflections on the Festival of Freedom* and *The Women's Seder Sourcebook: Rituals & Readings for Use at the Passover Seder.* Also see Bar/Bat Mitzvah for *The JGirl's Guide: The Young Jewish Woman's Handbook for Coming of Age.*

Travel

Israel—A Spiritual Travel Guide, 2nd Edition
A Companion for the Modern Jewish Pilgrim
By Rabbi Lawrence A. Hoffman 4¼ x 10, 256 pp, Quality PB, illus., ISBN 1-58023-261-2 **$18.99**
Also Available: **The Israel Mission Leader's Guide** ISBN 1-58023-085-7 **$4.95**

12 Steps

100 Blessings Every Day Daily Twelve Step Recovery Affirmations, Exercises for Personal Growth & Renewal Reflecting Seasons of the Jewish Year
By Rabbi Kerry M. Olitzky. Foreword by Rabbi Neil Gillman.
One-day-at-a-time monthly format. Reflects on the rhythm of the Jewish calendar to bring insight to recovery from addictions.
4½ x 6½, 432 pp, Quality PB, ISBN 1-879045-30-3 **$15.99**

Recovery from Codependence: A Jewish Twelve Steps Guide to Healing Your Soul
By Rabbi Kerry M. Olitzky 6 x 9, 160 pp, Quality PB, ISBN 1-879045-32-X **$13.95**

Renewed Each Day: Daily Twelve Step Recovery Meditations Based on the Bible
By Rabbi Kerry M. Olitzky and Aaron Z.
Vol. 1—Genesis & Exodus: 6 x 9, 224 pp, Quality PB, ISBN 1-879045-12-5 **$14.95**
Vol. 2—Leviticus, Numbers & Deuteronomy: 6 x 9, 280 pp, Quality PB, ISBN 1-879045-13-3 **$14.95**

Twelve Jewish Steps to Recovery: A Personal Guide to Turning from Alcoholism & Other Addictions—Drugs, Food, Gambling, Sex...
By Rabbi Kerry M. Olitzky and Stuart A. Copans, M.D. Preface by Abraham J. Twerski, M.D.
6 x 9, 144 pp, Quality PB, ISBN 1-879045-09-5 **$14.95**

About Jewish Lights

People of all faiths and backgrounds yearn for books that attract, engage, educate, and spiritually inspire.

Our principal goal is to stimulate thought and help all people learn about who the Jewish People are, where they come from, and what the future can be made to hold. While people of our diverse Jewish heritage are the primary audience, our books speak to people in the Christian world as well and will broaden their understanding of Judaism and the roots of their own faith.

We bring to you authors who are at the forefront of spiritual thought and experience. While each has something different to say, they all say it in a voice that you can hear.

Our books are designed to welcome you and then to engage, stimulate, and inspire. We judge our success not only by whether or not our books are beautiful and commercially successful, but by whether or not they make a difference in your life.

For your information and convenience, at the back of this book we have provided a list of other Jewish Lights books you might find interesting and useful. They cover all the categories of your life:

Bar/Bat Mitzvah	Life Cycle
Bible Study / Midrash	Meditation
Children's Books	Parenting
Congregation Resources	Prayer
Current Events / History	Ritual / Sacred Practice
Ecology	Spirituality
Fiction: Mystery, Science Fiction	Theology / Philosophy
Grief / Healing	Travel
Holidays / Holy Days	Twelve Steps
Inspiration	Women's Interest
Kabbalah / Mysticism / Enneagram	

Stuart M. Matlins, Publisher

Or phone, fax, mail or e-mail to: **JEWISH LIGHTS Publishing**
Sunset Farm Offices, Route 4 • P.O. Box 237 • Woodstock, Vermont 05091
Tel: (802) 457-4000 • Fax: (802) 457-4004 • www.jewishlights.com
Credit card orders: (800) 962-4544 (8:30AM–5:30PM ET Monday–Friday)
Generous discounts on quantity orders. SATISFACTION GUARANTEED. Prices subject to change.